The McGraw-Hill

Handbook of English Grammar and Usage

MARK LESTER AND LARRY BEASON

Tata McGraw-Hill Publishing Company Limited
NEW DELHI

McGraw-Hill Offices
New Delhi New York St Louis San Francisco Auckland Bogotá Caracas
Kuala Lumpur Lisbon London Madrid Mexico City Milan Montreal
San Juan Santiago Singapore Sydney Tokyo Toronto

Tata McGraw-Hill

Tata McGraw-Hill Edition 2005

Third reprint 2006
RZLLCDRKRZRDY

Reprinted in India by arrangement with The McGraw-Hill Companies, Inc., New York

Sales territories: India, Pakistan, Nepal, Bangladesh, Sri Lanka and Bhutan

Library of Congress Cataloging-in-Publication Data

Lester, Mark.
The McGraw-Hill handbook of English grammar and usage / Mark Lester and Larry Beason.
p. cm.
Includes index.
ISBN 0-07-144133-6
1. English language—Grammar—Handbooks, manuals, etc. 2. English language—Usage—Handbooks, manuals, etc.
PE1112.L463 2004
428.2—dc22 2004052404

ISBN 0-07-060115-1

Published by Tata McGraw-Hill Publishing Company Limited,
7 West Patel Nagar, New Delhi 110 008, and printed at
Pushp Print Services, Delhi 110 053

The McGraw-Hill Companies

Contents

Introduction

". . . You should say what you mean," the March Hare went on.

"I do," Alice hastily replied; "at least—at least I mean what I say—that's the same thing, you know."

"Not the same thing a bit!" said the Hatter. "You might just as well say that 'I see what I eat' is the same thing as 'I eat what I see!' "

—Alice in Wonderland

The March Hare sounds as though he might have been an English teacher! Whatever his profession, he is clearly aware that precision in one's language choices can be a serious matter.

Such precision is especially important in written communication. Writing, unlike conversation, allows you to refine your language before sharing it, and readers are well aware you have this "prep time" for writing. When we show our writing to others, there is an expectation of correctness and precision far beyond the expectations of day-to-day conversations. Mistakes that are routinely accepted in casual conversation are glaringly apparent in writing—or in formal speaking situations.

English teachers and March Hares are not the only ones who expect our language choices to be made carefully and correctly. Indeed, many businesspeople are far more demanding than English teachers when it comes to following grammar rules and preferences. Errors and poor decisions in regard to language can annoy readers of all sorts, can confuse people about what you are trying to say, and can lead your audience to question your credibility or professionalism.

Thus, we offer this book to help people improve their ability to follow the rules, conventions, and preferences associated with formal English.

This book is intended for various readers and needs. You might feel your skills in these areas need drastic improvement, or you might just need to brush up on a few matters.

Grammar books are commonplace. What makes this one different? Following are seven features that set this book apart:

- **Separating grammar and usage:** Part I focuses on the grammatical terminology used to describe language. Part II goes a step further by covering the rules and conventions—the "prescriptions" for proper language, or what you should and should not do in formal communication. Rather than conflate these two issues (description versus prescription), this book separates them so readers can pay attention to the parts that matter most to them.
- **A nontechnical approach:** You do not have to be a grammarian or linguist to use this book. Part I covers the technical aspects of grammar, but we assume our readers do not necessarily have a background in this area. More importantly, Part II does not rely on Part I or on previous knowledge of formal grammar.
- **Accessible, bottom-line information:** Part II in particular offers bottom-line definitions, hints, and rules that summarize the least you need to know about grammar and usage.
- **More than just the bottom line:** Most reference books on grammar stop with the bottom-line rules and with maybe an example or two. The problem is that almost every grammar rule is not self-explanatory. If it were, you would not need a book on grammar at this point in your life. Unlike most reference books on grammar, ours gives a thorough explanation so that you can better understand the rules, exceptions, and methods for correcting an error. Our goal is for you to know how to avoid problems so you will not need this or any other grammar book later. Thus, we provide enough information so you can truly understand and learn.
- **A focus on the most important aspects of grammar and usage:** To avoid overwhelming our readers, this book focuses on what matters the most. Neither Part I nor Part II covers *every* aspect of formal English.

Instead, Part I deals with the grammatical terminology and information that are most useful and common. Part II deals with the most serious or most frequent errors in formal English.

• **Clearly marked examples of correct and incorrect sentences:** People learn from examples, so we include plenty. But research indicates that many people who are given incorrect examples only remember how to create these errors. Often readers do not know that the examples are actually incorrect, or they only remember seeing mistakes, meaning all they learn is how to commit an error. In this book we clearly mark errors (with an X); other examples are correct. We attempt to include at least as many correct examples as errors.

• **A focus on traditional grammar with insights from modern approaches:** In school the most common approach to grammar is a traditional scheme based on certain parts of speech, functions, and definitions that, as a whole, are standard throughout the English-speaking world. Our book uses this system as a basis. However, along the way we draw on insights from other theories of grammar and language. For example, Part II is largely based on the notion that people use intuitive tips that tell them if they are putting a sentence together properly. This notion builds on modern grammatical theories that assume people learn a language by subconsciously drawing on particular tests and procedures. In other words, our book describes English in ways that might sound familiar to those who studied grammar in school, but we also draw on more recent perspectives of how people naturally learn and improve their language skills.

We thank you for your interest in this book and hope that it proves not only useful but interesting.

We also wish to thank several people who have helped with the writing and production of this book. In terms of publishing and production, we thank Executive Editor Christopher Brown, Production Manager Marisa L'Heureux, and Acquisitions Editor Holly McGuire. In terms of the writing, we thank our students, academic colleagues, and people in the business sector who have helped us learn more about what constitutes a "serious" language error and effective ways for avoiding these problems.

PART I

Grammar 101

The grammar section of this book is a practically painless explanation of how English grammar works. It presumes that the reader has little or no previous exposure to formal grammar. The grammar section covers all the conventional grammar terms and concepts that you are ever likely to encounter.

The approach in this book is substantially different from what you may have experienced back in junior high school for two reasons:

First, you are now a consenting adult who has actually chosen to learn something about grammar (as opposed to the normal junior high school audience). Therefore, the presentation is aimed at a much more sophisticated audience, one that values ideas, evidence, and explanations. Many of the ideas are presented deductively. That is, you are given numerous examples and tests that you can use to see for yourself how the rules actually work.

Second, today's grammar is substantially different from traditional classroom grammar. There have been quantum leaps in our understanding of what language is and how it works. While the general framework of this presentation is quite conventional, there are many places where traditional grammar has been supplemented with insights from modern linguistics. The resulting picture of English is both more comprehensive and in many ways simpler than what you might have experienced back in junior high school. Enjoy!

1

Parts of Speech

The fundamental building block of all language is the word. Words are classified into **parts of speech** according to the way words function in a sentence. It is important to realize that a word's part of speech is not inherent in the word itself but in the way the word is used. It is not unusual for a word to belong to more than one part of speech class depending on how the word is used. For example, the word *round* can be used as a noun, a verb, or an adjective:

Noun:	Should we get another *round*?
Verb:	The horses *round* the last post and head for home.
Adjective:	He put a small, *round* pebble in his pocket.

So, instead of asking the question, "What part of speech is X?," we should always ask the question, "What part of speech is X in this sentence?"

There are seven functional parts of speech: **nouns**, **verbs**, **adjectives**, **adverbs**, **pronouns**, **conjunctions**, and **prepositions**. There is also by some reckoning an eighth part of speech, **interjections**. Interjections are like asides or commentaries that are really not part of the actual grammar of a sentence. For example, *well* and *damn* in the following sentences are interjections:

Well, I don't know what to tell you.
Damn, I burned my fingers on that pan!

Because interjections, by definition, play no grammatical role in a sentence, we will ignore them from this point onward and concentrate on the remaining seven functional parts of speech.

Nouns

The word *noun* comes from a Latin word that means "name." Accordingly, nouns are often defined by their naming ability: a noun is a word used to name a person, a place, a thing, or an idea.

There are two types of nouns, **proper nouns** and **common nouns.** Proper nouns are the names of specific individuals or entities, while common nouns are the names of generic categories. Proper nouns are normally capitalized. (See Chapter 15 for a treatment of the sometimes confusing and arbitrary conventions for capitalizing proper nouns.)

Here are some examples of roughly corresponding proper and common nouns:

Proper Noun	Common Noun
Abraham Lincoln	president
Fred Flintstone	caveman
Garfield	cat
New Zealand	country
Rio Grande	river
Everest	mountain
Stone Age	period

Defining a noun as a "name" seems quite natural for proper nouns. However, the definition of *noun* as a "name" does not work as well for common nouns. It is not that common nouns are not names; they are. The problem is that the concept of "name" is so broad that it is easy to extend "name" to parts of speech that are not nouns. For example, *jump* is the "name" of an action and *blue* is the "name" of a color, but in the following sentences, *jump* is a verb and *blue* is an adjective:

The children tried to *jump* over the ditch.
The new dishes are *blue.*

Another way to identify common nouns is by taking advantage of a unique property of how they are used. Only common nouns are commonly and routinely modified by adjectives. Thus, if a word can be readily modified by an adjective, then that word must be a common noun. A particularly convenient adjective to use as a test word is *the.*

The *the* Test for Common Nouns

If *the* can be put immediately in front of a word and the result makes sense, then that word is a noun.

Let's apply the *the* test to the two example sentences we just saw. In the first example, when we put *the* in front of the word *jump*, the result is ungrammatical. (We will use X to show that we have intentionally produced an ungrammatical sentence.)

the
X The children tried to ^ *jump* over the ditch.

The failure of the *the* test shows us that the word *jump* is not being used as a noun in this sentence. (Remember that the *the* test is only relevant to this use of the word *jump* in this sentence. In another sentence, *jump* could be used as a noun.)

In the second example, when we put *the* in front of the word *blue*, the result is again ungrammatical:

the
X The new dishes are ^ *blue.*

The failure of the *the* test shows us that the word *blue* is not being used as a noun in this sentence.

The *the* test requires that the word *the* be immediately in front of the word being tested. The reason for this requirement is that other adjectives can separate *the* from the noun it is modifying. For example, in the phrase *the new dishes*, the word *the* is immediately in front of the adjective *new*. When you think about it for a second, it is easy to see that *the* is modifying the noun *dishes*, not the adjective *new*. We can confirm this by dropping the adjective. We can say *the dishes*. Just be sure to put *the* immediately in front of the word you want to test.

However, the *the* test for common nouns is not perfect. Some abstract common nouns are not used with *the*—for example, *honesty* in the following sentence:

Honesty is the best policy.

Saying ***The** honesty is the best policy* sounds odd, at best.

Outside of not being used with a few abstract nouns, the *the* test is a simple and highly reliable test. It also has the advantage of not giving false positives. That is, the test will never tell you something is a noun when it actually isn't.

Verbs

The traditional definition of *verb* is "a word used to express action or describe a state of being." As the definition implies, there are two different types of verbs: **action verbs** and **linking verbs** that describe the subjects. Here are some examples of each type:

Action Verbs	**Linking Verbs**
Donald *laughed*.	Donald *is* funny.
Jane *wrote* a novel.	The novel *became* a bestseller.
Erma *made* some soup.	The soup *smelled* wonderful.

As you can see, the verbs in the first column express some action that the subject of the sentence is carrying out. In the third example, for instance, Erma is engaged in the action of making soup. In the second column, however, the subjects are not doing anything. In the third example, for instance, the soup is not doing the smelling. Rather, the verb *smelled* is used to describe the soup. We will examine the distinction between action and linking verbs further in the section on verb phrases in Chapter 2. For now, we will ignore the distinction between action and linking verbs and concentrate on identifying verbs as a part of speech distinct from the other parts of speech.

The defining characteristic of all verbs is that verbs (and only verbs) have tenses: present, past, and future. Unless a word can be used in the present, past, and future tense, it is not a verb—no exceptions. Verbs come in two flavors: regular and irregular. Regular verbs form their past tenses in an absolutely *regular* way by adding *-ed* (sometimes just *-d* if the verb already ends in an *e*). Irregular verbs form their past tense in some other *irregular* way, often by changing the vowel of the verb. Here are two examples, one with the regular verb *remember* and the other with the irregular verb *forget*:

Present: Wilbur always *remembers* his mother's birthday.
Orville always *forgets* his mother's birthday.
Past: Wilbur *remembered* his mother's birthday this year.
Orville *forgot* his mother's birthday this year.
Future: Wilbur *will remember* his mother's birthday this year.
Orville *will forget* his mother's birthday this year.

The helping verb *will*, which we use to form the future tense, is a convenient test word for identifying verbs.

The *Will* Test for Verbs

If you can put *will* in front of a word and the result is grammatical, then that word must be a verb.

To see how simple and effective the *will* test is, let's apply it to the three uses of the word *round* from the beginning of the chapter:

Noun: Should we get another *round*?
Verb: The horses *round* the last post and head for home.
Adjective: He put a small, *round* pebble in his pocket.

Now let's apply the *will* test for verbs:

will
Noun: X Should we get another ^ *round*?

will
Verb: The horses ^ *round* the last post and head for home.

will
Adjective: X He put a small, ^ *round* pebble in his pocket.

As we would expect, the *will* test fails with the noun and the adjective but works with the verb.

Adjectives

Adjectives play two distinct roles: **noun modifiers** and **predicate adjectives.** As noun modifiers, adjectives always precede the nouns they modify. As predicate adjectives, adjectives follow linking (descriptive) verbs and describe the subject.

Here are some examples of both types.

Adjectives as noun modifiers (adjectives in italics, nouns in bold)
an awful **noise**
that dreadful old **man**
five golden **rings**
the special, deep-dish, Chicago-style **pizza**

Adjectives as predicate adjectives (adjectives in italics)
The play was *terrific.*
Harry sounded *excited.*
The crust turned *brown.*
Please remain *calm.*

We will deal with predicate adjectives as part of the broader discussion of verb phrases in Chapter 2 because we cannot talk about predicate adjectives without also discussing linking (descriptive) verbs in more detail. In this section, then, we will concentrate solely on adjectives as noun modifiers.

Here is a simple test for identifying modifying adjectives:

The Pair Test for Modifying Adjectives

If you can pair up a modifying word with a noun, then that word is an adjective.

Using the last example of adjectives used as noun modifiers from above, here is how the adjectives pair up with the noun they modify:

the special, deep-dish, Chicago-style **pizza**
the **pizza**
special **pizza**
deep-dish **pizza**
Chicago-style **pizza**

The pair test shows that each of the words can separately and independently modify the noun *pizza*. Therefore, they are all valid adjectives.

The pair test is helpful in distinguishing adverbs from adjectives. Here is an example:

that absolutely dreadful old man

Here is what happens when we apply the pair test:

that man
X absolutely man
dreadful man
old man

The pair test shows us that *absolutely* is not an adjective because it cannot modify the noun *man*. *Absolutely* is actually an adverb modifying the adjective *dreadful*.

Adjectives can be subdivided into two main classes: **determiners** and **descriptive adjectives.**

Determiners

Determiners are a diverse group of modifiers that precede descriptive adjectives. For example, *the* is a determiner and *old* is a descriptive adjective. We can say

the old house

but we cannot reverse the order and put the determiner after the descriptive adjective:

X old the house

There are at least five subclasses of determiners:

Articles: *the* (**definite**); *a* and *an* (**indefinite**)
Demonstratives: *this, that, these, those*
Number words: Cardinal numbers: *one, two, three* . . .
Ordinal numbers: *first, second, third* (plus other words indicating order: *first, last* . . .)

The terms *cardinal* and *ordinal* are easily mixed up. Here is a trick to remember which is which: the term *ordinal* refers to the *order* in which things occur: *first, second, third,* etc.

Possessives used as adjectives: *John's, Mary's* . . . (nouns) *my, your, his, her, its, our, their* (pronouns)

Part of speech is determined by function. When nouns and pronouns are used in their possessive forms, they are functioning as adjectives and are no longer classified as nouns and pronouns per se.

Quantifiers: *some, many, several* . . .

Descriptive Adjectives

Most, but not all, descriptive adjectives have **comparative** and **superlative** forms. Here are some examples of sentences with comparative and superlative adjectives (in italics):

Comparative: Fred took a *smaller* piece than I did.
Fred has a *more sensitive* personality than I do.

Superlative: Fred took the *smallest* piece.
Fred has the *most sensitive* personality of anybody I know.

As you can see, there are two different patterns for forming the comparative and superlative: one with *-er* and *-est*, the other with *more* and *most*. The *-er/-est* pattern goes back to Old English. The *more/most* pattern emerged in the Middle Ages and is probably a kind of translation of the way the comparative and superlative are formed in French. All one-syllable adjectives and some two-syllable adjectives (especially ones of native English origin) follow the *-er/-est* pattern. All three-syllable (or longer) adjectives and some two-syllable adjectives (especially ones of French origin) follow the *more/most* pattern.

Here are some more examples of each type:

***-er/-est* Pattern**	***more/most* Pattern**
brave, braver, bravest	ambitious, more ambitious, most ambitious
shy, shyer, shyest	serious, more serious, most serious
witty, wittier, wittiest	loyal, more loyal, most loyal
happy, happier, happiest	vicious, more vicious, most vicious

Descriptive adjectives can be easily combined, for example (descriptive adjectives in italics, nouns being modified in bold):

six *thin gray* **cats**
that *disgusting old* **man**
a *shiny new* **quarter**

Sometimes it is necessary to separate descriptive adjectives from each other by commas. The section on commas and adjectives in Chapter 11 gives a simple way to tell when to use (and not use) commas with multiple descriptive adjectives.

Adverbs

Adverbs are words that modify verbs, adjectives, or other adverbs. By far the most common use of adverbs is to modify verbs, so we will deal with them first.

Adverbs That Modify Verbs

Here are some examples of adverbs (in italics) that modify verbs (in bold):

> They **parked** the truck *yesterday*.
> They **loaded** the truck *there*.
> They **drove** the truck *carefully*.
> They **use** the truck *frequently*.

Adverbs that modify verbs have several characteristics that make them (relatively) easy to identify: they answer adverb questions, and they are movable.

> **The Adverb Question Test**
>
> If a word answers an adverb question (*when, where, how, why, how often*, etc.), then the word is an adverb that modifies the verb.

Here is the adverb question test applied to the example sentences (adverb question words in bold):

Adverb question:	**When** did they park the truck?
Answer:	Yesterday. (*Yesterday* is an adverb that modifies the verb.)
Adverb question:	**Where** did they load the truck?
Answer:	There. (*There* is an adverb that modifies the verb.)

Adverb question:	**How** did they drive the truck?
Answer:	Carefully. (*Carefully* is an adverb that modifies the verb.)
Adverb question:	**How often** do they use the truck?
Answer:	Frequently. (*Frequently* is an adverb that modifies the verb.)

The Adverb Movement Test

If a word can be moved to a different position in the sentence, then the word is an adverb that modifies the verb.

Here is the adverb movement test applied to the same example sentences (adverbs in italics):

Original:	They parked the truck *yesterday*.
Adverb moved:	*Yesterday* they parked the truck.
Original:	They loaded the truck *there*.
Adverb moved:	*There* they loaded the truck.
Original:	They drove the truck *carefully*.
Adverb moved (1):	*Carefully* they drove the truck.
Adverb moved (2):	They *carefully* drove the truck.
Original:	They use the truck *frequently*.
Adverb moved (1):	*Frequently* they use the truck.
Adverb moved (2):	They *frequently* use the truck.

As you can see, adverbs that modify the verb can usually be moved to the beginning of the sentence. Sometimes, depending on the particular adverb, they can be moved in front of the verb.

Adverbs That Modify Adjectives

Here are some examples of adverbs (in italics) that modify adjectives (in bold):

a *completely* **false** statement
some *rather* **unusual** ideas
a *terribly* **hot** afternoon

Adverbs that modify adjectives are immobile: they cannot be moved away from the adjective they modify. There is no simple, direct test for adverbs that modify adjectives, but there is a reliable negative test: the pair test for modifying adjectives. Because adverbs can never modify nouns, a modifying word that fails the pair test must be an adverb modifying an adjective. Here is the pair test used to identify adverbs that modify adjectives:

a completely false statement
a statement
X completely statement (*Completely* fails, therefore it is an adverb modifying *false.*)
false statement

some rather unusual ideas
some ideas
X rather ideas (*Rather* fails, therefore it is an adverb modifying *unusual.*)
unusual ideas

a terribly hot afternoon
an afternoon (We need to change *a* to *an* because the following word now begins with a vowel.)
X terribly afternoon (*Terribly* fails, therefore it is an adverb modifying *hot.*)
hot afternoon

Adverbs That Modify Other Adverbs

Here are some examples of adverbs (in italics) that modify other adverbs (in bold):

I always answer my calls *very* **promptly**.
The students answered the questions *quite* **easily**.

Harvard fought *rather* **fiercely**.
I did *even* **worse** on the test than I had expected.

Adverbs that modify other adverbs are easy to recognize. They are locked into place immediately in front of the adverbs they modify. Adverbs that modify other adverbs belong to a limited class of words that are sometimes called **intensifiers**: they emphasize the meaning of the adverb they modify.

Pronouns

Pronouns are divided into four subclasses: **personal**, **reflexive**, **indefinite**, and **demonstrative**.

Personal Pronouns

The conventional definition of *pronoun* is "a word used in place of one or more nouns." This definition captures the single most important use of pronouns—namely, to replace or represent a noun or nouns. Here is a simple example of pronouns replacing single nouns:

Tarzan wondered where *Jane* was.
He wondered where *she* was.

The pronoun *he* stands for or replaces *Tarzan* and ditto for *she* and *Jane*.

Here is an example where one pronoun replaces two nouns:

Tarzan and Jane were having a romantic dinner together.
They were having a romantic dinner together.

In this case, the pronoun *they* stands for or replaces two nouns: *Tarzan* and *Jane*.

The pronouns that literally replace specific nouns are called **third-person pronouns**. There are several third-person pronouns depending on the number, gender, and grammatical function of the nouns that are being replaced (i.e., whether they replace nouns being used as subjects, objects, or possessives). Here is a complete list:

THIRD-PERSON PRONOUNS

Grammatical Function	Singular	Plural
subject	he, she, it	they
object	him, her, it	them
possessive	his, hers, its	theirs

The subject and object forms are obvious, but the possessive is tricky because we need to distinguish between possessives being used as pronouns from similar possessives being used as adjectives. An example will show the difference:

Possessive pronoun: That book is *Jane's book.*
That book is *hers.*

In this first example, *hers* stands for the noun *book* (together with the possessive noun *Jane's*, which is being used as an adjective to modify the noun *book*).

Possessive adjective: That is *Jane's* book.
That is *her* book.

In this second example, both the possessive noun *Jane's* and the possessive pronoun *her* (which replaces *Jane's*) are used as adjectives to modify the noun *book*, but they are not used to replace or represent the noun *book*, so they are not pronouns. They are adjectives.

The distinction between the possessive pronoun *hers* and the possessive adjective *her* is a little easier to see in this pair of examples because they have different forms: *hers* (with the *s*) is a pronoun; *her* (without the *s*) is an adjective. This same distinction holds for *theirs* (pronoun) and *their* (adjective), but unfortunately the pronoun and adjective forms of *his* and *its* are identical, so good luck with these two.

Third-person pronouns belong to a larger family of pronouns called **personal pronouns**. There are two other members of the personal pronoun family: **first-person pronouns** and **second-person pronouns.** First- and second-person pronouns do not literally replace specific nouns the way that third-person pronouns do. First-person pronouns represent the speaker (or writer) of the sentence. Second-person pronouns represent the hearer (or reader) of the sentence. Here is an example:

I see *you.*

I (the speaker/writer) is a first-person pronoun. *You* (the hearer/reader) is a second-person pronoun.

Here is the complete set of first and second-person pronouns:

FIRST-PERSON PRONOUNS

Grammatical Function	Singular	Plural
subject	I	we
object	me	us
possessive	mine	ours

SECOND-PERSON PRONOUNS

Grammatical Function	Singular	Plural
subject	you	you
object	you	you
possessive	yours	yours

Reflexive Pronouns

Reflexive pronouns are a unique and easily recognizable group of pronouns that end in *-self* or *-selves.* Here is the complete list:

Person	Singular	Plural
first person	myself	ourselves
second person	yourself	yourselves
third person	himself	themselves
	herself	themselves
	itself	themselves

Reflexive pronouns must refer back to a specific noun (usually, but not always, the subject) in the same sentence. This noun is called the **antecedent** of the reflexive pronoun. The term *reflexive* comes from a Latin word meaning "bend back." The origin of the term may help you to remember that a reflexive pronoun must "bend back" to refer to its antecedent. For example, in the following sentence

The queen saw *herself* in the mirror.

the reflexive pronoun *herself* can only refer back to its antecedent *queen*.

Reflexive pronouns *must* have an antecedent in the same sentence. A common mistake is to use a reflexive pronoun as a way of avoiding the choice between a subject and object pronoun, for example:

X Snow White smiled at the dwarves and *myself*.

In this sentence, the writer was not sure whether to use *I* or *me*. The writer thought to duck the choice by using the reflexive *myself*. This is a mistake because there is no antecedent for *myself*. If the writer had stuck with *I* and *me*, the writer would have had a fifty-fifty chance of being right. But the reflexive without an antecedent is wrong 100 percent of the time. Here is the reflexive *myself* used correctly with an antecedent:

I smiled at *myself*.

The antecedent of *myself* is the subject pronoun *I*.

Indefinite Pronouns

A large number of pronouns refer to unspecified persons, things, or groups. Here are some common indefinite pronouns:

all	many	one
another	more	other
both	most	several
each	much	some

either	neither	such
few	none	

Here is an example of a sentence with two indefinite pronouns:

Many are called, but *few* are chosen.

It is easy to confuse indefinite pronouns with the same words used as adjectives. Remember: indefinite pronouns stand alone; adjectives modify nouns. Here is an example that illustrates the difference:

Indefinite pronoun: Popeye would like *some*. (The pronoun *some* stands alone.)

Modifying adjective: Popeye would like *some* spinach. (The adjective *some* modifies *spinach*.)

Another group of indefinite pronouns is made up of compounds of *any*, *every*, *no*, and *some* followed by *-body*, *-one*, and *-thing*:

	-body	-one	-thing
any	anybody	anyone	anything
every	everybody	everyone	everything
no	nobody	no one*	nothing
some	somebody	someone	something

Demonstrative Pronouns

Demonstrative pronouns are a group of four pronouns: *this*, *that*, *these*, and *those*. As with indefinite pronouns, these same words are often used as modifying adjectives. Again, the difference is that pronouns stand alone; adjectives modify nouns:

Demonstrative pronoun: Popeye would like *that*. (The pronoun *that* stands alone.)

Modifying adjective: Popeye would like *that* spinach. (The adjective *that* modifies *spinach*.)

* Note the spelling of the compound *no one*. All the others are written without a space.

Conjunctions

Conjunctions are words used to join (or conjoin—*conjunction*, get it?) words or groups of words. There are two fundamentally different types of conjunctions: **coordinating conjunctions** and **subordinating conjunctions.** Coordinating conjunctions are words like *and*, *but*, and *or* that join words or groups of words of equal status. Subordinating conjunctions join groups of words of unequal status. We will deal with subordinating conjunctions in Chapter 3 when we see how dependent clauses are built. For now, we will deal only with coordinating conjunctions.

There are seven single-word conjunctions. A helpful acronym for remembering them is FANBOYS:

For
And
Nor
But
Or
Yet
So

Here are some examples using coordinating conjunctions to join single words (the joined words are underlined):

Tarzan loves coconuts *and* bananas.
Jane wanted coconuts *or* bananas.
Tarzan's parents were poor *but* honest.

Here are examples using the remaining coordinating conjunctions to join groups of words (the joined groups of words are underlined):

Jane and Tarzan are in love, *yet* they still can't agree on their china pattern.
It was my turn to cook, *so* we had something simple.
We turned back, *for* it was getting dark.
I didn't want to leave, *nor* did anybody else.

There is a subgroup of coordinating conjunctions called **correlative conjunctions**. Correlative conjunctions are two-part conjunctions, for example, *both . . . and*; *either . . . or*; *neither . . . nor*; *not only . . . but also.* Here are some examples:

They had *both* cake *and* pie for dessert.
I had to *either* exercise more *or* eat less.
Not only was it a stupid movie, *but* it *also* lasted three hours.

Prepositions

Prepositions are "little words" such as *by*, *to*, *with*, *about*, *over*, etc. They are used to make **prepositional phrases**. Prepositional phrases consist of a preposition plus its object, which can be either a noun (with or without adjective modifiers) or a pronoun. Here are some examples of prepositional phrases (prepositions in italics, objects in bold):

in the **morning**
under the **bridge**
by **Shakespeare**
to **them**

Prepositions are part of a package deal. They are always bound together with their objects to form prepositional phrases. It is impossible to identify prepositions at the single-word, part-of-speech level in isolation from the rest of their package. Accordingly, we will postpone any further discussion of prepositional phrases until Chapter 2, where we will look at phrases in general and prepositional phrases in particular.

2

Basic Phrases

Phrases are grammatical building blocks (typically, but not always, multiword constructions) that act as a single part of speech unit. (As you will see, this definition of *phrase* differs a little from the definition of a phrase in traditional grammar.) In this chapter, we will examine four types of phrases: **noun phrases, appositive phrases, verb phrases**, and **prepositional phrases.**

All phrases contain a **head** that determines the nature of the phrase. The head of a noun phrase is a noun; the head of an appositive phrase is an appositive; the head of a verb phrase is a verb; and the head of a prepositional phrase is (surprise!) a preposition.

Noun Phrases

The term *noun phrase* is not widely used in traditional grammar. However, the distinction between a noun and a noun phrase is quite clearly made in traditional grammar, though in different terminology: **simple subject** and **complete subject**. A simple subject in traditional grammar corresponds to a head noun in modern grammar, and a complete subject corresponds to a noun phrase.

Traditional Grammar		Modern Grammar
simple subject	=	head noun
complete subject	=	noun phrase

In the examples that follow, the head (simple subject) is in italics and the noun phrase (complete subject) is underlined:

The well-dressed young *woman* glanced in the mirror.
The sleek new *car* in the driveway belongs to my grandmother.
The chilly November *rains* never seemed to let up.

Appositive Phrases

An **appositive phrase** is a phrase headed by an **appositive**. An appositive is a noun that follows another noun or pronoun to identify or explain it. Here is an example of a sentence containing an appositive (in italics):

She is going out with Richard, *a guy in her exercise class.*

The appositive is used to give information that helps identify who Richard is.

Appositive phrases are essentially special-purpose noun phrases. The appositive is the head noun, and the rest of the appositive phrase consists of modifiers of the noun, adjectives in front of the appositive noun, and modifying prepositional phrases following the appositive noun. Here are some examples with the appositive phrases in italics and the appositive heads in bold:

Atolls, *small coral* ***islands***, cover shallow tropical waters.
His car, *a hulking* ***SUV***, costs a fortune to fill up and rides like a tank.
The police went to his last address, *an old* ***hotel*** *in Denver*.

Notice that all the appositive phrases are set off from the rest of their sentences by commas: a pair of commas if the appositive phrase is in the middle of a sentence or a single comma if the appositive phrase is at the end of the sentence (as in the last example).

If the appositive phrase follows the subject noun phrase, we can move the appositive phrase to the beginning of the sentence. Appositive phrases moved out of their normal position following the noun phrase are sometimes called **inverted appositives**. Following is an example of a sentence containing an appositive phrase (in italics) that can be inverted:

Normal order: Emma, *the only child in the class with no cavities,* smiled proudly.
Inverted order: *The only child in the class with no cavities,* Emma smiled proudly.

There is one situation in which it is normal to invert the appositive phrase: when the subject noun phrase is a pronoun. Here are two examples (appositive phrases in italics):

A hopeless romantic, I always want movies to have a happy ending.
Always a sucker for a smile, he gave in to his daughter's request.

If we were to leave the inverted appositive phrases in their normal position following the nouns they explain, the results might or might not be grammatical, but they would certainly be odd:

? I, *a hopeless romantic,* always want movies to have a happy ending.
? He, *always a sucker for a smile,* gave in to his daughter's request.

The **?** at the beginning of a sentence indicates that the sentence is only marginally grammatical.

Essential and Nonessential Appositive Phrases

Up to this point, all the appositive phrases we have examined have been **nonessential.** Nonessential appositive phrases are not required to define the noun phrase they follow. That is, we can delete the appositive phrases and still be left with a meaningful noun phrase. For example, in the following sentence

Noel Coward wrote *Private Lives, his best-known play,* in 1930.

the appositive phrase *his best-known play* can be deleted without affecting the basic identity of the noun it follows:

Noel Coward wrote *Private Lives* in 1930.

Private Lives would still have been written by Noel Coward in 1930 even if we were not told that it is his best-known play. Even if the play were to be largely forgotten, it still would have been written by Noel Coward in 1930. Compare this example of a sentence containing a nonessential appositive with the following sentence, which contains an essential appositive:

My friend *Tim* works in the city.

Presumably, the writer of this sentence has more than one friend, so when we delete the appositive phrase *Tim*, we lose information critical to establishing the meaning of the noun phrase *my friend*:

My friend works in the city.

We have no idea which of the writer's friends works in the city.

The distinction between essential and nonessential appositive phrases is not so much a grammatical distinction as a judgment about what we can reasonably expect the reader to know. For example, compare the following sentences:

Nonessential: Homer, *the Greek poet*, was blind.
Essential: The Greek poet *Homer* was blind.

In the first sentence, the appositive phrase *the Greek poet* is nonessential because we can reasonably assume that everyone who can read without moving their lips knows who Homer was. The reader does not need the information in the appositive phrase to identify Homer. In the second sentence, on the other hand, the appositive phrase *Homer* is essential because the reader would not have any way of knowing *which* Greek poet the sentence was about:

? The Greek poet was blind.

A simple and reliable way to test whether an appositive phrase is essential or nonessential is to delete the appositive and see the effect on the noun phrase preceding the appositive phrase. If that noun phrase is still meaningful, then the appositive phrase is nonessential. If the meaning of that noun phrase is now inappropriately ambiguous, then the appositive phrase is essential.

Essential and nonessential appositive phrases are always distinguishable by their punctuation. Essential appositive phrases are *never* set off with commas. Nonessential phrases are *always* set off with commas.

Verb Phrases

A **verb phrase** is a phrase headed by a verb. The distinction between a verb head and verb phrase is quite clearly made in traditional grammar, though in different terminology: **simple predicate** and **complete predicate**. A simple predicate in traditional grammar is a verb head, and a complete predicate is a verb phrase.

Traditional Grammar		Modern Grammar
simple predicate	=	verb head
complete predicate	=	verb phrase

In the examples that follow, the verb head (simple predicate) is in italics and the verb phrase (complete predicate) is underlined:

The well-dressed young woman *glanced* in the mirror.
The sleek new car in the driveway *belongs* to my grandmother.
The chilly November rains never *seemed* to let up.

Most verb phrases consist of a verb head together with that verb's **complement**. A complement is whatever is required by a particular verb to make a complete sentence. For example, here is a sentence with the verb in italics and the complement in bold:

A truck driver *saw* **the accident**.

If we delete the complement, we get either a totally ungrammatical sentence or a new, unrelated sentence that does not mean the same thing as the original:

X The truck driver *saw*.

In other words, when we use the verb *see* with the meaning of "to observe," we need to express what it was that the subject saw.

As you recall from Chapter 1, the traditional definition of *verb* is "a word used to express action or describe a state of being." As the definition implies, there are two different types of verbs: **action verbs** and **linking verbs** that describe the subjects. Here are the examples from Chapter 1:

Action Verbs	**Linking Verbs**
Donald *laughed*.	Donald *is* funny.
Jane *wrote* a novel.	The novel *became* a bestseller.
Erma *made* some soup.	The soup *smelled* wonderful.

The terms *action* and *linking* are not very transparent. Part of the problem is with the term *action*. Certainly many action verbs express action. In the first example, Donald engaged in the action of laughing. In the second example, Jane engaged in the action of writing a novel. In the third example, Erma engaged in the action of making soup. So far, so good. However, many action verbs do not express action in any normal sense of the word. Here are some examples of actionless action verbs:

Fred *has* a new car.
Pat *forgot* his keys.
The garden *swarmed* with bees. (A classic example from a nineteenth-century grammarian.)

In the first example, Fred is not engaging in any overt action. The verb *has* seems to describe what Fred owns or possesses rather than tell us what Fred does. Compare that sentence with this sentence: *Fred bought a new car*. Here, Fred is clearly engaged in the action of buying. In the second example, the meaning of *forgot* is almost the opposite of any kind of action. Poor Pat didn't engage in the action of bringing his keys. In the third sentence, the garden is not engaged in the action of swarming—the bees are. The garden is not doing anything at all, yet this is still an action verb.

The problem these examples illustrate is that there is no good way to define the class of action verbs by meaning alone. Because action verbs constitute such a large and diverse class (99.9 percent of all verbs), it is impossible to find a single defining characteristic that will hold equally well for all action verbs.

The only really accurate definition is a negative one: action verbs are those verbs that are not linking verbs. Beginning with linking verbs works because the class of linking verbs is very small and has certain distinguishing characteristics, making it relatively easy to define. So, we will begin with linking verbs and then turn to action verbs.

Linking Verbs and Their Complements

The term *linking* refers to the relation between the complement of the linking verb and the subject. In linking verb sentences, the verb "links" the complement back to the subject. In other words, the complement must give some information about or description of the subject. Here are the three examples of linking verb sentences again:

Donald *is* funny.
The novel *became* a bestseller.
The soup *smelled* wonderful.

In the first example, the predicate adjective *funny* describes Donald's personality. In the second example, the noun phrase *a bestseller* tells us something about the success of the novel. In the third example, the predicate adjective *wonderful* tells us something about the nature of the soup.

Sometimes linking verbs are compared to equal signs. That is, we can replace the linking verbs with equal signs:

Donald = funny
the novel = a bestseller
the soup = wonderful

While the analogy of linking verbs to equal signs is not perfect, it does convey a sense of the special relationship between the complement and the subject in sentences with linking verbs. This relationship is completely absent in action verbs.

The complements of linking verbs are collectively called **subject complements**. The term *subject complement* comes from the fact that the complements of linking verbs must refer back to and describe the subjects. Two common subject complements are adjectives (called **predicate adjectives**) and noun phrases (called **predicate nominatives**). Here are examples of sentences that illustrate each type of subject complement (subject complements in italics):

Predicate adjective: Olive Oyl sounded *happy.*
Predicate nominative: Bluto is *a bully.*

Linking verbs have a unique grammatical feature that distinguishes them from all action verbs: only linking verbs can have predicate adjectives as complements.

If a verb can be used with a predicate adjective complement, then we know for certain that the verb is a linking verb. This extremely useful fact gives us a simple way to distinguish linking verbs from action verbs. If a verb can take a predicate adjective as a complement, then it must be a linking verb.

Linking verbs can also be followed by noun phrases. But even here, predicate nominatives, the type of noun phrase that follows a linking verb, are functionally different from the type of noun phrase that follows an action verb. Here is a pair of examples:

Linking verb: Alice *became* a successful writer.
Action verb: Alice *met* a successful writer.

The same noun phrase *a successful writer* follows the verbs in the two examples, so how can the complements be different? The complements are completely different in their relationship to their subjects. In the linking verb example, the predicate nominative *a successful writer* and the subject *Alice* must be one and the same person:

Alice = a successful writer

In the action verb example, the object *a successful writer* and the subject *Alice* cannot be the same person:

Alice ≠ a successful writer

By definition, predicate nominatives have two distinctive characteristics:

1. They are always complements of linking verbs.
2. They must identify or rename the subject—i.e., they must refer to the same person or thing as the subject.

There are only a handful of verbs that can be used as linking verbs. By far the most common is the verb *be*. Because the verb *be* is the most wildly irregular verb in English, it might be helpful to review its various forms:

FORMS OF *BE*

Present Tense

	Singular	Plural
first person	I *am*	we *are*
second person	you *are*	you *are*
third person	he/she/it *is*	they *are*

Past Tense

	Singular	Plural
first person	I *was*	we *were*
second person	you *were*	you *were*
third person	he/she/it *was*	they *were*

Future Tense

all persons and numbers	*will be*
present participle	*being*
past participle	*been*

Many common linking verbs are verbs of appearance or sense perception, for example:

Sight:	They *appeared* angry about something.
	Larry *looked* pleased with himself.
	Sam-I-am *seemed* a little sad today.
Sound:	The tenor *sounded* flat to me.
	The note *rang* true.

Smell: Some tropical fruit *smells* absolutely dreadful.
Taste: The fruitcake *tasted* stale.

The remaining common linking verbs describe the nature or condition of the subject, for example:

The cook always *gets* upset when someone complains about the food.
The kittens soon *grew* strong.
The patient *remained* weak.
Tarzan *stayed* angry about the incident with the coconuts.
The explorer *became* faint with hunger.
I *feel* terrific.
His face *turned* bright red.

Although all the verbs used in the preceding examples are linking verbs, some can also be used as action verbs. When they are used as action verbs, their meanings are completely different from when they are used as linking verbs. Here is an example using the verb *feel*:

A verb can act as linking or action verb depending on the context

Linking verb: The detective *felt* sick.
Action verb: The detective *felt* the victim's body for the missing gun.

In the first example, the linking verb *felt* is used to describe the detective. In the second example, the action verb *felt* tells us what the detective did: he or she engaged in the action of searching the body.

Notice also that the linking verb is followed by the predicate adjective *sick*, while the action verb is followed by an ordinary noun phrase object *the victim's body*. The noun phrase *the victim's body* cannot be a predicate nominative because it does not refer back to *detective*:

detective ≠ the victim's body

Action Verbs and Their Complements

Traditional grammar has a well-established terminology for the more common complements used with action verbs. Action verbs that have complements are called **transitive verbs.** Action verbs that have no complements are called **intransitive verbs.**

The distinction between transitive and intransitive verbs is widely recognized. For example, when you look up an action verb in the dictionary, you will find the following symbols right after the entry: *vt* or *vi.* The *vt* stands for *transitive verb*; the *vi* stands for *intransitive verb*. The only trouble with the terms is that it is easy to forget which is which. It may help to know that the terms come from the Latin preposition *trans*, which means "across." *Trans* also appears in the English words *transportation* and *transit.* A transitive verb "goes across" to its object. An intransitive verb does not "go across" because it does not have any object to go to.

Here are some examples of intransitive verbs (verbs in italics):

Sam *snores.*
Sally *sneezed.*
The children *snickered.*
All of the flowers *wilted* in the sun.

Notice the last example. *In the sun* is an optional adverb prepositional phrase. Because *in the sun* is not required by the verb to make a complete sentence, it cannot be a complement. Intransitive verbs can be followed by any number of optional adverbs.

We will now turn to a discussion of the various types of complements that transitive verbs can be used with.

Objects. By far the most frequent complement of a transitive verb is a noun phrase. (Recall that the term *noun phrase* is a collective term covering single nouns, nouns and their modifiers, and pronouns.) The noun phrase complement of an action verb is called an **object.** (The term **direct object** is also sometimes used. The two terms, *object* and *direct object*, are used interchangeably in most contexts.)

Here are some examples of transitive verbs with objects (transitive verbs in italics, objects in bold):

Simple Simon *met* **a pie-man,** going to the fair.
Simple Simon *bought* **a pie.**

Simple Simon really *liked* **it.**
Unfortunately, Simple Simon didn't *have* **any money to pay for it.**

Indirect and Direct Objects. A small but important subgroup of transitive verbs has not one but *two* objects. For these verbs, it is necessary to distinguish between an **indirect object** (abbreviated as **IO**) and a **direct object** (abbreviated as **DO**). When there are two objects, the indirect object always occurs before the direct object. Here are some examples with both object noun phrases underlined and labeled:

Sally gave the boss (IO) her report (DO).

John got the kids (IO) some pizza (DO).

When a sentence contains only a single object (as is the case with most transitive verbs), that object can also be called a *direct object.* However, an indirect object can never be used as the sole object in a sentence. That is, we can only have an indirect object when there is also a direct object.

Sentences with indirect objects have a somewhat peculiar feature that makes indirect objects (relatively) easy to identify.

The *to/for* Test for Indirect Objects

An indirect object can be turned into a prepositional phrase beginning with either *to* or *for* (depending on the verb). That prepositional phrase is then moved after the direct object.

Here is the *to/for* test applied to the two preceding example sentences:

Sally gave the boss (IO) her report (DO).
***to/for* test:** Sally gave her report *to* the boss.

IO DO
John got the kids some pizza.
***to/for* test:** John got some pizza *for* the kids.

Notice that in both examples two things have happened: (1) the two noun phrase objects have switched places: what was the indirect object now follows the original direct object; and (2) the preposition *to* or *for* has been inserted in between the two reversed noun phrases.

Objects and Object Complements. A few action verbs can have an **object** and an **object complement**. An object complement is a noun or descriptive adjective that follows an object and refers back to that object. Here are some examples:

Noun as object complement (object complements in italics, objects in bold)
Sally considered **John** *a fool.* (a fool = John)
The board named **him** *the new vice president for sales.* (the new vice president for sales = him)
They elected **Elaine** *treasurer.* (Elaine = treasurer)

Descriptive adjective as object complement (object complements in italics, objects in bold)
Keep the **room** *clean.* (*Clean* refers to *room.*)
They painted the **house** *white.* (*White* refers to *house.*)
The jury believed **him** *innocent.* (*Innocent* refers to *him.*)

Summary of Verb Complements in Traditional Grammar. Here is a summary, with examples, of the seven types of complements recognized in traditional grammar. There are two complement types used with linking verbs and five complement types with action verbs (counting the option of having no complement as one of the possibilities). The verbs are in italics, and complements are in bold:

Linking Verbs

Subject Complements:

1. **Predicate nominative** (a noun phrase that must refer back to the subject)

   Butch *became* **a football coach.**

2. **Predicate adjective** (a descriptive adjective that must refer back to the subject)

   Butch *was* **aggressive.**

Action Verb Complements:

3. No complement (an intransitive verb)

   Rudolph *smiled.*

4. **Object or direct object** (a single noun phrase)

   Santa *fed* **the reindeer.**

5. **Indirect and direct object** (two noun phrases)

   IO DO

   Santa *gave* **Rudolph a carrot.**

6. **Object and noun phrase (NP) object complement** (two noun phrases that must refer to the same person or thing)

   object NP object complement

   The committee *named* **Senator Blather chair.**

7. **Object and adjective object complement** (noun phrase object and an adjective that must refer back to that object)

   object adj. object complement

   The committee *believed* **Senator Blather capable.**

Prepositional Phrases

A **prepositional phrase** consists of a preposition head followed by a noun phrase object. Here is a way to represent the structure of a prepositional phrase:

prepositional phrase = preposition + noun phrase

The noun head inside the object noun phrase is called the **object of the preposition**. Here are several examples with the prepositions in italics and the object of the preposition in bold:

by the ***way***
after the ***meeting***
since this ***afternoon***
from ***you***

Here is a list of fifty common single-word prepositions:

about	but	over
above	by	past
across	concerning	since
after	down	through
against	during	throughout
along	except	till
among	for	to
around	from	toward
as	in	under
at	inside	underneath
before	into	until
behind	like	up
below	near	upon
beneath	of	with
beside	off	within
between	on	without
beyond	out	

In addition to the preceding list of common single-word prepositions, there are many multiple-word prepositions sometimes called **compound** or **phrasal prepositions**. Here are some examples of multiple-word prepositions with objects (prepositions in italics):

as of today
in addition to the assignment
next to me
in spite of your concerns
because of the budget
aside from all that
in place of Alice
on account of bad weather
in case of accident
on behalf of my friends

For the remainder of the chapter, we will concentrate on how prepositional phrases are used. In traditional grammar, prepositional phrases are always modifiers; that is, they are used as adjectives or as adverbs. Prepositional phrases used as adjectives modify nouns. Prepositional phrases used as adverbs modify verbs, predicate adjectives, or (occasionally) other adverbs.

Prepositional Phrases Used as Adjectives

We will call prepositional phrases used as adjectives **adjective prepositional phrases**. Adjective prepositional phrases can only be used to modify nouns. Here are two examples of adjective prepositional phrases (in italics) used to modify nouns (in bold):

The **book** *on the top shelf* needs to go back to the library tomorrow.
I hated the muggy **summers** *in Florida.*

You recall that, by definition, a noun phrase consists of a noun head together with *all* of its modifiers. When a prepositional phrase modifies a noun, then that prepositional phrase must also be part of the noun phrase that it modifies.

The following diagram shows how noun phrases are built with adjectives in front of the noun and prepositional phrases after the noun. The parentheses around *adjectives* and *adjective prepositional phrases* mean that they are optional. That is, a noun phrase must have a noun, but adjectives and prepositional phrases are optional.

(adjectives) + noun + (adjective prepositional phrases)
noun phrase

Because adjective prepositional phrases are part of the noun phrase, adjective prepositional phrases will also be scooped up and replaced along with the head noun by the third-person pronoun test. Here is the third-person pronoun test for noun phrases specifically tailored for prepositional phrases used as adjectives:

The Third-Person Pronoun Test for Adjective Prepositional Phrases

If a noun *and* a following prepositional phrase *together* can be replaced by a single third-person pronoun, then that prepositional phrase must be a modifier of that noun.

Here is the third-person pronoun test applied to the two earlier example sentences:

The **book** *on the top shelf* needs to go back to the library tomorrow.
It needs to go back to the library tomorrow.

I hated the muggy **summers** *in Florida*.
I hated them.

Here is a somewhat more complicated example that shows how useful the third-person pronoun test is for identifying adjective prepositional phrases:

We should eat the apples in the refrigerator first.

What is slightly tricky about this example is the word *first*. Is *first* part of the prepositional phrase or not? When we apply the third-person pronoun test, we can see that *first* is not part of the prepositional phrase because it is not replaced by the third-person pronoun *them*:

We should eat the apples in the refrigerator first.
We should eat them first.

Adjective Prepositional Phrases and Subject-Verb Agreement Errors. The ability to recognize adjective prepositional phrases modifying the subject noun is especially important in spotting and correcting a common source of subject-verb agreement errors. Here is an example:

X A group of middle-management leaders are to directly supervise employees.

The writer has erroneously made the verb (*are*) plural to agree with the nearest noun, *leaders*. This error occurred in part because the writer did not recognize that *leaders* is locked up inside the adjective prepositional phrase *of middle-management leaders*. *Leaders* is the object of the preposition *of* and as such cannot serve as the subject of a verb. The actual subject, of course, is the noun *group*, which is singular. Here is the third-person pronoun test applied to the corrected sentence:

A group of middle-management leaders *is* to directly supervise employees.
It *is* to directly supervise employees.

The third-person pronoun test makes it easy to see that the verb must be singular to agree with the third-person pronoun *it*. Learning to spot adjective prepositional phrases used to modify subjects is an important step in eliminating subject-verb agreement errors.

Prepositional Phrases Used as Adverbs

We will call prepositional phrases used as adverbs **adverb prepositional phrases**. Adverb prepositional phrases modify verbs, predicate adjectives, and other adverbs. Adverb prepositional phrases behave very much like ordinary, single-word adverbs. Nearly everything that we said about identifying single-word adverbs also applies to adverb prepositional phrases.

Adverb Prepositional Phrases Used to Modify Verbs. This is by far the most common use of adverb prepositional phrases. Here is the adverb movement test for adverbs adapted to adverb prepositional phrases:

> **The Adverb Movement Test for Adverb Prepositional Phrases**
>
> **If a prepositional phrase can be moved to a different position in the sentence, then that prepositional phrase is an adverb that modifies the verb.**

Following are some examples of sentences containing adverb prepositional phrases (in italics) that modify the verb with the adverb movement test applied:

They have classes in accounting *at our local community college.*
At our local community college, they have classes in accounting.

We all went to a movie *after dinner*.
After dinner, we all went to a movie.

The kids quit playing early *because of the heat*.
Because of the heat, the kids quit playing early.

Notice the use of commas in these three examples. When single-word adverbs or adverb prepositional phrases have been moved to the beginning of the sentence, we can set them off with commas. This use of commas with introductory elements is not strictly required. The general rule of thumb is to use commas with long and/or complicated introductory elements. However, it is never wrong to use the comma, and it is always helpful to the reader to do so. Therefore, we strongly recommend that you routinely use the comma with introductory elements, especially with adverb prepositional phrases.

Adverb Prepositional Phrases Used to Modify Predicate Adjectives. Predicate adjectives are often modified by adverb prepositional phrases. Here are some examples with the adverb prepositional phrases in italics and the predicate adjectives in bold:

He is **unlucky** *at love.*
I am **happy** *with my current job.*
We are all **ready** *for dinner.*
They were **wise** *beyond their years.*

Adverb prepositional phrases that modify predicate adjectives are easy to recognize. They cannot be mistaken for adjective prepositional phrases because there are no nouns for them to modify. They can't be mistaken for verb modifiers because they cannot be moved without sounding unnatural or odd. If they are moved, we would know what was meant, but we would just never say it that way:

? *At love*, he is unlucky.
? *With my current job*, I am happy.
? *For dinner*, we are all ready.
? *Beyond their years*, they were wise.

Adverb Prepositional Phrases Used to Modify Other Adverbs. Adverbs are sometimes modified by adverb prepositional phrases. Here are some examples with the adverb prepositional phrases in italics and the adverbs being modified in bold:

We got there **late** *in the evening.*
Our team scored **early** *in the first quarter.*

As you can see, this construction is limited. We can distinguish adverb prepositional phrases that modify adverbs from the much more common adverb prepositional phrases that modify verbs by the fact that the ones that modify adverbs cannot be moved without sounding unnatural:

? *In the evening*, we got there late.
? *In the first quarter*, our team scored early.

Again, we would probably understand what was meant by these sentences, but we would not normally say it that way.

3

Sentences and Clauses

Sentences

Sentences are the only groups of words that can stand alone to express complete thoughts. The key idea here is standing alone. Sentences are not dependent on some previous context or question to fill in grammatically significant missing pieces. For example, the following is a sentence because it can stand alone as a grammatically complete unit:

I would like a pizza with anchovies and pineapple.

We must be careful to distinguish sentences from **fragments**, which are only pieces of sentences. The problem is that, in context, fragments can be perfectly meaningful and grammatical. However, their meaningfulness and grammaticality is not their own. It is borrowed from other sentences. Here is an example of such a fragment in a dialogue:

Waiter: What would you like?
Customer: A pizza with anchovies and pineapple.

What the customer said is a fragment. The fragment makes sense only in the context of the dialogue. The fragment is a piece of telegraphic shorthand that borrows the rest of its meaning and grammar from the waiter's question. What the customer is really saying is this:

[I would like] a pizza with anchovies and pineapple.

Sentences never need to borrow from surrounding sentences to be grammatically complete.

Sentences also have a distinctive structure: they contain both a subject noun phrase and a verb phrase (or predicate, in traditional terms). In the example sentence just given, there is a subject noun phrase (NP) and a verb phrase:

subject NP · verb phrase

I would like a pizza with anchovies and pineapple.

The fragment *a pizza with anchovies and pineapple* lacks both a subject and a complete verb phrase.

Sentences Classified by Purpose

Sentences are used in four different ways. Up to this point, we have only looked at sentences used to make statements. But there are other ways to use sentences, for example, to ask questions, to issue commands, or to make exclamations. We will now examine in turn each of the four possible uses.

Declarative Sentences. Declarative sentences are used for making statements. Declarative sentences are always punctuated with periods. Here are some examples:

This is a declarative sentence.
Declarative sentences can be positive or negative.
Even if they contain dependent clauses, declarative sentences are always punctuated with a period.

Interrogative Sentences. Interrogative sentences are used for asking questions. Interrogative sentences must be punctuated with question marks. Here are some examples:

Do you know what an interrogative sentence is?
No, what are they?
Why did you ask?

Imperative Sentences. Imperative sentences are used to issue commands. Imperative sentences are not defined by their punctuation but by their grammar. Imperative sentences must have an understood *you* as the subject. They may be punctuated with either periods or exclamation points. Here are some examples:

Go away.
Cut it out!
Stop it.

Each of these examples has an implied *you* as the subject:

You go away.
You cut it out!
You stop it.

Exclamatory Sentences. Exclamatory sentences are actually declarative sentences that are punctuated with exclamation points for emphasis. Here are some examples:

I can't believe I ate the whole thing!
This is really an exclamatory sentence!
Sally has no cavities!

Declarative and interrogative sentences are easy to recognize, but imperative and exclamatory sentences can be confusing because both can be punctuated with exclamation points. A mnemonic trick is to remember that exclamatory sentences can only be punctuated with exclamation points. The other thing to remember is that imperatives must have an understood *you* as the subject.

Clauses

A clause can be either of two types of structures:

1. **Independent clause** (or **main clause**), which can stand alone
2. **Dependent clause** (or **subordinate clause**), which is a clause that cannot stand alone and must be attached to or included within an independent clause

To cut down on terminological clutter, we will not use the redundant terms *main* and *subordinate* from now on. Instead, we will use only *independent* and *dependent*.

A sentence must contain at least one independent clause, but, in addition, a sentence may also contain one or more dependent clauses. We can think of a sentence as having this formula:

sentence = independent clause + (dependent clauses)

The parentheses around *dependent clauses* indicate that dependent clauses are optional.

Here is an example of a sentence containing a dependent clause (in italics) modifying the independent clause:

Louise takes her lunch *whenever she has to attend a noon presentation.*

The clause *whenever she has to attend a noon presentation* is an adverb clause that modifies the verb *takes.*

The independent clause can stand alone as a complete sentence, but the dependent clause cannot:

Independent clause:		Louise takes her lunch.
Dependent clause:	X	Whenever she has to attend a noon presentation.

Despite differences in their ability to stand alone, clauses (both independent and dependent) are set apart from all other grammatical structures by one key characteristic: clauses must have subject-verb agreement. Here are the subjects (in bold) and the verbs (in italics) from the preceding example:

Independent clause:		**Louise** *takes* her lunch.
Dependent clause:	X	Whenever **she** *has* to attend a noon presentation.

In the independent clause, the verb *takes* agrees with its subject *Louise*, and in the dependent clause, the verb *has* agrees with its subject *she*.

Most of the remainder of this chapter will focus on dependent clauses.

There are three different types of dependent clauses: **adverb clauses, adjective clauses**, and **noun clauses**. As you can probably deduce from their names, each of the three types of dependent clauses acts as a single part of speech. Adverb clauses do what adverbs always do: they modify verbs, adjectives, and other adverbs. Adjective clauses modify nouns (and, once in a great while, pronouns). Noun clauses play the basic roles that noun phrases play: they act as subjects, objects, and predicate nominatives.

All dependent clauses have the same basic structure. They all begin with special introductory "flag" words that signal the fact that the following clauses are dependent clauses, not freestanding independent clauses. These special flag words have different names according to the type of dependent clause they introduce. (Noun clauses are unique in that they have not just one but two types of flag words.) Here are examples of each type (introductory flag words underlined, dependent clauses in italics):

Type of Dependent Clause	Term for Introductory Flag Word	Example
Adverb clause	Subordinating conjunction	*Whenever it rains,* our creek runs over.
Adjective clause	Relative pronoun	The creek *that runs by our house* floods.
Noun clause	*That* type	The problem is *that our creek floods.*
	Wh- type	We saw *what the flooded creek did.*

We will now look at each of the three types of dependent clauses in detail.

Adverb Clauses

Adverb clauses must begin with a **subordinating conjunction**. As an overview, here are examples of adverb clauses in the three roles that they can play: modifying verbs, adjectives, and other adverbs. The adverb clauses are in italics, and the subordinating conjunctions are in bold:

Modifying verbs:	I ordered a whole pizza ***because*** *I had skipped lunch.*
	Give me a call ***if*** *I can help you.*
Modifying adjectives:	I am sorry ***that*** *we missed you last night.*
	The movie was even worse ***than*** *I had feared.*
Modifying other adverbs:	I answered more sharply ***than*** *I had intended.*
	We did better ***than*** *we thought we would.*

Adverb Clauses That Modify Verbs. Adverb clauses that modify verbs are by far the most common type of adverb clause. This type of adverb clause also has the largest number of subordinating conjunctions. While each individual subordinating conjunction has its own specific meaning, it is possible to group them by broad categories. Here is a list of the more common subordinating conjunctions classified by meaning (note that many subordinating conjunctions are compounded of more than one word):

Time

after
as
as soon as
before
even after
even before
since (meaning "from when")
until

when
whenever
while

Place
everyplace
everywhere
where
wherever

Manner
as
as if
as though

Cause
as
because
inasmuch as
since
so that

Condition
if
on condition that
provided that
unless

Concession
although
even though
though

Following are some examples of adverb clauses illustrating the different categories of subordinating conjunctions (adverb clauses in italics, subordinating conjunctions in bold):

Time:	I had finished my popcorn ***before*** *the movie even started.*
	The theater gets really quiet ***when*** *the movie starts.*
Place:	We found broken glass ***where*** *the accident had occurred.*
	The lamb followed Mary ***everywhere*** *she went.*
Manner:	They talked about us ***as if*** *we were not even there.*
	I parked the car ***as though*** *nothing had happened.*
Cause:	Sue needs the key ***because*** *she has to lock up tonight.*
	We left the game early ***since*** *it was getting pretty one-sided.*
Condition:	I wouldn't do that ***if*** *I were you.*
	Fred will go to the meeting ***unless*** *you want to go yourself.*
Concession:	Fred went to the meeting, ***although*** *he didn't want to.*
	We went to dinner, ***even though*** *none of us were very hungry.*

For the most part, we do not use a comma before adverb clauses. The three subordinating conjunctions of concession—*although*, *even though*, and *though*—are exceptions to this rule. Adverb clauses beginning with these words are always set off with commas. (The use of the comma probably reflects the fact that the clauses following these subordinating conjunctions are contrary to what we might expect to follow from the meaning of the independent clause.)

Adverb clauses that modify verbs behave very much like single-word adverbs. As you recall, one of the easiest tests for single-word adverbs that modify verbs is the adverb movement test, here slightly modified to apply to adverb clauses:

The Adverb Clause Movement Test

If a clause can be moved to the beginning of the sentence, then that clause is an adverb that modifies the verb.

Here is the adverb clause movement test applied to the preceding examples of adverb clauses. Note that with the exception of adverb clauses that employ subordinating conjunctions of manner—*as*, *as if*, and *as though*—the adverb clause movement test is highly reliable:

Time:		***Before** the movie even started*, I had finished my popcorn.
		***When** the movie starts*, the theater gets really quiet.
Place:		***Where** the accident had occurred*, we found broken glass.
		***Everywhere** she went*, the lamb followed Mary.
Manner:	X	***As if** we were not even there*, they talked about us.
	?	***As though** nothing had happened*, I parked the car.
Cause:		***Because** she has to lock up tonight*, Sue needs the key.
		***Since** it was getting pretty one-sided*, we left the game early.
Condition:		***If** I were you*, I wouldn't do that.
		***Unless** you want to go yourself*, Fred will go to the meeting.
Concession:		***Although** he didn't want to*, Fred went to the meeting.
		***Even though** none of us were very hungry*, we went to dinner.

Also note that when adverb clauses are moved to the first position of the sentence, they are *always* followed by commas. This use of the comma is obligatory. According to a large study of college writing, leaving off the comma after an introductory adverb clause is the single most common punctuation error among college students.

Adverb Clauses That Modify Adjectives. Adverb clauses can only modify predicate adjectives, not adjectives used to modify following nouns. As you may recall, predicate adjectives follow linking verbs. For example, in the sentence *Sally was sad*, *sad* is a predicate adjective following the linking verb *was*. Adjectives used to modify following nouns cannot themselves be modified by adverb clauses. In the sentence *Sally sang a sad song*, *sad* is not a predicate adjective. *Sad* modifies the following noun *song*. There are two slightly different patterns depending on the form of the predicate adjective being modified. If the predicate adjective is not in its comparative form (that is, if it is in what is technically called its **base** form), then the conjunctive adverb is *that*. If the predicate adjective is in its comparative form, then the conjunctive adverb is *than*. Here are some examples of both patterns (adverb clauses in italics, predicate adjectives in bold):

Base-form predicate adjective + (*that*) + independent clause
We were **glad** *(that) you could come.*
I am **afraid** *(that) it might rain this afternoon.*
Harvard was **certain** *(that) it could beat Oklahoma in football.*

As the parentheses around *that* indicate, we can drop the conjunctive adverb *that* from the adverb clause. In most situations, dropping the flag word from any dependent clause is rather unusual. Dropping the *that* makes it somewhat harder to recognize the adverb clause for what it is since the normal subordinating conjunction flag word is missing. Nevertheless, dropping the *that* is both grammatical and common. Here are the same example sentences again, this time without the *that*. Notice how normal the sentences seem:

We were **glad** *you could come.*
I am **afraid** *it might rain this afternoon.*
Harvard was **certain** *it could beat Oklahoma in football.*

Comparative-form predicate adjective + *than* + independent clause
It is **later** *than you think it is.*
The dinner was **more formal** *than I had expected it to be.*
The movie was **more frightening** *than the book was.*

Recall from Chapter 1 that comparative adjectives are formed in two ways: with *-er* endings (*soon, sooner; hard, harder*) or with *more* (*beautiful, more beautiful; upset, more upset*). Adverb clauses modify both forms of comparative adjectives equally well.

Adverb Clauses That Modify Other Adverbs. Adverb clauses that modify other adverbs follow exactly the same pattern as adverb clauses that modify comparative adjectives: the adverb being modified must be in its comparative form, and the subordinating conjunction is *than* and cannot be deleted. Here are some examples:

Comparative-form adverbs + *than* + independent clause
I answered **more sharply** *than I had meant to.*
"Star Trek" ships went **faster** *than any had gone before.*
The forest fire spread **more rapidly** *than the crews had anticipated.*

Adjective Clauses

Adjective clauses (also called **relative clauses**) have only a single function: to modify nouns. As with adverb clauses, adjective clauses begin with a distinctive flag word that signals the beginning of the clause. In the case of adjective clauses, the flag words are a special group of pronouns called **relative pronouns**. The list of relative pronouns is mercifully short:

who
whom
whose
that
which

Here are examples of all five relative pronouns (adjective clauses in italics, relative pronouns in bold):

The sportscaster ***who** is on Channel 7* has never picked a winner yet.
She married a man ***whom** she had met at work.*
I contacted the person ***whose** car I bumped into.*

I finally read the book ***that*** *you told me about.*
I finally read the book ***which*** *you told me about.*

Adjective clauses are relatively (pardon the pun) easy to identify for several reasons. First, there are only five relative pronouns to remember. Second, adjective clauses are locked into place immediately following the nouns they modify, so they can hide, but they can't run. Third, as you might expect, the third-person pronoun test provides a powerful tool for identifying adjective clauses.

Here is the third-person pronoun test slightly modified for adjective clauses:

The Third-Person Pronoun Test for Adjective Clauses

If a noun *and* a following clause are *both* replaced by a single third-person pronoun, then that clause must be an adjective clause modifying that noun.

Following is the third-person pronoun test applied to the five examples from above:

The sportscaster ***who*** *is on Channel 7* has never picked a winner yet.
He/She has never picked a winner yet.

She married a man ***whom*** *she had met at work.*
She married him.

I contacted the person ***whose*** *car I bumped into.*
I contacted him/her.

I finally read the book ***that*** *you told me about.*
I finally read it.

I finally read the book ***which*** *you told me about.*
I finally read it.

Adjective clauses are not built the same way that adverb clauses are. In adverb clauses the flag words that introduce adverb clauses are subordinating conjunctions. The subordinating conjunctions are followed by "bound" independent clauses. The subordinating conjunctions are in front of (and outside) the "bound" independent clauses. In adjective clauses, however, the relative pronouns are *inside* (and part of) the "bound" independent clauses. In the first example,

The sportscaster ***who*** *is on Channel 7* has never picked a winner yet.

the relative pronoun *who* is the subject of the verb *is* inside the adjective clause. In the second example,

She married a man ***whom*** *she had met at work.*

the relative pronoun *whom* is the object of the verb *met* inside the adjective clause.

Adjective clauses have one feature that can make them a little more difficult to recognize: under certain circumstances (described a little later) the relative pronoun that begins an adjective clause can be deleted. The role that the relative pronoun plays *inside* the adjective clause governs when a relative pronoun may or may not be deleted.

We can see the differences in roles most easily in the *who-whom-whose* family of relative pronouns:

who = the subject of the adjective clause
whom = an object of the verb or of a preposition in the adjective clause
whose = a possessive pronoun modifying the noun that follows it in the adjective clause

Here are some further examples of the uses of *who-whom-whose* with commentary on the roles of the relative pronouns (relative clauses in italics, relative pronouns in bold):

Who: I met with the real estate agent ***who*** *sold us our house.*
(*Who* is the subject of the verb *sold* in the adjective clause.)
The woman ***who*** *introduced herself* is my sister-in-law.
(*Who* is the subject of the verb *introduced* in the adjective clause.)

Whom: I met with the real estate agent ***whom** you recommended.* (*Whom* is the object of the verb *recommended.*)
The woman ***whom** you asked me about* is my sister-in-law. (*Whom* is the object of the preposition *about.*)

Whose: The umpire motioned to the player ***whose** helmet had come off.* (*Whose* is a possessive modifying the noun *helmet.*)
The driver ***whose** turn was next* drove onto the ramp. (*Whose* is a possessive modifying the noun *turn.*)

The basic rule of relative pronoun deletion is this: only relative pronouns playing the roles of objects can be deleted; relative pronouns playing the other roles of subjects or possessives cannot be deleted.

Here are examples of valid deletion involving *whom*:

Whom: I met with the real estate agent ***whom** you recommended.* (*Whom* is retained.)
I met with the real estate agent *you recommended.* (*Whom* is deleted.)

Whom: The woman ***whom** you asked me about* is my sister-in-law. (*Whom* is retained.)
The woman *you asked me about* is my sister-in-law. (*Whom* is deleted.)

The deletion of *whom* seems perfectly routine. In conversation, we may actually prefer to delete the *whom* because *whom* may sound a little stuffy or overly formal.

Now let's see what happens when we try to delete *who* and *whose*:

Who: I met with the real estate agent ***who** sold us our house.* (*Who* is retained.)
X I met with the real estate agent *sold us our house.* (*Who* is deleted.)
The woman ***who** introduced herself* is my sister-in-law. (*Who* is retained.)
X The woman *introduced herself* is my sister-in-law. (*Who* is deleted.)

Whose: The umpire motioned to the player ***whose*** *helmet had come off.* (*Whose* is retained.)

X The umpire motioned to the player *helmet had come off.* (*Whose* is deleted.)

The driver ***whose*** *turn was next* drove onto the ramp. (*Whose* is retained.)

X The driver *turn was next* drove onto the ramp. (*Whose* is deleted.)

As you can see, the deletion of *who* and *whose* creates completely ungrammatical sentences.

That and *which*, the two remaining relative pronouns, are a little harder to work with because, unlike *who* and *whom*, they do not have endings that tell us whether they are being used as subjects or objects. Nevertheless, they follow the same basic rules about deletion: if they play the role of object, they may be deleted. However, if they play the role of subject, they cannot be deleted. Here are some examples of *that* and *which* playing both roles (adjective clauses in italics, *that* and *which* in bold):

Subject: The car ***that*** *was in the left lane* suddenly put on its brakes.
Barney's car, ***which*** *was in the left lane*, suddenly put on its brakes.

When we attempt to delete *that* and *which*, the results are predictably ungrammatical because *that* and *which* are the subjects of the verb *was*:

X The car *was in the left lane* suddenly put on its brakes.

Object: The car ***that*** *I was driving* got a flat tire.
My son's car, ***which*** *I was driving*, got a flat tire.

As expected, *that* and *which* may be deleted because they are objects of the verb *driving*:

The car *I was driving* got a flat tire.
My son's car *I was driving* got a flat tire.

Restrictive and Nonrestrictive Adjective (Relative) Clauses. Adjective clauses come in two flavors: **restrictive** and **nonrestrictive**. As the name *restrictive* implies, adjectives have the power to restrict or limit the meaning of the nouns they modify. Here is an example from above of an adjective clause used restrictively:

The car ***that*** *I was driving* got a flat tire.

A major part of the function of the adjective clause *that I was driving* is to identify which car got a flat tire—it was the car that I was driving, as opposed to the car that somebody else was driving. Adjective clauses that play this defining or restricting role are called, not surprisingly, restrictive clauses.

Nonrestrictive adjective clauses, conversely, do not have this defining function. Nonrestrictive adjective clauses give information that can be interesting or even highly significant, but the information does not serve to define which noun it is that we are talking about. Here is an example of a sentence containing a nonrestrictive adjective clause (in italics):

My Uncle Harry, *who is an absolute loony*, always overstays his welcome.

Now, my Uncle Harry would still be my Uncle Harry even if he were not an absolute loony. In other words, the information in the adjective clause (interesting as it is) does not serve to tell us which Uncle Harry we are talking about. I only have one Uncle Harry. The fact that he is an absolute loony does not serve to distinguish one Uncle Harry from another. Therefore, the adjective clause is nonrestrictive.

The distinction between restrictive and nonrestrictive clauses affects the choice between *that* and *which*. In nonrestrictive clauses, *which* is nearly always used now instead of *that* (though this was not always the case). For example, compare the following uses of *which* and *that* in a nonrestrictive clause. Notice how strange the use of *that* sounds:

Our house, *which* we just repainted, was damaged in the storm.
? Our house, *that* we just repainted, was damaged in the storm.

In restrictive clauses, the matter is not so clear-cut. Historically, *that* and *which* were always used interchangeably, as in the following quote from the Authorized (King James) Version of the Bible (1611):

> Render therefore unto Caesar the things *which* are Caesar's; and unto God the things *that* are God's.

However, the increasingly strong preference for *which* in nonrestrictive clauses led commentators at the end of the nineteenth century to advocate using *that* in restrictive clauses so that restrictive and nonrestrictive clauses would be consistently marked: *that* in restrictive clauses and *which* in nonrestrictive.

Most style sheets and editors (including the editors of this book) strongly recommend using only *that* in restrictive clauses. In fact, many published writers use *which* in restrictive clauses. (One study found that fully 25 percent of the uses of *which* in edited, published writing are used to introduce restrictive clauses.)

Bottom line? Because the folks who use both *that* and *which* in restrictive clauses don't care which you use, you might as well use only *that* in restrictive clauses to make happy the folks who do care (often deeply).

We distinguish restrictive and nonrestrictive clauses in writing by putting commas around the nonrestrictive ones. The trick, of course, is knowing when adjective clauses are nonrestrictive. The section "Commas with Adjective Clauses" in Chapter 11 deals with this problem in detail.

Noun Clauses

Noun clauses are the most complicated and sophisticated of the three types of clauses. Children learn to use noun clauses substantially later than the other two types of clauses. Abstract and technical writing abounds in noun clauses. Noun clauses give us the ability to take a whole sentence and compact it down into a unit that we can use as a subject or an object in the independent clause. Noun clauses are a bit of a double-edged sword. The ability to use noun clauses is one of the hallmarks of sophisticated writing. However, overuse of noun clauses leads to leaden, deadly dull writing. (Think of textbooks in education.)

A noun clause is a dependent clause used as a noun phrase. Noun clauses can play the basic noun phrase roles of subject, object of verbs, object of prepositions, and predicate nominative, for example (noun clauses in italics):

Subject:	*What he does for a living* is a big mystery.
Object of verb:	I know *that you are right.*
Object of preposition:	We were aware of *what we needed to do.*
Predicate nominative:	That is *what we wanted.*

Because noun clauses always play the role of noun phrases, they can be identified the same way that noun phrases are: by the third-person pronoun test. Noun clauses have another property that we can take advantage of: they are always singular. This means that we can always replace noun clauses with singular third-person pronouns. Furthermore, because noun clauses are always a kind of abstraction, we can replace them with the pronoun *it*. Here is the third-person pronoun test modified for noun clauses:

The *It* Test for Noun Clauses

If a clause can be replaced by the pronoun *it*, then that clause is a noun clause.

Following is the *it* test applied to the four preceding example sentences:

Subject:	*What he does for a living* is a big mystery.
	It is a big mystery.
Object of verb:	I know *that you are right.*
	I know *it.*
Object of preposition:	We were aware of *what we needed to do.*
	We were aware of *it.*
Predicate nominative:	That is *what we wanted.*
	That is *it.*

Noun clauses, like the other two types of clauses, have flag words that signal the beginning of the clause. Noun clauses are a bit different from the other two types of clauses in that there are two different sets of flag words, creating two slightly different kinds of noun clauses. Strangely enough, neither set of flag words has a conventional name in traditional grammar. In many modern grammar books they are called ***that* type** and ***wh-* type** (for reasons that will soon become apparent). Accordingly, the two different types of noun clauses are called ***that* type noun clauses** and ***wh-* type noun clauses.**

The two different groups of noun clauses behave the same way, but how the two types of clauses are constructed is different. In *that* type noun clauses, the flag word is *outside* the "bound" independent clause (as in adverb clauses). In *wh-* type noun clauses, the flag word is *inside* the "bound" independent clause (as in adjective clauses). For this reason, we will discuss the two groups separately.

***That* Type Noun Clauses.** By far the most common flag word in this group is *that*. The other three are *if*, *whether*, and *whether or not*. Here are examples of *that* type noun clauses playing all four noun phrase roles (noun clauses in italics, flag words in bold):

Subject:	***Whether or not*** *it rains* will determine our destination.
Object of verb:	We wondered ***if*** *we should go to the party.*
Object of preposition:	We couldn't decide about ***whether*** *we should leave.*
Predicate nominative:	The plan is ***that*** *we will reconvene after lunch.*

That type noun clauses are built like adverb clauses in that the flag word is put in front of a "bound" independent clause, and the flag word plays no grammatical role inside the "bound" independent clause:

that type noun clause = *that* type flag word + "bound" independent clause

The flag word *if* poses a special problem. Noun clauses beginning with *if* are easily confused with adverb clauses, which can also begin with *if*.

Here are a pair of examples of the two different kinds of clauses, both beginning with *if* (clauses in italics, flag words in bold):

Noun clause:	I don't know ***if*** *I can come.*
Adverb clause:	I will meet you there ***if*** *I can come.*

As you can see, these two *if* clauses are absolutely identical in wording. What is not identical is their relationship to the independent clause. Fortunately, we have reliable tests for both types of clauses that clearly show the differences between the uses of the *if* clauses in the two sentences.

For noun clauses, we have the third-person pronoun test:

Noun clause:	I don't know ***if*** *I can come.*
Third-person pronoun test:	I don't know ***if*** *I can come.*
	I don't know *it.*

When we apply the third-person pronoun test to the adverb clause, the result is ungrammatical because the *it* is replacing an adverb clause, not a noun clause:

I will meet you there ***if*** *I can come.*
X I will meet you there *it.*

Conversely, when we apply the adverb clause movement test to both sentences, the noun clause fails and the adverb clause passes:

Noun clause:	I don't know ***if*** *I can come.*
Adverb clause movement test:	X ***If*** *I can come,* I don't know.

As we would expect, the adverb clause moves quite naturally:

Adverb clause:	I will meet you there ***if*** *I can come.*
Adverb clause movement test:	***If*** *I can come,* I will meet you there.

***Wh-* Type Noun Clauses.** *Wh-* type noun clauses got their peculiar name from the fact that nearly all the flag words happen to begin with the letters *wh*. *Wh-* words are unique among flag words in that they belong to different parts of speech. Here are the most common *wh-* words classified by their parts of speech. Notice that many of the *wh-* words can be compounded with *-ever*:

Nouns	
what	whatever
who	whoever
whom	whomever
Adjectives	
whose	
which	whichever
Adverbs	
when	whenever
where	wherever
why	
how	however

The last two words on the list, *how* and *however*, do not actually begin with *wh-*. We will treat them as honorary members of the *wh-* family. The following is a set of *wh-* type noun clauses in the four main noun roles (noun clauses in italics, *wh-* words in bold):

Subject:	***Whatever** you decide* is fine with us.
Object of verb:	I know ***where** we can get a good pizza.*
Object of preposition:	We were aware of ***which** choices were open to us.*
Predicate nominative:	The situation is ***what** we expected it would be.*

Wh- type noun clauses are built like adjective clauses in that *wh-* words (like relative pronouns in adjective clauses) are inside the "bound" independent clause. Thus, the *wh-* word must play some grammatical role within the "bound" independent clause. Let us look again at the four example sentences, this time focusing on the grammatical role of the flag word:

***Whatever** you decide* is fine with us. (*Whatever* is the object of the verb *decide.*)

I know ***where** we can get a good pizza.* (*Where* is an adverb of place modifying the verb *get.*)

We were aware of ***which** choices were open to us.* (*Which* is an adjective modifying the noun *choices*, the subject of the verb *were open.*)

The situation is ***what** we expected it would be.* (*What* is the predicate nominative complement of the verb *be.*)

The distinction between the function of the *wh-* word inside the noun clause and the function of the noun clause as a whole in relation to the rest of the independent clause can be quite confusing. For example, in the following sentences, which is correct, *whoever* or *whomever*?

We will sell it to ***whoever** bids the highest.*
We will sell it to ***whomever** bids the highest.*

At first glance, we might think the answer is *whomever* because *whoever* is the object of the preposition *to*. Wrong! The right answer is *whoever.* The object of the preposition *to* is not the *wh-* word, but the *entire* noun clause *whoever bids the highest.* Inside the noun clause, *whoever* is the subject of the verb *bids*. We might imagine the sentence this way:

We will sell it to [noun clause].

Think of noun clauses as islands. Their internal grammatical relationships are not affected by anything that takes place off the island.

Using Conjunctive Adverbs to Join Independent Clauses

Conjunctive adverbs are words used to show how the ideas in the second of two closely related sentences relate to the meaning of the ideas in the first sentence. Conjunctive adverbs can be roughly sorted into three groups depending on how the second sentence is related to the first sentence:

1. The ideas in the second sentence expand or elaborate on the ideas in the first sentence (what we have called the "In Addition" group of conjunctive adverbs).

2. The ideas in the second sentence spell out the results or consequences of the first sentence (what we have called the "As a Consequence" group of conjunctive adverbs).

3. The ideas in the second sentence are somewhat contrary to what you might expect to follow from the first sentence (what we have called the "On the Other Hand" group of conjunctive adverbs).

Here are examples of the common conjunctive adverbs arranged by meaning:

In Addition	As a Consequence	On the Other Hand
again	accordingly	however
also	consequently	nevertheless
besides	hence	nonetheless
further	then	otherwise
furthermore	therefore	still
moreover		
similarly		

Here are some examples of independent clauses joined by one example of each type of conjunctive adverb (in bold):

In addition:	John was in an accident; **furthermore**, it was his third car crash this year.
As a consequence:	John was in an accident; **consequently**, he will miss work for several days.
On the other hand:	John was in an accident. **However**, he was not injured.

The first thing to notice in these examples is the punctuation. The first of each of the two independent clauses in the examples is punctuated with either a semicolon (;) or a period. It is not correct to use a comma to join two independent clauses without a coordinating conjunction. The presence of the conjunctive adverb changes nothing. Conjunctive adverbs are not conjunctions. They are adverbs, and adverbs by themselves have no power to join independent clauses with a comma. Just using a comma (with or without a conjunctive adverb) to join independent clauses is a common punctuation error called a **comma splice**. Also notice that conjunctive adverbs are always followed by commas.

Conjunctive adverbs are easily confused with subordinating conjunctions—flag words used to signal the beginning of adverb clauses. Here are two sentences that illustrate the problem (flag words in bold):

Conjunctive adverb:	John was in an accident; **consequently**, he took drivers' education.
Subordinating conjunction:	John was in an accident **after** he took drivers' education.

How can we tell which flag word is the conjunctive adverb and which is the subordinating conjunction without memorizing tediously long lists of flag words? The adverb clause movement test is a simple and completely reliable way of telling them apart. When we apply the test to the two sentences, we get completely different results:

Adverb clause movement test

Conjunctive adverb:	John was in an accident; **consequently**, he took drivers' education.
	X **Consequently**, he took drivers' education, John was in an accident.
Subordinating conjunction:	John was in an accident **after** he took drivers' education.
	After he took drivers' education, John was in an accident.

As you can see, the independent clause beginning with the conjunctive adverb *consequently* cannot be moved in front of the first independent clause because it is not an adverb clause. Conversely, the adverb clause beginning with *after* moves quite easily.

Conjunctive adverbs have another property that helps distinguish them from subordinating conjunctions. Conjunctive adverbs are adverbs, and, as is often the case with adverbs, they can be moved around inside their clauses. They can be moved next to the verb and sometimes to the end of their clause. Here are some new example sentences containing conjunctive adverbs (in bold) with the conjunctive adverb moved:

The accident ruined the experiment; **moreover**, some equipment was damaged.
The accident ruined the experiment; some equipment, **moreover**, was damaged.
The accident ruined the experiment; some equipment was damaged, **moreover**.

The accident ruined the experiment; **therefore**, I had to start all over again.
The accident ruined the experiment; I had, **therefore**, to start all over again.
The accident ruined the experiment; I had to start all over again, **therefore**.

The accident ruined the experiment; **nevertheless**, I could still see that it would work.
The accident ruined the experiment; I could still see, **nevertheless**, that it would work.
The accident ruined the experiment; I could still see that it would work, **nevertheless**.

The punctuation is essentially the same no matter where the conjunctive adverb is. The two sentences must still be separated by either a period or a semicolon, and the conjunctive adverb must be set off from the rest of its sentence by commas.

When we attempt to move a subordinating conjunction around inside its clause, the result is completely ungrammatical:

John was in an accident **after** he took drivers' education.
X John was in an accident he took **after** drivers' education.
X John was in an accident he took drivers' education **after**.

Sentences Classified According to Structure

Traditional grammar has a special terminology for describing the clause structure of sentences. If a sentence consists of a single independent clause with no dependent clauses, it is called a **simple sentence**. If a sentence contains two or more independent clauses but no dependent clauses, it is called a **compound sentence**. If a sentence contains a single independent clause and one or more dependent clauses, it is called a **complex sentence**. If a sentence contains two or more independent clauses and at least one dependent clause, it is called a **compound-complex sentence**. We may represent these various configurations as follows:

simple sentence = independent clause
compound sentence = independent clause + independent clause
complex sentence = independent clause + dependent clause(s)
compound-complex sentence = independent clause + independent clause + dependent clause

Here are examples of the four possibilities:

independent clause

Simple sentence: The elves were unhappy with Santa.

independent clause 1 / independent clause 2

Compound sentence: The elves were unhappy with Santa, and the reindeer were considering a class-action lawsuit.

independent clause / dependent clause

Complex sentence: The elves were unhappy with Santa because they had to work during the Christmas season.

independent clause 1 independent clause 2

Compound-complex sentence: The elves were unhappy with Santa, and the reindeer were considering a class-action lawsuit because Rudolph got preferential treatment.

dependent clause

4

Verb Forms

Tense

Tense is one of the most confusing (and confused) terms in English grammar. Part of the confusion is that *tense* refers, often quite inconsistently, either to verb form or to verb meaning. We will keep the two ways of looking at verbs—form and meaning—separate. A metaphor from chemistry may (or may not) be helpful here. Think of verb forms as the six basic elements that make up the verbal system. Some of these six basic elements can stand alone as meaningful verb expressions. Others can only exist when combined with another basic element in a sort of verb molecule. For example, what traditional grammar calls the **future tense** is such a molecule. Here is an example of a sentence containing a future tense (in italics):

I *will go* to the grocery store on my way home.

The future actually consists of two elementary verb components: *will*, a present tense form, and *go*, a base form.

We begin by looking first at verb forms and then turn to how these forms are used to create meaning.

Verb Forms

All verbs (with the exception of **modal verbs**, which will be discussed a little later) have six different forms. The six forms are listed here and illustrated by the regular verb *walk* and the irregular verb *swim*:

	Base Present	Past	Infinitive	Present Participle	Past Participle
walk	walk, walks	walked	to walk	walking	walked
swim	swim, swims	swam	to swim	swimming	swum

Base Form. The **base form** is the dictionary-entry form of the verb. For example, if you looked up the past form *swam* in the dictionary, the dictionary would refer you to the base form *swim*. At first, it may seem difficult to tell base forms from present forms because in nearly all cases, they are identical. However, there is one verb whose base form is completely different from its present form: the verb *be*:

Base: *be*
Present: I *am*
you *are*
he/she/it *is*
we/you/they *are*

We can use the fact that the base form of *be* is different from all its present forms to determine when base forms are used.

There are two quite common places where the base form is used: (1) in imperative sentences and (2) in the future tense.

Here are some examples of imperative sentences (verbs in italics):

Go away!
Oh, *stop* that!
Answer the question.

When we use the verb *be* in imperative sentences, we can see that the base form is used:

Be good!
Be prepared.
Be careful what you wish for.

If we attempt to use any present form of *be*, the results are clearly ungrammatical:

X *Are* good!
X *Is* good!
X *Am* good!

The future tense is formed by using the verb *will* followed by a verb in its base form. Here are some examples of future tenses (base forms in italics):

We will *walk* to the restaurant.
The kids will *swim* in the pool this afternoon.

We can show that the verbs following *will* are in the base form by again using the verb *be*:

Santa will *be* upset with Rudolph again.

Present forms of *be* are impossible after *will*:

X Santa will *are* upset with Rudolph again.
X Santa will *is* upset with Rudolph again.

Present Form. With the exception of the verb *be*, the **present** is formed in the following manner:

third-person singular = base + *s*
all other persons and numbers = base

For example:

Third-person singular:	he/she/it *walks, swims*
All other persons and numbers:	*walk, swim*

As noted, the verb *be* follows a completely different pattern in the present form.

Past Form. There are two ways of forming the **past: regular** and **irregular**. The regular verbs form their past by adding *-ed* or *-d* to the base form:

Base Form	**Past Form**
pass	passed
cough	coughed
smile	smiled

Originally, all irregular verbs formed the past by using a different vowel sound in the past form from the vowel used in the base form. A number of verbs still preserve this ancient way:

Base Form	**Past Form**
dig	dug
freeze	froze
ring	rang
see	saw

Some irregular verbs became hybrids by keeping their historic vowel changes but adding the regular verb *-ed* or *-d* ending:

Base Form	**Past Form**
sell	sold
tell	told

Some verbs have a vowel change but add a *-t* rather than *-ed* or *-d*:

Base Form	**Past Form**
keep	kept
think	thought

Some one-syllable verbs that end in *-t* or *-d* have a past that is exactly the same as the base (or present) form. For example, here is the verb *put*, first used in the present form and then in the past:

Present: I always *put* suntan lotion on when I go out.
Past: I *put* suntan lotion on yesterday, but I still got burned.

Here are more examples of verbs that follow this pattern:

Base Form	**Past Form**
bet	bet
cost	cost
rid	rid
shut	shut

A few verbs have remarkably irregular past forms. The verbs *go* and *be* share a peculiar feature: their past forms come from completely different words than their base form comes from. The past of *go* is *went*. *Went* is related historically, not to the verb *go*, but to the verb *wander* and the now rare verb *wend*, as in to *wend* one's way. Likewise, *was* and *were*, the past forms of the verb *be*, are from a verb historically unrelated to *be*. *Was* and *were* are doubly exceptional in that they are the only past forms that change to agree with the subject:

I, he, she, it	*was*
we, you (both singular and plural), they	*were*

Infinitive Form. The **infinitive** is also completely regular. It consists of *to* plus the base form. Here are some examples:

Base Form	**Infinitive**
answer	to answer
go	to go
be	to be

Present Participle Form. The **present participle** is completely regular in that all present participles are formed by adding *-ing* onto the base form. Here are some examples:

Base Form	**Present Participle**
talk	talking
be	being
sing	singing

However, the rules of spelling sometimes cause the present participle to be spelled differently than the base form. For example, the doubled-consonant rule will apply to some base forms ending in a single consonant, as seen in *hop, hopping; hit, hitting.*

Past Participle Form. There are two kinds of **past participles: regular** and **irregular.**

Regular past participles are formed by adding *-ed* or *-d* to the base form, just the same way that regular past forms are. The past and past participles of regular verbs are thus identical:

Past Form	Past Participle Form
snored	snored
shouted	shouted
laughed	laughed

So, how can we tell past verb forms from past participles? Only by the way they are used. Past verb forms are always used by themselves. Past participles can only be used after the helping verbs *have* or *be* (in some form), for example:

Past (in italics):	We *reported* the accident promptly.
Past participle (in italics):	We had *reported* the accident as soon as it happened.
	The accident was *reported* as soon as it happened.

When we use irregular verbs in similar sentences, we can see overt differences between the past and the past participles:

Past (in italics):	We *saw* the accident.
Past participle (in italics):	We had *seen* the accident on our way in.
	The accident was *seen* by everybody.

The past participle of irregular verbs historically ended in *-en* or *-n.* Many past participles preserve this old pattern, some without a vowel change, some with a vowel change:

Base Form	Past Participle
fall	fallen
see	seen
freeze	frozen
be	been

Other irregular verbs have lost the *-en* or *-n* and form the past participle in a variety of other ways:

Base Form	Past Participle
tell	told
have	had
bring	brought

The same group of one-syllable verbs ending in *-d* or *-t* whose past forms are identical to the base form also have past participles that do not change. That is, their past participle form is the same as their base and past forms:

Base Form	Past Form	Past Participle Form
hit	hit	hit
rid	rid	rid
put	put	put

Modal Verbs. Finally, there is an exceptional group of five verbs called **modals** that doesn't follow any of the patterns already discussed. For complicated historical reasons, the modals do not have the full range of verb forms. Accordingly, they are sometimes called "defective" verbs. They have both present and past forms (most of them do, anyway) but nothing else. Modals have no base forms, no infinitive forms, no present participle forms, and no past participle forms. Here are the present and past forms of the five modals:

Present Form	Past Form
can	could
may	might
must	—

Present Form	**Past Form**
shall	should
will	would

The present forms are themselves highly unusual in that they have no third-person singular *-s*. For example, we can say

He can go.
She will leave.

but not

X He cans go.
X She wills leave.

(Trivia item: notice that *must* has no past form. It is the only verb in English to have a present but no past.)

Modals are **helping verbs**. They are quite limited in how they can be used. Modals can never be used alone. They can only be used in combination with a following verb in the base form, for example (modals in italics, base verbs in bold):

You *can* **do** it.
They *must* **be** careful.
You *should* **know** better.

Using Verb Forms to Create Meaning

In traditional grammar, English is said to have six tenses. In traditional grammar, there are three **simple tenses** (**present, past**, and **future**) and three **perfect tenses** (**present perfect, past perfect**, and **future perfect**). Here are the six tenses with examples:

Simple Tenses	**Perfect Tenses**
Present Tense	**Present Perfect Tense**
I *walk*	I *have walked*
I *swim*	I *have swum*

Past Tense	**Past Perfect Tense**
I *walked*	I *had walked*
I *swam*	I *had swum*
Future Tense	**Future Perfect Tense**
I *will walk*	I *will have walked*
I *will swim*	I *will have swum*

We will now discuss in a little more detail how the six tenses are built and what they mean.

Simple Tenses. The simple tenses are not called "simple" because they are easy. Historically, the term "simple" was used to distinguish the meaning of the three simple tenses from the three perfect tenses. The simple tenses (generally) refer to actions that take place at a single moment in time—at the present time, at a past moment in time, or at a future moment in time. The three perfect tenses, on the other hand, deal with actions that span a period of time.

Present tense. The **present tense** is the present form of a verb. Despite its name, the present tense form of verbs does not really mean present time. In fact, most action verbs actually sound rather odd when used in the present tense, for example:

? I *walk* now.
? I *run* now.

If we want to talk about something happening at the present moment, we do not use the present tense at all; instead, we use what is called the **progressive** (described in more detail later):

I *am walking* now.
I *am running* now.

There are two main uses of the present tense: (1) to make statements of fact and (2) to make generalizations. Here are some examples of statements of fact and generalizations (present tense verbs in italics):

Statement of fact

Two plus two *equals* four.
Gold *dissolves* in mercury.
Annapolis *is* the capital of Maryland.

Generalizations

Liver *is* disgusting.
The new Saab *is* the best-looking car on the road.
Fast-food restaurants *exploit* their employees.
I *shop* at Safeway.

Notice the last example, *I shop at Safeway.* We often use the present tense for generalizations about habitual actions. When we say, "I shop at Safeway," it does not mean that I am in the process of shopping at Safeway at this moment. It means that it is my custom to shop at Safeway. The sentence is still valid even if I have not stepped foot inside a Safeway store in weeks.

Both statements of fact and generalizations are essentially timeless. Statements of fact sound particularly odd if they are tied to a particular moment. For example, the statement

Two plus two *is* four now.

makes it sound as though this fact is only temporary—tomorrow, two plus two might be something else. Even statements that are not universally true are still true for an indefinite period of time. For example, the statement

I *hate* liver.

implies that this statement is valid for the foreseeable future.

One consequence of the fact that English reserves the use of the present tense for timeless statements of facts and generalizations is that technical and scientific writing, which is primarily concerned with statements of facts and generalizations, is normally written in the present tense.

Past tense. The **past tense** is the past form of the verb. The past tense, obviously, is used to describe events that took place in past time. However, there is more to the use of the past tense than this statement would imply. Because the present tense is preempted for making timeless statements of fact and generalizations, the past tense becomes the primary vehicle for all narration that deals with time-bounded events. For this reason, nearly all stories and novels are written in the past tense.

Future tense. The **future tense** is formed by the present form of the helping verb *will*, followed by a verb in its base form, for example (*will* in italics, base verbs in bold):

The meeting *will* **be** tomorrow at four.
I *will* **see** you there later.
I *will* **go** to Seattle tomorrow.

As you may recall, *will* is only one of a group of verbs called **modals**. All of the modals can be used to talk about the future. In this respect, *will* is no different than the other four modals. The only reason that traditional grammar singled out *will* from the other modals is that *will* was the best single modal for translating the Latin future tense into English. However, all of the modals can be used equally as well for talking about the future. Here are examples of the remaining four present tense modals used for the future (modals in italics):

I *can* go to Seattle tomorrow.
I *may* go to Seattle tomorrow.
I *must* go to Seattle tomorrow.
I *shall* go to Seattle tomorrow.

Modal verbs are anomalous in many ways. For historical reasons, the terms *present* and *past* have a different meaning when applied to modals. The terms *present* and *past* refer to the historical *forms* of the modals, not their meaning. *Could*, for example, is the historical past tense form of *can. Might* is the historical past tense form of *may*, and so on. However, the terms *present* and *past* do not mean time at all. Even the so-called past tense modals can be used to talk about the future:

I *could* go to Seattle tomorrow.
I *might* go to Seattle tomorrow.
I *should* go to Seattle tomorrow.
I *would* go to Seattle tomorrow if I could afford it.

In many ways, it makes sense to broaden the meaning of *future tense* to include all of the modals, not just *will*.

Perfect Tenses. The **perfect tenses** consist of the helping verb *have* in some form followed by a verb in the past participle form. Let us first look at what the term *perfect* means in traditional grammar. To begin with, *perfect* does not mean "terrific." The term *perfect* comes from the Latin phrase *per factus*, meaning "completely done" or "completely finished." The term *perfect* was used to describe three verb tenses in Latin. They were called perfect, or perfected, tenses because each of the three tenses dealt with actions that spanned a period of time. The action was begun at one time and then completed or finished (get it? *perfected*) at or before a second time.

The basic idea of the traditional concept of tense is that there is a fundamental division between the time relationships in the three simple tenses and the time relationships in the three perfect tenses.

The action in the simple tenses takes place at a single point or moment in time. In the present tense, it is a present moment in time. In the past tense, it was at a past moment of time. In the future tense, it will be at a future moment of time.

The perfect tenses, on the other hand, deal with actions that span a period of time. The present perfect tense deals with an action that began in the past and continues up to the present time. The past perfect deals with an action that began at a more distant point in the past and ended at a more recent point in the past. The future perfect deals with an action that begins in the present or in the near future and ends by some more distant point of time in the future.

Present perfect tense. The **present perfect tense** is formed by the present tense of the helping verb *have* followed by a second verb in the past participle form, which we can summarize as follows:

present perfect = *have/has* + past participle

We use the present perfect to describe actions that have occurred continuously or repeatedly from some time in the past right up to the present moment (sometimes with the implication that these actions will continue into the future). Here are some examples (present perfect in italics):

Their phone *has been* busy for half an hour.
The kids *have watched* cartoons all afternoon.
The choir *has sung* that hymn a hundred times.

The fundamental difference between the present perfect and the past tense is that the present perfect emphasizes the continual or repeated nature of a past action across a span of time, while the past tense describes a single-event action that is now over and done with. To see the difference, compare the following sentences:

Present perfect:	Elliot *has lived* in Chicago for ten years.
Past:	Elliot *lived* in Chicago for ten years.

The present perfect sentence tells us two things: (1) that Elliot has lived in Chicago continuously for ten years and (2) that Elliot still lives in Chicago now. The sentence also implies that Elliot will continue to live in Chicago for the foreseeable future. The past tense sentence tells us that while Elliot lived in Chicago for ten years, he does not live in Chicago anymore. His presence in Chicago is over and done with.

A second use of the present perfect describes a recent past event that still affects the present. Here are some examples:

I'm sorry, Ms. Smith *has stepped* away from her desk for a moment.
Sam *has lost* his car keys.

In both cases, an event that was begun in the past continues in effect and very much still influences the present moment.

Past perfect tense. The **past perfect tense** is formed by the past tense of the helping verb *have* followed by a verb in the past participle form:

past perfect = *had* + past participle

We use the past perfect when we want to emphasize the fact that a particular event in the past was completed *before* a more recent past-time event took place. Here are three examples with commentary (past perfect in italics):

I *had stepped* into the shower just when the phone rang.

In this example, two things happened: (1) the speaker stepped into the shower and (2) the phone rang. The speaker is using the past perfect to emphasize the inconvenient order of the two past-time events.

When we bought the house last year, it *had been* empty for ten years.

In this example, the past perfect is used to emphasize the fact that the house had been empty for the ten-year period *before* it was bought.

They'*d had* a big fight before they broke up.

In this example, the past perfect sequences two events: (1) a big fight and (2) a breakup. Here, the past perfect implies that not only did these two events happen in this order, but there is probably a cause-and-effect connection between them. That is, their big fight may have caused their subsequent breakup.

Future perfect tense. The **future perfect tense** is formed by the future tense of the helping verb *have* followed by a verb in the past participle form:

future perfect = *will have* + past participle

We use the future perfect tense when we want to emphasize the "no-later-than" time of the completion of a future action. Compare the meaning of the following sentences, the first in the future tense, the second in the future perfect tense:

Future:	We *will break* for lunch around 12:30.
Future perfect:	We *will have broken* for lunch by 12:30.

The future tense sentence merely states when some future action will take place. The future perfect sentence puts a "no-later-than" time limit on when the action will have been completed. We could break for lunch at noon or even 11:00, but in any event, we will have broken for lunch no later than 12:30.

Here are some more examples of the future perfect tense:

The train *will have left* by the time we get to the station.
The paint *will have dried* by tomorrow morning.
The snowplows *will have cleared* the roads before we get to the lodge.

The Progressive

The term **progressive** is used to describe a set of verb constructions that stand apart from the system of six tenses that have already been described. The term aptly describes the main characteristic of the progressive constructions. We use the progressive to emphasize that the action of the verb is in progress or ongoing at a particular moment of time. There are three types of progressives: a **present progressive**, a **past progressive**, and a **future progressive**. All three types of progressive are built in the same way: a form of the helping verb *be* is followed by a verb in the present participle form. We will now examine each of them in turn.

Present Progressive

The **present progressive** is formed by the present tense of the verb *be* followed by a verb in the present participle form:

present progressive = *am/are/is* + present participle

Here are some examples of sentences using the present progressive (helping verbs in italics, present participles in bold):

I *am* **working** on it even as we speak.
We *are* **waiting** to hear from the boss.
It*'s* **raining** like anything.

We use the present progressive when we want to emphasize that some action is in progress at the present moment.

Past Progressive

The **past progressive** is formed by the past tense of the verb *be* followed by a verb in the present participle form:

past progressive = *was/were* + present participle

Here are some examples of sentences using the past progressive (helping verbs in italics, present participles in bold):

I *was* **working** on it when you called.
We *were* **waiting** to hear from the boss.

We use the past progressive when we want to emphasize that some action was in process at a moment or period of past time.

Future Progressive

The **future progressive** is formed by the future tense of the verb *be* followed by a verb in the present participle form:

future progressive = *will be* + present participle

Here are some examples of sentences using the future progressive (helping verbs in italics, present participles in bold):

I *will be* **working** on it all next week.
It *will be* **raining** by the time we get there.

We use the future progressive when we want to emphasize that some action will be in process at some moment or period in the future.

"Tensed" Verbs

We will end this section on tense with an important generalization about how sentences and clauses are built. Sentences and clauses differ from phrases in one fundamental way: sentences and clauses have verb phrases (or predicates) that begin with a **"tensed" verb**. A "tensed" verb is a verb in either the present or past tense form. As we will see in Chapter 5, certain types of phrases also contain verb phrases, but their phrases do not have a "tensed" verb. Compare the following examples:

Sentence:	Barbara *rejected* the offer.
Gerund phrase:	Barbara's *rejecting* the offer [surprised everyone.]
Infinitive phrase:	For Barbara *to reject* the offer [surprised everyone.]

The first example is a sentence because it contains a "tensed" verb—the past tense *rejected.* While the two phrases contain essentially the same information as the sentence, they are clauses, not sentences, because they do not contain a "tensed" verb. The gerund phrase contains a verb in the present participle form (*rejecting*), and the infinitive phrase contains a verb in the infinitive form (*to reject*).

In any noncompounded verb phrase, there can be only one "tensed" verb. If there are multiple verbs in the verb phrase, only the first verb can be "tensed." Here are examples of the various multiple-verb constructions in italics with the "tensed" verbs in bold:

Future:	George ***will*** *get* the pizza. (*Will* is present tense.)
Present perfect:	George ***has*** *got* the pizza. (*Has* is present tense.)
Past perfect:	George ***had*** *got* the pizza. (*Had* is past tense.)
Future perfect:	George ***will*** *have* got the pizza. (*Will* is present tense.)
Present progressive:	George ***is*** *getting* the pizza. (*Is* is present tense.)
Past progressive:	George ***was*** *getting* the pizza. (*Was* is past tense.)
Future progressive:	George ***will*** *be getting* the pizza. (*Will* is present tense.)

The Passive Voice

In traditional grammar, all verbs occur in one of two **voices: active voice** or **passive voice**. The active voice is the normal state of affairs. Nearly all the sentences that we have examined in this book up to this point have been in the active voice. In the active voice, the subject of a sentence is either the doer of the action (with action verbs) or the topic of the sentence (with linking verbs). In a passive voice sentence, the subject is the recipient of the action. Compare the following sentences:

Active voice:	Rudolph washed the sled.
Passive voice:	The sled was washed by Rudolph.

In the active sentence, *Rudolph* (the subject) is doing the action of washing. In the corresponding passive sentence, *the sled* (the subject) is not doing anything. Instead, the sled is the recipient of the action of washing.

Passives have a unique structure that makes them easily recognizable (once you know what to look for). Passives must contain the helping verb *be* (in some form) followed by a past participle. The following is the formula for all passive voice sentences:

passive voice = *be* (in some form) + past participle

The form the helping verb *be* takes depends on the rest of the sentence. *Be* can appear in any of the three simple tenses (*be* in italics, past participles in bold):

Present passive:	Usually, the sled *is* **washed** by Rudolph.
Past passive:	The sled *was* **washed** by Rudolph.
Future passive:	The sled *will be* **washed** by Rudolph.

Be can appear as the past participle *been* in the three perfect tenses:

Present perfect passive:	The sled has *been* **washed** by Rudolph.
Past perfect passive:	The sled had *been* **washed** by Rudolph.
Future perfect passive:	The sled will have *been* **washed** by Rudolph.

Be can appear as the present participle *being* in present and past progressive constructions:

Present progressive passive:	The sled is *being* **washed** by Rudolph.
Past progressive passive:	The sled was *being* **washed** by Rudolph.

The third possibility, the future progressive passive, is actually grammatical, but it is so awkward that it is rarely used:

? The sled will be *being* **washed** by Rudolph when Santa comes.

To see why we use the passive, let us take another example of corresponding active and passive voice sentences:

Active voice:	John amused Mary.
Passive voice:	Mary was amused by John.

In the active voice sentence, the focus of the sentence is on what the subject, *John*, did: he amused Mary. In the passive voice sentence, the focus is shifted away from the original subject, *John*, and instead is refocused on what happened to the original object, *Mary*: she was amused.

In the passive voice sentence, the original subject can be retained as the object of the preposition *by*. However, because the whole point of using the passive voice is to shift emphasis onto the original object and away from the original subject, it is quite common to delete the *by* phrase that contains the original subject. According to one study, about 85 percent of the passive sentences in nonfiction books and articles do not retain the *by* phrase.

Sometimes we use the passive precisely because we do not know (or care) what the subject of the active sentence is. For example, we would certainly prefer the following passive voice sentence with the *by* deleted:

My cell phone was made in Taiwan.

to the corresponding active voice version:

Somebody in Taiwan made my cell phone.

Here are some more active voice sentences with their passive voice counterpoints (verbs in italics, *by* phrases deleted):

Active voice: Everybody *expects* the announcement at any moment.
Passive voice: The announcement *is expected* at any moment.

Active voice: Somebody *suspended* the search at nightfall.
Passive voice: The search *was suspended* at nightfall.

Active voice: Somebody *based* the movie on a bestselling novel.
Passive voice: The movie *was based* on a bestselling novel.

The passive has a certain negative connotation for several reasons. First, the passive can be used evasively, to avoid naming the person actually responsible for an action. When a politician uses the passive sentence "Mistakes were made," you can be sure that the choice of the passive was deliberate. Second, writers can fall into the habit of using the passive where the active voice would be more vivid and, well, less passive. One of the first lessons in any writing class is making students aware of their needless use of the passive.

Phrasal Verbs

All languages have ways of making new words. English has a rich set of mechanisms for creating new words by compounding verbs with prepositions. The oldest form of verb compounding fuses the preposition onto the beginning of the verb, creating a new verb, for example (prepositions in italics):

*by*pass
*down*play
*over*throw
*under*stand
*up*set
*with*draw

Beginning in the Middle Ages, English developed a second way of forming verb compounds—compounding a verb with a following preposition. We will call verb plus preposition compounds **phrasal verbs**. Over time, phrasal verbs have evolved to become the major source of new verbs in English. The best reference work on phrasal verbs is the *Longman Dictionary of Phrasal Verbs.* To give you some idea of how common phrasal verbs are, the *Longman Dictionary of Phrasal Verbs* has more than twelve thousand entries! Phrasal verbs are actually more numerous than nonphrasal verbs.

To get a sense of what phrasal verbs are like, here is a sentence that contains one type of phrasal verb (in italics):

Susan *turned down* the offer.

The key idea of phrasal verbs is that the verb plus preposition compound acts as a single semantic and grammatical unit. For example, we can paraphrase the meaning of *turned down* with the single verb *rejected*:

Susan *rejected* the offer.

The two sentences, *Susan turned down the offer* and *Susan rejected the offer*, mean exactly the same thing. The grammar of the two sentences is also identical. In both cases, the noun phrase *the offer* is the object of the verb.

5

Verbals

Question: When is a verb not a verb? Answer: When it is a verbal.

A verbal is a participle or an infinitive verb form used as another part of speech—a noun, an adjective, or an adverb. A phrase headed by a verbal is a verbal phrase. Before we do anything else, we need to distinguish between verb phrases and verbal phrases.

- **Verb phrases:** Verb phrases *must* contain a "tensed" verb—either a present or past tense verb that agrees with the subject of its clause. All verb phrases, in short, must exhibit subject-verb agreement.
- **Verbal phrases:** Verbals do not have present or past tense forms. Therefore, verbals *cannot* enter into subject-verb agreements. This is true even when a verbal phrase actually does have an expressed subject (more about this later).

There are three types of verbal phrases, called **gerund phrases**, **participial phrases**, and **infinitive phrases**. The following table is an overview that gives all three types of verbal phrases. For each type, the table gives the verb form, its part of speech, and an example.

TYPES OF VERBAL PHRASES

Type of Phrase	Verb Form	Part of Speech	Example (in italics)
gerund phrase	present participle	noun	*Eating ice cream* gives me a headache.
participial phrase	present participle	adjective	The girl *eating ice cream* is my daughter.

Type of Phrase	Verb Form	Part of Speech	Example (in italics)
	past participle	adjective	Ice cream *eaten too quickly* gives people headaches.
infinitive phrase	infinitive	noun	I love *to eat ice cream.*
	infinitive	adjective	The place *to get ice cream* is Harry's.
	infinitive	adverb	You must go to Harry's *to get good ice cream.*

We will now turn to an examination of each of the three types of verbal phrases.

Gerund Phrases

Gerund phrases are phrases headed by a **gerund**, the present participle form of a verb used as a noun phrase. As with other phrases, gerund phrases can consist of just a single word (the gerund head by itself) or multiple words (the gerund head together with modifiers and/or complements). Here are examples of single-word and multiple-word gerund phrases used as subjects (gerund phrases in italics, gerunds in bold):

Single-word gerund phrase: ***Smiling*** doesn't cost you anything.
Multiple-word gerund phrase: ***Smiling*** *at people* doesn't cost you anything.

Gerund phrases can be used in all four major noun roles: subjects, objects of verbs, objects of prepositions, and predicate nominatives. Here are some examples of gerund phrases in each role (gerund phrases in italics, gerunds in bold):

Subject: ***Winning*** *the game* is not everything.
Answering *my e-mail* always seems to take all morning.

Object of verb: I hate ***cleaning*** *out the garage.*
The kids enjoy ***taking*** *long walks in the country.*

Object of preposition:	Naturally, Fred was upset about ***missing*** *his flight.*
	After ***watching*** *some TV*, we went to bed.
Predicate nominative:	His main activity is ***watching*** *daytime TV.*
	Part of the problem is ***working*** *in such poor light.*

Because gerund phrases always play the role of noun phrases, and gerund phrases are always singular, there is a simple and highly reliable test for them:

The *It* Test for Gerund Phrases

If a phrase headed by a present participle verb can be replaced by the pronoun *it*, then that phrase is a gerund phrase.

Here is the *it* test applied to the earlier sample gerund phrases (gerund phrases in italics, gerunds in bold):

Subject

Winning *the game* is not everything.
It is not everything.

Answering *my e-mail* always seems to take all morning.
It always seems to take all morning.

Object of verb

I hate ***cleaning*** *out the garage.*
I hate it.

The kids enjoy ***taking*** *long walks in the country.*
The kids enjoy it.

Object of preposition

Naturally, Fred was upset about ***missing*** *his flight.*
Naturally, Fred was upset about it.

After ***watching** some TV*, we went to bed.
After it, we went to bed.

Predicate nominative
His main activity is ***watching** daytime TV*.
His main activity is it.

Part of the problem is ***working** in such poor light.*
Part of the problem is it.

The importance of the *it* test is shown in the last two examples, where the gerund phrases are playing the roles of predicate nominatives. At first glance, the sequence *is* plus present participle looks like a present progressive, as in this sentence:

Ralph *is ironing* his shirts.

We can confirm the results of the *it* test by changing the supposed present progressive into a simple past tense. If the present progressive analysis had been correct, the present tense paraphrases should be grammatical, but they are not:

His main activity *is watching* daytime TV.
X His main activity *watched* daytime TV.

Part of the problem *is working* in such poor light.
X Part of the problem *worked* in such poor light.

A sentence with a true present progressive can be paraphrased using a past tense:

Ralph *is ironing* his shirts.
Ralph *ironed* his shirts.

Gerund phrases are really compacted forms of complete sentences. In all the examples we have examined so far, the original subject has been deleted, though it is often easy to tell what the implied subject of the verb underlying the gerund is. For example, in this sentence:

> *Spilling the soup on the guest of honor* embarrassed the waiter terribly.

the subject of the verb underlying the gerund *spilling* is not actually stated. However, it is strongly implied that it was the waiter who did the spilling. We can rewrite the sentence and overtly state the subject:

> *The **waiter's** spilling the soup on the guest of honor* embarrassed him terribly.

When we retain the subject of the verb that underlies the gerund, that subject is called the **subject of the gerund**. Here are several more examples of gerund phrases with subjects of the gerund retained (gerund phrases in italics, subjects of the gerund in bold):

> ***Alice's** finishing the report on time* was greatly appreciated.
> We ate ***Fred's** first attempt at gourmet cooking* in tense silence.
> I was worried about ***my** going on too long.*

Notice that the subject of the gerund in all the examples is in the possessive form. This is the normal rule for formal writing. Failure to use the possessive is a common error in formal writing. When the subject of a gerund is not used in the proper possessive form, the construction is called a **fused participle.**

Participial Phrases

Participial phrases are phrases headed by either a **present participle** or a **past participle.** The sole function of participial phrases is to modify nouns. Single-word participles behave like adjectives and go in front of the words they modify, for example (participles in italics):

Present Participles	**Past Participles**
winning smile	*sanded* floors
blushing maidens	*concerned* parents
boring teachers	*bored* teachers

Notice that the participles in the last pair of examples are exact opposites in meaning. A *boring* teacher is a teacher who bores his or her students. A *bored* teacher is a teacher whose students bore him or her. Participles are derived from verbs. The nouns that the participle modify play different roles depending on which type of participle is used. With present participles, the noun being modified is the *subject* of the verb underlying the participle:

winning smile (The smile is doing the winning.)
blushing maidens (The maidens are doing the blushing.)
boring teachers (The teachers are doing the boring.)

With past participles, on the other hand, the noun being modified is the *object* of the verb underlying the participle:

sanded floors (Somebody sanded the floors.)
concerned parents (Something concerned the parents.)
bored teachers (Something bored the teachers.)

(Grammar factoid: many languages have only a single form of the participle, not two—a present and a past participle—as English does. When speakers of those languages learn English, they have trouble seeing the difference in meaning between the two participle types and often use the two participle forms in English interchangeably and thus often incorrectly.)

Multiword participial phrases—participles together with modifiers and/or complements—follow the nouns they modify. Here are some examples of participial phrases (participial phrases in italics, participles in bold, nouns being modified underlined):

Present participial phrases
The reporters ***covering*** *the accident* interviewed the survivors.
The man ***wearing*** *the silly hat* is my cousin.
The incident amused the people ***waiting*** *in line.*

Past participial phrases

The houses ***located*** *on the floodplain* all suffered extensive damage.

The quote was from a play ***written*** *by Shakespeare.*

The data ***required*** *for the report* was not available on the Internet.

Because participial phrases function as noun modifiers, they are easily identified by the pronoun replacement test, here slightly modified for participial phrases:

The Pronoun Replacement Test for Participial Phrases

If a noun and a following phrase containing a participle are *both* replaced by a pronoun, then that phrase is a participial phrase modifying that noun.

Here is the pronoun replacement test applied to the same sentences from earlier:

Present participial phrases

The reporters ***covering*** *the accident* interviewed the survivors.

They interviewed the survivors.

The man ***wearing*** *the silly hat* is my cousin.

He is my cousin.

The incident amused the people ***waiting*** *in line.*

The incident amused them.

Past participial phrases

The houses ***located*** *on the floodplain* all suffered extensive damage.

They all suffered extensive damage.

The quote was from a play ***written*** *by Shakespeare.*

The quote was from it.

The data ***required*** *for the report* was not available on the Internet.

It was not available on the Internet.

Restrictive and Nonrestrictive Participial Phrases

Participial phrases are really a kind of reduced adjective clause. Like adjective clauses, participial phrases can be used in either restrictive or nonrestrictive ways. All of the examples of participial phrases we have seen to this point have been restrictive. Here are examples of nonrestrictive present and past participial phrases (participial phrases in italics):

Present participial:	Scrooge, *muttering under his breath*, returned to work.
Past participial:	Scrooge, *upset by Tiny Tim's insolence*, vowed revenge.

As you can see, nonrestrictive participial phrases are set off with commas, just as nonrestrictive adjective clauses are.

Dangling Participles

Nonrestrictive participial phrases do have one feature that is unique among noun modifiers: participial phrases can be moved away from the nouns they modify. They are often moved to the beginning of the sentence, for example:

Present participial:	*Muttering under his breath*, Scrooge returned to work.
Past participial:	*Upset by Tiny Tim's insolence*, Scrooge vowed revenge.

The fact that participial phrases can be moved away from the nouns they modify creates the condition for a peculiar grammatical error known as a **dangling participle**. A participle is said to dangle when it is not properly attached to the noun that it apparently modifies. When a participial phrase is moved to the beginning of the sentence, we assume that the participial phrase modifies the subject—the nearest noun. This is the case in the two preceding example sentences. However, when the participial phrase does not literally modify the subject, then the participle is dangling. Here is an example of a dangling participle (participial phrase in italics):

X *Wrapped in beautiful paper*, Scrooge gave Tiny Tim his Christmas surprise.

What the writer meant to say, of course, was that Tiny Tim's Christmas surprise was wrapped in beautiful paper. What he actually said, though, was that Scrooge was wrapped in beautiful paper. (Dangling modifiers are discussed in detail in Chapter 10.)

Infinitive Phrases

Infinitive phrases are phrases headed by an **infinitive** used as a noun, an adjective, or an adverb. An infinitive is *to* plus the base form of a verb, for example:

to go
to eat
to be
to transform

An **infinitive phrase** consists of an infinitive head by itself or an infinitive head together with modifiers and/or complements.

The distinctive form of infinitives makes infinitive phrases easy to recognize. The catch is that infinitive phrases, unlike gerund phrases (nouns) and participial phrases (adjectives), can be used as more than one part of speech (nouns, adjectives, or adverbs).

Like gerund phrases, infinitive phrases can also have subjects. The **subject of the infinitive** is formed by retaining the subject of the verb as the object of the preposition *for*. Here are some examples of infinitive phrases with subjects in the three roles that infinitive phrases can play (infinitive phrases in italics, subjects of the infinitive in bold):

Noun: *For* ***Popeye*** *to turn down spinach* was a bit surprising.

Popeye is the subject of the infinitive *to turn down.* That is, *Popeye* is the person turning down the spinach.

Adjective: The route *for **you** to take* is I-95.

You is the subject of the infinitive *to take.* That is, *you* are the person who should take I-95.

Adverb: *For **the druggist** to fill my prescription*, I need a doctor's note.

The *druggist* is the subject of the infinitive *to fill.* That is, the *druggist* is the one who will fill my prescription.

Infinitive Phrases Used as Nouns

Infinitive phrases (with or without subjects) can play three of the major noun phrase roles (infinitive phrases in italics):

Subject:	*To learn a foreign language* takes a lot of practice.
Object of verb:	I wanted *to learn a foreign language.*
Predicate nominative:	All I wanted was *for him to finish his project.*

As was the case with the gerund phrases, infinitive phrases are always singular and can thus be replaced by the pronoun *it.* Here is the *it* test for infinitive phrases:

The *It* Test for Infinitive Phrases Used as Nouns

If an infinitive phrase can be replaced by *it,* then that infinitive phrase is being used as a noun phrase.

Subject:	*To learn a foreign language* takes a lot of practice.
	It takes a lot of practice.
Object of verb:	I wanted *to learn a foreign language.*
	I wanted to learn it.
Predicate nominative:	All I wanted was *for him to finish his project.*
	All I wanted was it.

(Grammar factoid: the one common noun role that infinitives cannot play is the object of a preposition. For example, compare the following sentences, one with a gerund phrase used as the object of a preposition, and one with an infinitive phrase as the object of a preposition [phrases in italics]:

Gerund object of preposition:		Scrooge worried about *getting rich.*
Infinitive object of preposition:	X	Scrooge worried about *to get rich.*

The gerund phrase seems perfectly acceptable as the object of a preposition, but the infinitive phrase is totally unacceptable. Probably the reason that infinitive phrases cannot be used after prepositions is that historically the *to* that begins an infinitive is itself a preposition. So, a preposition plus *to* would give us two noncompounded prepositions in a row—a linguistic no-no.)

Infinitive Phrases Used as Adjectives

Infinitive phrases (with or without subjects) can be used to modify nouns. Here are some examples (infinitive phrases in italics, infinitives in bold, nouns being modified underlined):

The need ***to sleep*** was nearly overpowering.
We marked the items ***to be** put on sale.*
Here is a list of drugs *for women **to avoid** during pregnancy.*

As you would expect, the modifying infinitive phrases can be readily identified by the pronoun replacement test, here slightly modified for infinitive phrases:

The Pronoun Replacement Test for Infinitive Phrases Modifying Nouns

If a noun and a following infinitive phrase are *both* replaced by a pronoun, then that phrase is an infinitive phrase modifying that noun.

Here is the pronoun replacement test applied to the preceding example sentences:

The need ***to sleep*** was nearly overpowering.
It was nearly overpowering.

We marked the items ***to be*** *put on sale.*
We marked them.

Here is a list of drugs for women ***to avoid*** *during pregnancy.*
Here is a list of them.

Infinitive Phrases Used as Adverbs

Infinitive phrases (with or without subjects) can be used to modify verbs or predicate adjectives. Both adverb uses are quite common.

Adverb Infinitive Phrases Used to Modify Verbs. Here are several examples of adverb infinitive phrases modifying verbs (infinitive phrases in italics, infinitives in bold):

I stayed up all night ***to finish*** *my book.*
They sold the bonds ***to invest*** *in Tootsie Roll stock.*
We finally moved into a hotel *for the kids* ***to get*** *some sleep.*

Adverb infinitive phrases modifying verbs behave just like all other adverbs modifying verbs: they answer adverb questions (especially *why* questions), and they can be moved to the beginning of the sentence:

Answer *why* questions
Why did I stay up all night? *To finish my book.*
Why did they sell the bonds? *To invest in Tootsie Roll stock.*
Why did we finally move into a hotel? *For the kids to get some sleep.*

Moved to the beginning of the sentence
To finish my book, I stayed up all night.
To invest in Tootsie Roll stock, they sold the bonds.
For the kids to get some sleep, we finally moved into a hotel.

A particularly easy and reliable test for adverb infinitive phrases that modify verbs is to put *in order* in front of the infinitive (*in order* is underlined):

I stayed up all night <u>in order</u> ***to finish*** *my book.*
They sold the bonds <u>in order</u> ***to invest*** *in Tootsie Roll stock.*
We finally moved into a hotel <u>in order</u> *for the kids* ***to get*** *some sleep.*

Though they are not nearly as common as dangling participles, infinitives used as adverbs can also dangle. The cause of the problem with adverb infinitives is exactly the same as with dangling participles. When an adverb infinitive is moved to the beginning of the sentence, the implied subject of the infinitive must be the same as the subject of the independent clause. Here are several examples of dangling adverb infinitives (in italics):

X *To sail a small boat safely*, the weather must be stable.

It sounds like the weather is sailing the boat.

X *To qualify for the election*, a valid ID card must be shown.

It sounds like the ID card is doing the qualifying.

Adverb Infinitives Used to Modify Predicate Adjectives. Here are several examples of adverb infinitive phrases modifying predicate adjectives (infinitive phrases in italics, infinitives in bold, predicate adjectives being modified underlined):

We are ready ***to go***.
I am anxious ***to start*** *packing for our trip.*
They are ready *for us* ***to come*** *in for dinner now.*

There is no positive test for identifying infinitive phrases that modify predicate adjectives. The only thing that infinitives modifying predicate adjectives could possibly be confused with is infinitive phrases modifying verbs. However, infinitive phrases modifying verbs have several positive tests that infinitives modifying predicate adjectives will fail. The easiest way to distinguish between the two uses of adverb infinitives is to see if the adverb infinitive can move. If it can, it modifies the verb; if it cannot, it modifies the predicate adjective. Infinitive phrases modifying predicate adjectives are locked into position following the predicate adjectives they modify, for example:

We are ready ***to go***.
X ***To go***, we are ready.

I am anxious ***to start*** *packing for our trip.*
X ***To start*** *packing for our trip*, I am anxious.

They are *ready for us* ***to come*** *in for dinner now.*
X *For us* ***to come*** *in for dinner now*, they are ready.

PART II

How to Find and Correct Mistakes

The first part of this book focused on the fundamental ways that English can be classified, explained, and analyzed. This first part was primarily descriptive, in that we simply laid out the ways English can be described. However, this second part is more prescriptive. In other words, we now focus on the correctness and the preferences that people have for formal English, especially written English. These preferences deal with what most people think of as the "rules" of English. Most, but not all, such rules are based on a logic intended to create more effective, consistent communication.

Unlike many grammar books written for people who want only to know the right answer in just a few seconds, our book offers more thorough explanations, while attempting to be as concise as possible.

Our hope is that, first, a thorough explanation will help you understand a given concept well enough that you will not need to consult another grammar book in the future. By understanding an issue in more than a superficial way, you will be more likely not to just follow a rule but to understand the basis of the rule.

We also believe that a thorough explanation will help you with the various exceptions, nuances, and finer points of a grammatical issue. Many books offer only simple rules and simple sentences as examples. However, most people have to apply rules in complex situations. We believe our explanations avoid over-oversimplifying matters and deal instead with the real sorts of problems that writers in particular must face in school, in the workforce, and even in their personal writing.

This second part of the book does not examine every grammatical error or problem that exists. Rather, we focus on the ones that are most common or cause writers and readers the most problems. Special attention is given to punctuation, especially the comma, because this aspect of writing leads to a considerable number of problems and questions for most people.

Pay special attention to our discussions on how you can avoid the problems covered. Rather than just offering self-explanatory rules, we offer general suggestions on how to detect and/or correct grammatical problems. These and other portions of our discussion attempt to draw on intuitive, commonsensical suggestions instead of overloading readers with linguistic jargon.

Finally, remember that this book, like most grammar reference books, is intended for a range of people in various contexts. We focus on the rules that serve as the basis for more specific style guides and preferences that evolve in particular professions, organizations, or vocations. It is normal for a group of people to take general rules (for grammar, dress, or any sort of human behavior) and tailor these. In other words, this book can only cover what most people prefer in terms of formal American English, but keep in mind that you will find some readers who, for better or worse, have more specific rules and preferences.

6

Writing Complete Sentences

This brief chapter is important for two reasons. First and most obviously, this chapter helps you avoid three major types of errors: fragments, fused sentences, and comma splices. Second, this chapter—especially the section on fragments—introduces you to some basic concepts that you should understand in order to avoid other types of problems and errors. In particular, recognizing a complete sentence is a necessary skill for avoiding a range of punctuation and sentence-structure problems.

These three sections have one major concept in common: all three deal with the notion of a complete sentence. The "Fragments" section applies to any sort of sentence, while "Fused Sentences" and "Comma Splices" focus on a common structure known as a **compound sentence**. In essence, a compound sentence results when two (or more) sentences are combined into one.

1. Fragments: A **fragment** is a group of words that cannot stand alone as a grammatically complete sentence. Even though fragments are common in speech and informal writing, they are considered one of the most serious types of errors in formal writing. In this section, we provide a formal definition of *fragment* and discuss some of the problems with the definition as most people seem to understand (or remember) it. This section also provides a useful tip for detecting fragments (the "I realize" tip).

2. Fused sentences: A **fused sentence** is a serious error that occurs when writers incorrectly attempt to combine two sentences. More specifically, the sentence has nothing at all separating these two groups of words, as in this example:

X A fire alarm sounded everyone ran out of the building.

We describe how you can avoid this error by first understanding that such a sentence is a compound sentence—a sentence made up of what could possibly be two sentences.

3. Comma splices: Like a fused sentence, a **comma splice** results when a writer does not correctly join two separate sentences. A comma splice is also considered a serious error in formal writing, but—unlike a fused sentence—at least the writer has used something to separate the two parts. However, you cannot use just a comma to separate them. Following is an example of a comma splice:

X A fire alarm sounded, everyone ran out of the building.

This section describes how you can easily correct a comma splice by putting a coordinating conjunction immediately after the comma. The most common coordinating conjunctions are *and*, *but*, and *or*.

Fragments

Most people have at least some idea of what a sentence fragment is—or have had a teacher write "frag" in red ink on their otherwise pristine papers. A **fragment** is a group of words that cannot stand alone as a grammatically complete sentence.

Fragment:	Because I said you can't leave the house.
Complete sentence:	You cannot go to the mall because I said you can't leave the house.

Grammar Tip: "I Realize"

Most complete sentences can be preceded with "I realize" and still sound fine. Fragments, however, will sound strange.

A more technical (and accurate) description of how to recognize a complete sentence is given in the following, but this "I realize" tip is a nontechnical means of recognizing most complete sentences and fragments. The tip draws on your intuitions of what seems to be a complete sentence in English, so it does not work well if your first language is not English.

Complete Sentence		**Sounds OK**
Brian forgot his keys.	*becomes*	I realize Brian forgot his keys.
We did not win the lottery.	*becomes*	I realize we did not win the lottery.
It rained heavily.	*becomes*	I realize it rained heavily.

Fragment		**Sounds Strange**
X Whatever.	*becomes*	X I realize whatever.
X Rolling down the hill.	*becomes*	X I realize rolling down the hill.
X Since the beginning of time.	*becomes*	X I realize since the beginning of time.

What's the Problem?

Several studies have shown that fragments are among the most annoying (if not *the* most annoying) types of errors that can be committed in formal writing. Even though fragments are common in speech and can be effective if used at the right time and place in written communication, many people do not believe a fragment is a complete thought. Indeed, many fragments lack a subject and a verb. Without a subject and a verb, a sentence is unlikely to communicate a complete idea.

In fact, fragments are so annoying to readers that you have to wonder how they could appear in the first place. Shouldn't these errors be so obvious that we recognize and delete them? Obviously, the answer is no. Bothersome fragments still manage to creep into most people's writing sooner or later, perhaps because some fragments seem like complete thoughts (while some people's complete sentences do not seem to reflect much thought at all).

Avoiding the Problem: Looking for Subjects and Verbs

Keep both of these ideas in mind to avoid fragments:

1. **Every complete sentence must have a subject and a verb.**
2. **Some fragments do have a subject and a verb, but they are still fragments because they start with a flag word that indicates what comes afterward is not a separate sentence.**

Requirement #1: A Subject and Its Verb

A complete sentence needs a subject and a verb that goes back to this subject. The subject is a person, place, or thing. It will be made up of a noun or a pronoun. The verb is something that the subject is doing, or the verb is a verb (such as *is*) that is not an action but is still linked to the subject to form a complete sentence.

Complete sentences (main subjects underlined once, their verbs underlined twice)

The busy executive ate lunch in her office.
She wrote this story in college.
Neil Armstrong received an annual salary of about $30,000 when he first walked on the moon.
Billy the Kid was twenty-one when he was killed.

Fragments

X Eating lunch in her office. (*Who* was eating?)
X A story from college. (*What* happened?)
X An annual salary of about $30,000. (*What* happened?)
X Killed when he was twenty-one. (*Who* killed *whom*?)

Requirement #2: No Improper Use of a Flag Word

Some words (usually called **subordinating conjunctions**) indicate that a dependent (subordinate) clause, rather than a complete sentence, is about to appear. That is, these flag words let us know that the next group of words the reader will see cannot stand as a complete sentence—even if they contain a subject and a verb. Notice how the following examples (dependent clauses) cannot stand by themselves as complete sentences despite having subjects and verbs:

Fragments: flag word subject + verb

X **When** the next train arrives.

X **Because** her boss was evil.

X **Whenever** you leave.

X **Because** the photocopier is being misused.

Grammar Tip: Checking *Because* Sentences

One common type of fragment begins with *because*. Double-check sentences that begin with *because* to make sure they are complete.

You can start a sentence with *because* if there is an independent clause later in the sentence, as in these complete sentences:

Because her boss was evil, Margaret found a job elsewhere.

Because the photocopier is being misused, our manager is unhappy with us.

In the next example, however, there is no independent clause coming after the "because" clause. Thus, this example is a fragment:

X Because I said that it is time to go.

Avoiding the Problem: Moving the Fragment

Almost every fragment is supposed to be part of the sentence right before it. To fix most fragments, move the fragment so it is part of the preceding sentence.

If you detect a fragment, see if you can correct the error by combining it with the previous sentence:

Sentence + Fragment		**Correction**
I will leave. When the next train arrives.	*becomes*	I will leave when the next train arrives.
She decided to quit. Because her boss was evil.	*becomes*	She decided to quit because her boss was evil.
You should lock the door. Whenever you leave.	*becomes*	You should lock the door whenever you leave.
We saw Dr. West. Who lives next door.	*becomes*	We saw Dr. West, who lives next door.

Punctuating the Correction

As you can see in the last corrected example, sometimes you need a comma to separate what used to be a fragment. Depending on your own writing style, you might discover that most of your corrections would require such a comma.

The best advice we can give is *not* to put a comma before the former fragment—unless you know why you should. (See "Commas with Adjective Clauses" in Chapter 11 to understand why the example just cited needs a comma.) If in doubt, do not use the comma. Or rewrite the correction entirely so you can keep the same ideas but put them into a sentence you know for certain how to punctuate.

Summary

- A complete sentence must have a subject that has a verb.
- Certain types of flag words introduce a subject and a verb, but these words are dependent clauses, not complete sentences.
- Most fragments result from a punctuation problem. That is, the fragment should not be set off as a complete sentence. The period right before the fragment should either be deleted or replaced by a comma so that the fragment becomes one with the preceding sentence.

Fused Sentences

A **fused sentence** is a sentence that has nothing at all separating one independent clause from another. An **independent clause** is a group of words able to stand alone as a complete sentence. Following is an example of a fused sentence:

X A parade is being held it should be enjoyable.

At first glance, you might think the sentence is chaotic. Here it is again with each independent clause underlined, revealing that the problem is indeed the result of putting two such clauses together with nothing to separate them:

Independent clause + independent clause

X A parade is being held it should be enjoyable.

What's the Problem?

The term *fused sentence* is used to describe this error because two clauses are merged (fused) into one—not a bad idea, except that readers need to know where one clause stops and the other begins. A fused sentence is a compound sentence that has gone wrong. That is, the writer understandably wants to combine two sentences but fails to provide proper punctuation between the two former sentences. (See Chapter 3 for more on compound sentences.)

Following are two more fused sentences. The second is particularly annoying because it is hard to tell if the word *today* describes the first or second part of the sentence.

X Walt Disney created the character Mickey Mouse Disney also provided the cartoon character's voice in the early days.

X We need to talk today I am lonely.

> **Period Test**
>
> If you can place a period in a sentence and create two complete sentences, then you must use something to separate the two parts of the original sentence.

Notice how a period can be placed in roughly the middle of each of the fused sentences already given:

Fused sentence: X A parade is being held it should be enjoyable.
Two sentences: A parade is being held. + It should be enjoyable.

Fused sentence: X Walt Disney created the character Mickey Mouse Disney also provided the cartoon character's voice in the early days.
Two sentences: Walt Disney created the character Mickey Mouse. + Disney also provided the cartoon character's voice in the early days.

Fused sentence: X We need to talk today I am lonely.
Two sentences: We need to talk today. + I am lonely.
We need to talk. + Today I am lonely.

As you can see, each of these fused sentences consists of two sentences. A fused sentence is a serious problem, so we want to stress that you must use something to separate what could be two (or more) separate sentences.

Correcting a Fused Sentence

Once you detect a fused sentence, you can correct it in numerous ways. Here are three common methods:

1. Separate the fused sentence into two sentences. Avoid relying on just this one method to fix or avoid errors such as fused sentences. The result could be a series of short, choppy, dull sentences.

Fused Sentence		**Correction**
X I was sleepy I had to stay awake.	*becomes*	I was sleepy. I had to stay awake.

2. Use a comma plus *and*, *but*, *or*, or another coordinating conjunction. This is the most common means of correcting a fused sentence. (See Chapter 1 for more information on coordinating conjunctions.)

Fused Sentence		**Correction**
X I was sleepy I had to stay awake.	*becomes*	I was sleepy, but I had to stay awake.

3. Use a semicolon. This approach works when you do not want a word coming between the two parts of the sentence. (See Chapter 13 for more on semicolons.)

Fused Sentence		**Correction**
X I was sleepy I had to stay awake	*becomes*	I was sleepy; I had to stay awake.

Summary

- A fused sentence is a serious error. It results when there is nothing in a sentence to separate two independent clauses.
- To confirm a sentence is fused, see if you can put a period in the sentence to create two complete sentences. If so and if there is nothing in the original sentence separating these two parts, then there is a fused sentence.
- To correct a fused sentence, you can (1) break the fused sentence into two sentences, (2) separate the two parts with a comma plus a coordinating conjunction, or (3) separate the two parts with a semicolon.

Comma Splices

A **comma splice** is a sentence in which *only* a comma is used to separate what could be two separate sentences. In other words, a comma is incorrectly used by itself to separate independent clauses in a compound sentence, as seen in this example:

X Snow White arrived late, she has a bad habit of being tardy.

A comma can be used to help create a compound sentence, but the sentence would need more than just a comma to be correct.

What's the Problem?

A comma splice is not much better than a fused sentence, which is a compound sentence having absolutely nothing (not even a comma) separating independent clauses. True, at least a comma splice has something separating the two clauses, but commas have so many functions in English that a comma alone does not let readers understand the structure of a compound sentence. Other cues are needed so that readers can better interpret the compound sentence.

Avoiding the Problem

If you can place a period in a sentence and create two complete sentences, then you cannot use *just* a comma to separate the two parts. Either add a coordinating conjunction or change the comma to a semicolon.

First, notice how the following comma splices could be divided into two sentences, confirming that each of the original sentences is indeed a compound sentence:

Comma Splice	=	Two Sentences
X Fish travel in schools, whales travel in pods.	=	Fish travel in schools. + Whales travel in pods.
X Your report is late, we were depending on you.	=	Your report is late. + We were depending on you.

X Tennessee Williams is the name of a famous play-wright, he was born in Mississippi.	=	Tennessee Williams is the name of a famous playwright. + He was born in Mississippi.

These examples are relatively simple. A comma splice can be confusing when there are other commas in the sentence. Following is such an example. The circled comma creating the comma splice is incorrect, but the other commas are correctly used.

X When I was fourteen, my father gave me a large, strange painting, it attempted to capture the likeness of Colonel William Travis, an ancestor who died at the Alamo.

Correcting a Comma Splice

Once you determine there is a comma splice, the error can be corrected in several ways. Here are three common methods:

1. Separate the comma splice into two sentences. Avoid relying on this one method to avoid comma splices. The result could be a series of dull, choppy sentences. However, note how the long comma splice above is a good candidate for this correction method.

X When I was fourteen, my father gave me a large, strange painting, it attempted to capture the likeness of Colonel William Travis, an ancestor who died at the Alamo.

When I was fourteen, my father gave me a large, strange painting. It attempted to capture the likeness of Colonel William Travis, an ancestor who died at the Alamo.

2. Follow the comma with *and*, *but*, *or*, or another coordinating conjunction. This is the most common means of correcting a comma splice. (See Chapter 1 for more information on coordinating conjunctions.)

X Fish travel in schools, whales travel in pods.
Fish travel in schools, but whales travel in pods.

3. Replace the comma with a semicolon. This approach works best when you do not believe the sentence sounds right with a coordinating conjunction. A semicolon does not need a coordinating conjunction to separate two independent clauses. (See Chapter 13 for more on semicolons.)

X Your report is late, we were depending on you.
Your report is late; we were depending on you.

Summary

- A comma splice is an error. It results when only a comma is used to separate two independent clauses.
- To confirm there is a comma splice, see if you can replace the comma with a period to create two complete sentences. If so, the original sentence is indeed a comma splice and should be corrected.
- To correct a comma splice, you can (1) break the sentence into two sentences, (2) separate the two parts with a comma plus a coordinating conjunction, or (3) separate the two parts with a semicolon.

7

Subject-Verb Agreement

In order for a sentence to be a sentence, and for a clause to be a clause, the first verb in the sentence and clause must agree in number with the subject. By *agree* we mean that the number of the verb must match the number of the subject. For example, a singular subject must be paired with the corresponding singular form of the verb, and a plural subject must be paired with the corresponding plural form of the verb, as in the following (subjects in bold, verbs in italics):

Singular: That **apple** *looks* like a Gala.
Plural: Those **apples** *look* like Galas.

The sections in this chapter deal with the three main situations in which writers are most likely to make subject-verb agreement errors:

1. Agreement with lost subjects: This section shows you how to monitor for subject-verb agreement when the subject phrase is so long or complicated that the actual subject can get lost and the verb mistakenly agrees with a word that is not the actual subject, for example:

X The cost of all the repairs we needed to make *were* more than we could afford.

In this example, the writer has lost track of the subject and has made the verb *were* agree with the plural noun *repairs*. The actual subject is the singular noun *cost*:

The **cost** of all the repairs we needed to make *was* more than we could afford.

2. The mysterious case of *there is* and *there was*: A surprising number of subject-verb errors involve sentences that begin *there is* or *there was*. Part of the problem is that in sentences of this type, the subject actually follows the verb, for example:

X There *is* usually some **leftovers** in the freezer.

The verb is singular, but the actual subject is plural, so the verb also needs to be in the plural form:

There *are* usually some **leftovers** in the freezer.

3. Agreement with compound subjects: A compound subject is a subject with two noun phrases joined by a coordinating conjunction. This section deals with a number of subject-verb agreement problems posed by compound subjects. The most common problem is the failure to use a plural verb when the compound subjects are joined with *and*, for example:

X Good planning and careful execution *is* necessary for success.

The verb is singular, but a compound subject joined by *and* requires a plural verb:

Good planning and **careful execution** *are* necessary for success.

Agreement with Lost Subjects

The most common cause of **subject-verb agreement error** is when the writer has lost track of what the subject actually is and has made the verb agree with the wrong thing. To a great extent, the causes of this type of error are the length and complexity of the subject noun phrase. The longer and more grammatically complex the subject noun phrase portion of the sentence is, the more likely we are to misidentify the subject.

Part of the reason for this is the way our brain processes linguistic information. Most of us can hold five to seven words verbatim in short-term memory. If the subject noun phrase portion of the sentence is longer than five to seven words (or even fewer words if the subject noun phrase is grammatically complicated), our brains automatically recode the noun phrase in a simplified form. Here is an example:

X A group of yachts with brightly colored banners flying in the wind were entering the harbor.

This sentence contains a subject-verb agreement error. The verb *were* agrees with *yachts* rather than with the actual subject *group*. In the research literature on grammatical errors, this type of mistake is so common that it has its own name: the **nearest-noun agreement error**. When we recode a long and/or complex subject noun phrase into long-term memory, we tend to remember only the semantically strongest noun that is nearest the verb. In the case of the example sentence just given, the semantically strongest noun nearest the verb is *yachts*.

Here is a psycholinguistic experiment that you can perform at home. Read the example sentence to someone. Then after a minute or so, ask the person what the sentence was about. The odds are very strong that the person will remember the sentence as being about yachts. Very few people will remember the sentence being about a *group* of yachts.

There are few subject-agreement errors in short sentences because the subject and the verb are either side by side or close together. So, one way to avoid subject-verb agreement errors is to write like third graders with short subject noun phrases. However, because we want to write sentences with adult-level complexity, we need to understand what it is about longer and/or more complex subject noun phrases that makes them hard to monitor for subject-verb agreement.

Understanding the mechanisms for expanding the subject noun phrase is the key to gaining control of the nearest-noun agreement error. Subject noun phrases (and all other noun phrases, for that matter) can be expanded in two ways. The first way is relatively trivial: we can put additional adjectives in front of the subject noun. A much more important way of expanding the subject noun phrase is to add postnoun modifiers. Basically, we make subject noun phrases longer and more complex by adding one or more of these three postnoun modifiers: **adjective prepositional phrases, adjec-**

tive clauses, and **participial phrases**. Here are examples of all three types of postnoun modifiers (in italics) applied to the basic sentence *Birds sing*:

Adjective prepositional phrase:	Birds *in the forest* sing.
Adjective clause:	Birds *that are in the forest* sing.
Participial phrase:	Birds *living in the forest* sing.

As you can see, the effect of each of these postnoun modifiers is to push the subject noun *birds* apart from the verb *sing*.

When multiple postnoun modifiers are combined, the subject noun and the verb end up at a considerable distance from each other. This is what happened in our original example sentence. The subject *group* is separated from the verb by two prepositional phrases and a participial phrase:

subject | prepositional phrase 1 | prepositional phrase 2 | participial phrase

A **group** *of yachts* *with brightly colored banners* *flying in the wind*

Consciously checking any sentence for subject-verb agreement always begins with finding the verb and then locating the subject to see that they agree. To check for nearest-noun type subject-verb agreement errors, we need to jump backward from the verb to the actual subject, skipping over all the intervening postnoun modifiers. Our natural tendency is to look at the first noun or pronoun on the left side of the verb for a possible match. This is a mistake. We do not want to cycle back through the sentence from right to left, checking each noun or pronoun as we go for possible subject-verb agreement.

Here is a helpful test for locating the subject when there is a long and/or complex subject noun phrase:

The Lost Subject Test

Jump from the verb back to the *first* eligible noun in the clause or sentence, ignoring any nouns or pronouns in introductory phrases. Test that noun or pronoun for subject-verb agreement.

Here is the lost subject test applied to the original example sentence:

X A group of yachts with brightly colored banners flying in the wind were entering the harbor.

Begin by locating the verb *were*. Next, jump back to the beginning of the sentence, ignoring all the intervening nouns. The first eligible noun (also, in this case, the first noun) is *group*. Unless something remarkable is going on in the sentence, this is going to be the actual subject. Test the verb with that first noun to see if there is valid subject-verb agreement:

X A *group were* entering the harbor.

In this case, we can see that there is a subject-verb agreement error, which we then correct:

A *group was* entering the harbor.

The full, corrected sentence reads as follows:

A *group* of yachts with brightly colored banners flying in the wind *was* entering the harbor.

Here is the lost subject test applied to a second example:

X The number of accidents caused by drunk drivers dramatically increase at night.

The first step is to identify the verb (in italics):

The number of accidents caused by drunk drivers dramatically *increase* at night.

The next step is to apply the lost subject test and jump to the first eligible noun or pronoun in the sentence (now also in italics):

The *number* of accidents caused by drunk drivers dramatically *increase* at night.

Next, check for subject-verb agreement:

X The *number increase* at night.

Clearly, there is a subject-verb agreement error that needs to be corrected:

The *number* of accidents caused by drunk drivers dramatically *increases* at night.

The lost subject test has one tricky bit. The test identifies the first *eligible* noun or pronoun in the clause. The reason for this qualification is that often sentences or clauses begin with introductory adverb prepositional phrases that contain nouns or pronouns. The nouns and pronouns in introductory adverb prepositional phrases are not eligible to enter into subject-verb agreement. Here is an example of such a sentence:

X In our last three games, the average margin of our losses *have* been two points.

The first noun in the sentence is *games*, the object of the preposition *in*. Nouns inside prepositional phrases are locked up inside the prepositional phrases and are therefore ineligible for subject-verb agreement. Accordingly, when we apply the lost subject test, we ignore the ineligible noun *games* and look at the next noun:

X The average *margin have* been two points.

We have now identified a subject-verb agreement error, which we would correct as follows:

In our last three games, the average *margin* of our losses *has* been two points.

In actual practice, introductory adverb prepositional phrases are so easy to recognize that they pose little practical problem in using the lost subject test.

One final point about the lost subject test: despite the fact that all of our examples so far have been sentences, the actual wording of the test is that it applies to clauses as well as to sentences. The term *clause* is broader than the term *sentence*. Sentences are just one type of clause—an independent clause. The lost subject test works equally well for subject-verb agreement in dependent clauses as for subject-verb agreement in independent clauses. Here is an example of the lost subject test applied to a dependent clause:

X Harold told them that his cottage in one of the new seaside developments *were* not damaged in the storm.

To apply the lost subject test, we must jump from the verb *were* to the first eligible noun or pronoun *in its clause*. (Remember, clauses are like Gilligan's Island—you can't get off.) The first eligible noun in its clause is *cottage*:

X His *cottage were* not damaged in the storm.

Clearly, there is a subject-verb agreement error, which we would correct as follows:

His *cottage was* not damaged in the storm.

The entire sentence would now read this way:

Harold told them that his *cottage* in one of the new seaside developments *was* not damaged in the storm.

Summary

The most common cause of subject-verb error is when the verb agrees with the nearest semantically strong noun rather than with the more distant actual subject. Anytime you have a sentence or clause with a long or complicated subject noun phrase, it is probably worth your while to check for lost subject error. Jump from the verb to the first noun in the sentence or clause. Pair that noun up with the verb to see if it makes sense as the subject. The odds are that it is the actual subject. If it does not make a valid subject, work your way across the subject noun phrase from left to right until you find the actual subject. It won't be far.

The Mysterious Case of *There Is* and *There Was*

Nearly every language has a construction called an **existential**. Existential sentences are used for pointing out the existence of something. In English, existential sentences use the adverb *there* plus a linking verb (usually a form of *be*). Here are some examples (*there* plus linking verbs in italics):

Waiter, *there is* a fly in my soup.
There was an old woman who lived in a shoe.
There seems to be a problem with my bill.
Houston, *there's* a problem.

The grammar of existential sentences is somewhat unusual in that the actual subject *follows* the verb. Here are the example sentences again, this time with the verbs in italics and the subject nouns in bold:

Waiter, there *is* a **fly** in my soup.
There *was* an old **woman** who lived in a shoe.
There *seems* to be a **problem** with my bill.
Houston, there*'s* a **problem**.

We can prove that the nouns following the verbs are actually subjects by making the nouns plural. When we do so, the verbs must change to agree with the changed nouns:

Waiter, there *are* **flies** in my soup.
There *were* some old **women** who lived in a shoe.

There *seem* to be some **problems** with my bill.
Houston, there*'re* some **problems.**

One of the authors of this book and his students did a study of subject-verb agreement errors found in the writing of college freshmen. Somewhat to our surprise, a substantial number of subject-verb agreement errors involved existential sentences. Even more surprising, the errors fell into a distinct pattern.

Following are two groups of subject-verb errors involving existential sentences. The first group is representative of more than 98 percent of the errors we found. The second group is representative of a kind of error that made up less than 2 percent of the errors. Look at the two groups, and see if you can figure out what the errors in each group have in common (existential verbs in italics, subjects in bold):

Group A: almost all errors were like this
X There *is* dozens of **books** piled on the carpet.
X There *was* some old **dishes** that looked usable.
X There *seems* to be **noises** coming from the backyard.
X There *was* still many **jobs** to be done.

Group B: errors like this were quite uncommon
X There *are* a big **lake** on the other side of the mountain.
X There *appear* to be no **solution.**
X There *were* a bright **light** shining in the trees.

Do you see the pattern? The common error is using a singular verb with a plural subject. The uncommon error is the reverse: using a plural verb with a singular subject. (Didn't you find the second group to be so odd as to seem almost un-English?)

Clearly, something is going on here. All things being equal, we would expect roughly as many errors with singular subjects as with plural subjects. Some other factor must be intervening to cause the distribution of errors to be so skewed. Something makes it much more likely for us to make a subject-verb agreement error in existential sentences when the subject is plural than when the subject is singular.

The answer seems to be in English speakers' perception of how existential sentences are built. Apparently, people increasingly think of the existential *there* not as an adverb but as the actual subject of the sentence. The existential *there* has become like the pronoun *it*—an invariant singular that requires a verb with a third-person singular *-s*. This analysis would explain why errors of plural subjects with singular verbs are so common and the reverse error of singular subjects with plural verbs is so rare. If *there* is perceived as a singular subject, then all verbs in existential sentences must also be singular to agree, regardless of the number of the noun following the verb.

If this analysis is correct, then we have a conflict between what sounds right in casual, spoken English and what is technically correct in formal, written English. Maybe at some point in the future, existential *there* will be fully accepted as the grammatical subject of its sentence. But until that happy time, we need to monitor existential sentences for subject-verb agreement.

What we have learned about existential *there* gives us a considerable advantage in knowing exactly what kind of error to look for:

The Existential *There* Test

When a sentence contains an existential *there*, check the noun following the linking verb to see if it is plural. If it is, then make sure the verb agrees with it.

Following are some sentences containing existential *there*:

X There is millions of stars in our galaxy.

The noun after the linking verb is *millions*. Because *millions* is plural, we must make the verb agree:

There *are* millions of stars in our galaxy.

X There was several movies that we wanted to see.

The noun after the linking verb is *movies*. Because *movies* is plural, we must make the verb agree:

There *were* several movies that we wanted to see.

X I didn't like the ending because there was far too many loose ends that were not tied up.

In this sentence, the existential is in the dependent clause *there was far too many loose ends*. Whether the existential is in an independent clause or in a dependent clause, the rule still holds: look for the noun following the linking verb. In this case, the subject is *loose ends*. Because the subject is plural, we must change the verb to agree:

I didn't like the ending because there *were* far too many loose ends that were not tied up.

X There is an old flashlight and some batteries in the drawer.

This sentence is a little more complicated because we have a compound subject—*flashlight and some batteries*. We must change the verb to make it agree with the compound subject:

There *are* an old flashlight and some batteries in the drawer.

Summary

Existential sentences are so prone to subject-verb error that you should monitor each one. Look at the noun *following* the existential verb to see if it is plural. If it is, check to make sure the verb is in agreement with that plural subject.

Agreement with Compound Subjects

A **compound subject** is formed when two (or more) subjects are joined by a **coordinating conjunction**. The coordinating conjunctions normally used to join subjects are the following:

Single-Word Conjunctions	**Correlative Conjunctions**
and	both . . . and
or	either . . . or
	neither . . . nor

Following are examples of each (coordinating conjunctions in italics, compound subjects underlined):

Larry *and* Holly are coming to the meeting.
A pencil *or* a pen is all that you will need.
Both Donner *and* Blitzen were really fed up with the fat guy.
Either Fred *or* Louise is scheduled to be there.
Unfortunately, *neither* I *nor* my husband is able to come.

The rules for subject-verb agreement with compound subjects are different, depending on the coordinating conjunction used. For *and* and the correlative conjunction *both . . . and*, the compound subject requires a plural verb.

Compound subjects formed with any of the three remaining coordinating conjunctions (*or*, *either . . . or*, *neither . . . nor*) are governed by a more complicated rule: the verb agrees *only* with the second of the two subjects. Here are some examples (coordinating conjunctions in italics, compound subjects underlined, verbs in bold):

One truck *or* three cars **are** all that the ferry can carry at one time.

The verb *are* agrees with *cars*, the second (and closer) of the two subjects in the compound subject. Now see what happens when we reverse the two noun phrases in the compound subject:

Three cars *or* one truck **is** all that the ferry can carry at one time.

Now the verb is singular to agree with *truck*.

Either Aunt Sarah *or* the Smiths **are** picking you up.

The verb is plural to agree with the plural subject *Smiths.* Here are the two subject noun phrases reversed:

Either the Smiths *or* Aunt Sarah **is** picking you up.

Now the verb is singular to agree with *Aunt Sarah.*

Neither the banks *nor* the post office **is** open today.

The verb is singular to agree with *the post office*, the second of the two noun phrases. Here are the two subjects reversed:

Neither the post office *nor* the banks **are** open today.

Now the verb is plural to agree with *banks.*

Compound subjects joined with *and* or the correlative *both . . . and* would seem to be no-brainers. They always take plural verbs, don't they? Most of the time they do, but there are three exceptions, which we have labeled "*one and the same,*" "*each and every,*" and "*bacon and eggs.*"

One and the Same

Occasionally, we will use a compound subject in which the two nouns refer to the same person or thing. In this situation, we use a singular verb. Here is an example (compound underlined, verb in italics):

My neighbor and good friend Sally *has* lived here for years.

In this sentence, *my neighbor* and *good friend Sally* are one and the same person. Because there is only one person, the verb is singular.

Here are two more examples:

His pride and joy *was* a restored Stanley Steamer.
His son and heir *is* an accountant in Burbank.

Each *and* Every

When the modifier *each* or *every* is used to modify a compound subject, the verb is singular. *Each* and *every* seem to have an implicit paraphrase of *each one* and *every one* that requires a singular verb. Here are two examples of *each* and two examples of *every* (verbs in italics, compounds underlined, *each* and *every* in bold):

Each: **Each** senator and representative on the committee *has* one vote.
Each boy and girl *takes* a turn at drawing names.

Every: **Every** senator and member of congress *has* exactly one vote.
It seems that **every** town, country, and village *has* an Oak Street.

Bacon and Eggs

When compound subjects joined by the coordinating conjunction *and* form a well-recognized single unit, then they are used with a singular verb. Here are some clear-cut examples of well-recognized single units (verbs in italics, compounds underlined):

Bacon and eggs *is* still the standard American breakfast.
Drinking and driving *is* the major cause of accidents.
The bow and arrow *is* found in virtually every traditional culture.
Thunder and lightning always *scares* my dog to death.

The most common source of error in sentences with compound subjects joined with *and* is writers' overgeneralizing the *bacon and eggs* rule. That is, writers tend to think of *all* compound subjects joined with *and* as units and thus use a singular verb with all of them.

However, unitary compounds like *bacon and eggs* are the exception, not the rule. From a purely logical standpoint, one could make a case that all compounds joined with *and* are units of some sort. It's too bad the conventions of English grammar are pretty insensitive to logic! The fundamental rule is that compound subjects joined with *and* require a plural verb. So, unless there is a compelling reason to override the fundamental rule, always use a plural verb with compound subjects joined with *and*. The following test will help you decide whether or not compound subjects joined with *and* should be used with singular or plural verbs:

The Pronoun Replacement Test for Compound Subjects Joined with *And*

Whenever *and* is used to join compound subjects, see whether you can replace the compound subject with the pronoun *they* or *it*. If *it* really seems preferable to *they*, then use a singular verb. Otherwise, always use *they*.

Here are some example sentences, which may or may not be correct as is (verbs in italics, compound subjects underlined):

The pencils and some paper *is* on the desk.

Would you prefer (a) or (b)?

(a) *They* are on the desk. (*They* = the pencils and some paper)
(b) *It* is on the desk. (*It* = the pencils and some paper)

Here, the choice seems quite clear. The compound subject *the pencils and some paper* does not seem to be enough of a well-established unit to be replaced by *it*. Therefore, the sentence needs to be corrected:

The pencils and some paper *are* on the desk.

Our genetic makeup and our personal experience *makes* us who we are.

Would you prefer (a) or (b)?

(a) *They* make us who we are. (*They* = our genetic makeup and our personal experience)

(b) *It* makes us who we are. (*It* = our genetic makeup and our personal experience)

Genetic makeup and *personal experience* together make a kind of natural unit, but because they are not any kind of a fixed or recognizable phrase, *they* seems a much better pronoun substitute for the phrase. Accordingly, we need to correct the original sentence:

> Our genetic makeup and our personal experience *make* us who we are.
>
> What we see and what we get *is* not always the same thing.
>
> Would you prefer (a) or (b)?
>
> **(a)** *They* are not always the same thing. (*They* = what we see and what we get)
>
> **(b)** *It* is not always the same thing. (*It* = what we see and what we get)

In this example, we have a more complicated compound subject that combines two noun clauses. Despite the fact that *what we see* and *what we get* are both recognizable phrases, they are not phrases normally yoked together as a single unit. Therefore, *they* is preferable, so the sentence needs to be corrected:

> What we see and what we get *are* not always the same thing.

Summary

Compound subjects cause a surprising number of subject-verb agreement errors. The single most common error is treating a compound subject joined by *and* or *both . . . and* as a single unit that takes a singular verb. Unless the compound subject is a well-established phrase like *bacon and eggs*, use a plural verb. There are two other main exceptions to this rule:

1. If the compound subject is modified by *each* or *every*, then the verb is singular.
2. If the noun phrases joined by the compound refer to one and the same person or thing, then the verb is singular.

If the compound is *or*, *either . . . or*, or *neither . . . nor*, then the verb agrees with the nearest subject.

8

Pronoun Problems

A **pronoun** is a word that takes the place of a noun. Pronouns normally have very little meaning by themselves. They are general words that can be used to refer to various types of things, objects, people, places, and ideas.

The best-known pronouns are **personal pronouns**. These include *she, he, we, our, it,* and *they*. However, there are other categories of personal pronouns as well. Some other common pronouns are *which, who, somebody, something, each, this, that,* and *these.*

Pronouns are an indispensable part of the English language. In fact, most languages have a part of speech similar to the English pronoun. Because they are used in diverse ways, various rules developed over the years to help distinguish one type of pronoun from another. This chapter includes a discussion of some basic properties of pronouns, but we focus on the most common or most bothersome types of problems that can occur with pronouns.

1. *I* or *me*? *she* or *her*? *he* or *him*? *they* or *them*? The title of this section is a bit wordy, but a technical description of the issue seems to lose most readers. In essence, this section focuses on choosing the correct form (case) of a personal pronoun. Unlike nouns, personal pronouns usually take a different form or shape depending on the word's function in a particular sentence.

Note how the same personal pronoun takes on different shapes in each sentence (pronouns underlined):

Dan told me that I could not leave my car here.
Somebody needs to tell him that he should mind his own business.

In general, most people have few problems using the correct form of a pronoun. However, errors in this regard have a much greater chance of occurring in certain types of sentence structures than in others. This section describes such common structures (especially those involving a pronoun and a coordinating conjunction) and offers tips and strategies for correcting errors involving pronoun form.

2. *Who, whom, or that*? This section focuses on errors and issues involving three types of pronouns: *who*, *whom*, and *that*. One issue is whether to use *who* or *whom* in a particular sentence. The other issue—often considered less serious—is when to use *that* rather than the other two pronouns. These are actually two distinct matters even though both involve the same three pronouns.

The pronouns *who* and *whom* are really not interchangeable despite their shared meanings and functions. You should use *who* when the pronoun has a subject function, saving *whom* for the object function. We provide a more accessible way to understand this complex issue. Following are two correct uses of these pronouns (underlined):

I do not know who is ready to eat.
You forget to whom you are speaking.

Even though modern usage allows *that* to be used in various ways, the conventional rule of thumb is you should not use *that* to refer to humans; rather, you should use *that* only when referring to ideas, animals, or inanimate objects. In this first sentence, *that* is incorrectly used to refer to a specific person. The second sentence correctly uses *who* to refer to the teacher.

X Mavis saw the teacher that once gave her an F in English.
Mavis saw the teacher who once gave her an F in English.

3. Vague pronouns: As noted earlier, pronouns have little if any meaning by themselves. One way they mean something is by taking the place of an earlier noun (or another pronoun). Here, the pronoun *it* refers back to *boat*:

Pat saw a boat she wanted, but it cost far too much.

Not all pronouns have to refer back to such a noun (for instance, the pronoun *everyone* does not). This section applies to various types of pronouns that do refer to a previous word. The basic rule is that such pronouns must clearly refer back to a noun or pronoun. However, we focus on the three pronouns that seem to account for the vast majority of vague pronoun errors: *this*, *that*, and *it*.

4. Reflexive pronouns: problems with "*-self*" and "*-selves*" words: One type of pronoun is the reflexive pronoun. This category includes the "*-self*" and "*-selves*" pronouns, such as *myself*, *herself*, and *ourselves*. These are common words that usually do not lead to significant problems. However, this section describes various problems that do occur with reflexive pronouns.

One serious problem involves using reflexive pronouns that do not truly exist, at least not in formal English. There are no such words as *hisself* and *theirselves*. The correct forms are *himself* and *themselves*.

Another problem arises when people mistakenly use a reflexive pronoun when another pronoun, such as *me* or *I*, should be used. Here is an example of such an error:

X Sean made a dessert for Carol and myself.

This section briefly notes also that reflexive pronouns are often overused. They should be used when something does something to itself:

He also burnt himself in the process.

5. Pronoun agreement errors: Some pronouns refer back to a previous word (an **antecedent**). Personal pronouns such as *he* and *she* must always have an antecedent. Such pronouns must logically refer back to their antecedents so that they are in agreement about matters such as gender or number.

One problem is that certain pronouns seem to be plural (more than one) yet actually are singular. In the following example, *everybody* is singular. However, a later pronoun that refers back to *everybody* is plural, creating a pronoun agreement error.

X Everybody will need to return their forms on time to be considered for the job.

Pronouns and antecedents also agree in terms of gender. For instance, a "female" pronoun should refer to a "female" antecedent. A related issue involves avoiding sexist pronouns. In particular, do not use pronouns such as *he* and *his* when referring to both men and women. We offer a simple suggestion for avoiding such problems altogether.

I or *Me*? *She* or *Her*? *He* or *Him*? *They* or *Them*?

A **pronoun** is a word used in place of a noun. There are several different types of pronouns, but the most commonly known is the **personal pronoun** (see Chapter 1). Some personal pronouns are *I, she, he, they, it,* and *you.*

Personal pronouns are unlike any other type of pronoun (or noun, for that matter) in the English language. The peculiarities of the "shape-shifting" personal pronoun often lead to errors when people use an incorrect form. (Some people refer to this matter as **case**.) The problem stems not just from the fact that personal pronouns change their appearance depending on how they are used but also from the fact that personal pronouns do not share the same rules for how they change. The most common errors occur when people mistakenly make the wrong choice when choosing between four pairs: *I* versus *me, she* versus *her, he* versus *him*, and *they* versus *them.*

A personal pronoun might change in appearance a little, greatly, or not all, depending on how the pronoun is used. For example, *I* becomes *me* when it is receiving action rather than giving it:

I chased our dog. *becomes* Our dog chased me.

Personal pronouns are not consistent in the way such changes occur. Note, for example, that the pronoun *you* would not change shape if it replaced *I* and *me* in the pair of examples just given.

Though not required to understand the focus of this section, the table that follows includes a complete listing of personal pronouns and how they change shape depending on their function.

PERSONAL PRONOUNS AND THEIR FORMS

	Singular	Plural
Subject form	I	we
	you	you
	he, she, it	they
Object form	me	us
	you	you
	him, her, it	them
Possessive form	my, mine	our, ours
	your, yours	your, yours
	his, her, its	their, theirs

I *Versus* Me, She *Versus* Her, He *Versus* Him, *and* They *Versus* Them

Fortunately, not all pronouns lead to problems related to form. The four pairs most involved in such errors are *I* versus *me*, *she* versus *her*, *he* versus *him*, and *they* versus *them*. Following are sample errors with the incorrect pronoun underlined:

X Colleen and him traveled to Birmingham this weekend.
X The identity of the masked assailant is known only to you and he.
X It is up to they to decide who can leave.
X The committee elected Jean and I cochairs for next year.
X It was me who called.

As illustrated, the errors can involve different sentence structures, making it more difficult to learn the correct rule. Fortunately, there is a rule that applies to these diverse situations. First, we will cover the technical guideline, and then we will offer a simpler approach.

Avoiding the Problem: A Technical Explanation

Use the subject form when the pronoun is either the subject of a verb or the subject complement. Use the object form when the pronoun has any other function.

More on Subject and Object Forms

The **subject form** of a personal pronoun is what the name suggests: the form you use when the pronoun is the subject of a verb, as in the following (pronoun underlined):

I went to work early.

The **object form** is the form you use when a pronoun is receiving an action, as here:

Sarah called me.

The subject and object forms actually do more than act as subjects or recipients of actions. However, half of the problem can be solved by understanding *which* forms you should associate with these two terms.

Subject Form	**Object Form**
I	me
he	him
she	her
they	them

Grammar Tip: Subject and Object Forms

The subject form of any pronoun is what you would use to fill in the blank in a sentence such as "_______ ran." The object form is what you would use in a sentence such as "The ball hit _______."

Consider the technical rule again. Use the subject form when the pronoun is the subject of the sentence, as shown in the following (pronouns underlined):

Colleen and he traveled to Birmingham this weekend.
Yesterday, they went to work early.
Shirley and I arrived just in time to catch the plane to Denver.

The rule also states that you should use the subject form when the pronoun is a subject complement, which is a fancy way of saying the pronoun comes right after a verb such as *is*, *am*, *are*, *was*, or *were*. Following are examples of pronouns correctly used in this way (underlined):

It was I who called.
The person you want is he.

Needless to say, following the formal rule in such sentences seems stuffy (even awkward). In informal English, many people do not follow the rule in regard to subject complements, and usually nobody complains.

The other half of the technical rule indicates you should use the object form in other situations. That is, if the pronoun is not a subject (or a subject complement), use the object form (underlined):

The identity of the masked assailant is known only to you and him.
It is up to them to decide who can leave.
The committee elected Jean and me cochairs for next year.

Only in the last example is the object form the recipient of an action (a direct object), but the object form is used correctly in all three sentences.

Avoiding the Problem: A Less Technical Explanation

If a verb appears right after the pronoun, use the subject form. If there is not a verb immediately afterward, use the object form. This hint will work most of the time.

More on Verbs After the Pronoun

The technical rule given earlier is best in that it is more complete, but this second approach should work 90 percent of the time and is easier to apply.

Following are three examples already used. Note how the pronoun (underlined once) is followed by the verb (underlined twice), meaning you should indeed use the subject form:

Colleen and he traveled to Birmingham this weekend.
Yesterday, they went to work early.
Shirley and I arrived just in time to catch the plane to Denver.

As noted, looking for a verb after the pronoun does not work with subject complements. In *It was I who called*, *I* is formally correct even though *I* is not followed by a verb. As seen in these next two examples, you could also have an adverb between a pronoun and its verb. Technically, a verb does not come immediately after each pronoun in these examples, but the tip should work with such sentences if you realize the adverbs are optional and could be deleted or moved elsewhere.

Colleen and he reluctantly traveled to Birmingham this weekend.
Yesterday, they almost went to work early.

As stated, use the object form when the pronoun is not followed by a verb. Notice how the next examples are followed by nothing at all or by something that is *not* a verb. You do not have to know what part of speech does appear right afterward, as long as you know it is not a verb. Here, though, we have indicated what type of word (if any) comes after the pronoun:

The identity of the masked assailant is known only to you and me.

part of an infinitive

It is up to them to decide who can leave.

noun

The committee elected Jean and me cochairs for next year.

Grammar Tip: Pronouns in Compound Structures

If you are using a pronoun in a compound structure, reword the sentence using just the pronoun. This test sentence will help make sure you are using the right form in the original.

As illustrated in earlier examples, a frequent situation involving pronoun errors is when the pronoun is part of a compound structure (most commonly, when *and* is used to combine the pronoun with a noun or another pronoun). For some reason, people will use an incorrect form when they would never do so if the pronoun were used by itself. That is the basis of our second tip: reword the sentence so you use only the pronoun in the original sentence. The resulting test sentence will not read properly if you are using the incorrect pronoun, as in the following (pronouns underlined):

Original Sentence with Error		**Test Sentence**
X Colleen and him traveled to Birmingham this weekend.	*becomes*	X Him traveled to Birmingham this weekend.
X Shirley and me arrived just in time to catch the plane to Denver.	*becomes*	X Me arrived just in time to catch the plane to Denver.
X The committee elected Jean and I cochairs for next year.	*becomes*	X The committee elected I cochair for next year.

The test sentences sound ridiculous, but the original sentences contain the same mistake. To correct the originals, use the same pronoun you would use if the pronoun were used alone. Following are corrections of these errors:

Colleen and he traveled to Birmingham this weekend.
Shirley and I arrived just in time to catch the plane to Denver.
The committee elected Jean and me cochairs for next year.

Summary

- Personal pronouns have subject and object forms.
- Four pairs of pronouns cause the most problems in regard to choosing the correct form: *I* versus *me*, *she* versus *her*, *he* versus *him*, and *they* versus *them*.
- Use the subject form when the pronoun is (1) the subject of a verb or (2) a subject complement.
- Use the object form when the pronoun has another function.
- A simpler guideline is to use the subject form when a verb appears right afterward. Otherwise, use the object form.
- Be careful when using personal pronouns in a compound structure. Use the same form you would if the pronoun appeared by itself.

Who, *Whom*, or *That*?

Who, *whom*, and *that* are pronouns. A **pronoun** is a word used in place of a noun. Actually, *that* can be other parts of speech as well, but its use as a pronoun causes some confusion. In these examples, the pronouns (underlined) are all used correctly:

You are speaking to whom?
Ricardo is a person whom we can trust.
I know who left early on Monday.
Who is ready?

Though a subject of debate, most modern reference books on grammar indicate this example of *that* is correct:

? We all need a leader that will improve morale.

What's the Problem?

There are two common errors involving these three pronouns, but both involve deciding which pronoun should be used in a particular sentence. The first and more significant error deals with choosing *who* or *whom*. The second is mistakenly using *that* when one of the other two pronouns should be used. (The pronouns *whoever* and *whomever* are also confused with one another, though they are used much less often. The following discussion applies to these two pronouns as well.)

> **Avoiding the Problem: *Who* Versus *Whom***
>
> Use the subject form *who* when the pronoun is used as the subject for a verb. Use the object form *whom* when the pronoun has any other function. Sometimes you must move the pronoun around to determine its function.

Who *Versus* Whom

Like some personal pronouns, *who* takes on a different shape when used as a direct object or any function besides a subject. Most people realize there is a difference between *who* and *whom*; the problem is remembering which form goes with what function. One solution is simply to remember the rule: use the subject form only when the pronoun is a subject. (See Chapter 7 for information on subjects and verbs.) In these examples, note how the pronoun (underlined once) is the subject of the verb (underlined twice):

I know <u>who</u> <u>left</u> early on Monday.
<u>Who</u> <u>is</u> ready?

> **Grammar Tip: A Verb Afterward**
>
> If the pronoun is quickly followed by a verb, use *who*.

This tip will work most of the time because a subject is normally followed immediately by a verb, as seen in the two examples just given. (It is possible, though, to have an adverb such as *almost* coming between a subject and its verb.)

The object form *whom* is used in other situations. In the following sentences, *whom* is not followed by a verb and is not the subject of a verb. Thus, *whom* is the correct choice.

You are speaking to <u>whom</u>?
Ricardo is a person <u>whom</u> we can trust.

The second example is harder to analyze because *whom* is out of order. Even though the sentence is correct, our intuition tells us *whom* should come after *trust*, for *whom* is the object (the direct object) of the act of trust. You do not have to worry about where *whom* is placed, however, if you follow the "verb afterward" tip. Is there a verb right after *whom*? No, so do not use *who*.

Grammar Tip: *Him* and *Whom*

Both *him* and *whom* end in the letter *m*, and both are object forms. Use *whom* only when *him* (not *he*) would be the appropriate choice. You might have to move words around and look only at part of the sentence to apply this tip.

This second tip is gimmicky, but it works. Even when *whom* refers to a female in your sentence, use *him* in a paraphrase. If *him* works, use *whom*. If *him* does not work, use *who*.

In these two examples, *him* would be the better choice, meaning *whom* is appropriate:

Original Sentence	Test Sentence
You are speaking to <u>whom</u>?	You are speaking to <u>him</u>.
Ricardo is a person <u>whom</u> we can trust.	We can trust <u>him</u>.

To apply this tip, focus on the part of the sentence involving the pronoun. In the first example, you might as well consider all of the sentence, but in the second example you have to look just at the part of the sentence in which the pronoun is either a subject or an object.

Consider the reverse of this tip: when *he* works better than *him*. Here are two instances where *him* clearly does not work, meaning *who* is indeed correct:

Original Sentence	**Test Sentence**
I know who left early on Monday.	X Him left early on Monday.
Who is ready?	X Him is ready.

Avoiding the Problem: *That* Versus *Who/Whom*

Avoid using *that* to refer to actual people. Instead, use *who* or *whom*. Most readers consider it acceptable, however, to use *that* when referring to a category or type of person.

That *Versus* Who/Whom

Up until near the end of the last century, it was considered incorrect to use *that* to refer to people, but the rules have eased, at least in regard to certain types of sentences. Still, we suggest you never use *that* to refer to a particular person or persons. In the following errors, *that* is used to refer back to specific individuals (a boy and a physician):

X You should thank the boy that returned your lost dog.
X Dr. Dolittle is a physician that I strongly recommend.

Some people use *that* to avoid having to choose between *who* and *whom*. Once you understand the rule governing the use of *who/whom*, you know the correct versions of the preceding sentences are as follows:

You should thank the boy who returned your lost dog.
Dr. Dolittle is a physician whom I strongly recommend.

As mentioned, the rules have recently relaxed—somewhat. Most grammar textbooks and style guides still indicate you *must* use *who* or *whom* when referring to specific people. But a number also indicate you can use *that* to refer to a category or type of person, as seen here:

? We all need a leader that will improve morale.
? Any worker that arrives late will be given a warning.

In both examples, *that* refers back to a type of person, not to someone in particular. Therefore, *that* is an acceptable choice for many readers. But what if your readers do not approve of *that* used in this way, or what if you use *that* when you incorrectly believe it refers to a type of person (a term that is not altogether clear at times)? For these reasons, we suggest you avoid using *that* at all to refer to people.

Save *that* for inanimate objects, animals, ideas, etc. These examples are perfectly fine uses of *that*:

We all need a system that will improve morale.
Any payment that arrives late will be returned.

Summary

- The pronouns *who* and *whom* are not interchangeable, for *who* is the subject form while *whom* is the object form.
- Use *who* when it is the subject of a verb; otherwise, use *whom*.
- Usually, you can look at the word right after the pronoun to determine which form to use. Use *who* if there is a verb right afterward; use *whom* otherwise.
- You can also associate *whom* with *him* (both end in the letter *m*). Use *whom* when *him* makes better sense. Use *who* when *he* works best.
- Avoid using *that* to refer back to people, although some readers consider it acceptable to use *that* if it refers to an abstract category of people.

Vague Pronouns

As explained earlier, a **pronoun** is a word that takes the place of a noun. Many people associate the term *pronoun* with words such as *he, she, it, you*, and *they*. However, there are other types of pronouns as well, such as *everybody, which, who, whom, each, that*, and *this*.

Some—but not all—pronouns "bend back" to refer to a previous noun or pronoun. That is, some pronouns derive their meaning by referring back to an **antecedent**. In this example, the pronoun *it* bends back to refer to the word *dog*:

> My dog knew it was in trouble for eating our lunch.

If *it* did not have an antecedent, the pronoun would not have meaning. In the next example, the pronoun *this* means something *only* if readers connect the pronoun with the antecedent (*wallet*):

> I found your missing wallet. Put this in your pocket right now!

Pronouns that often (or always) require antecedents include the following:

this	that	these	those	both	some	many	most	
he	she	him	they	them	which	who	either	which

As we will discuss shortly, the guidelines and suggestions in this section apply to various pronouns, but we will focus on three particular pronouns: *this, that*, and *it*.

What's the Problem?

Pronouns that require an antecedent must *clearly* refer back to a previous noun or pronoun. When they fail to do so, a **vague pronoun** results, meaning that the writer or speaker is not communicating effectively. The blame tends to be placed on the vague pronoun, but usually the source of the problem is the lack of a clear antecedent.

In this example, the underlined pronoun does not clearly refer back to one noun or pronoun:

X I had to run outside even though the weather was terrible, and it was bad.

Does *it* refer to the weather, to running outside, or to both? True, we understand the basic idea of the sentence, and the statement might be fine in informal communication when precision is not so important. Nonetheless, the rule is that you should avoid vague pronouns in formal writing—or in any situation when you want to communicate your ideas as exactly as possible.

Avoiding the Problem

If a pronoun needs an antecedent, make sure the pronoun refers back to the nearest logical noun or pronoun.

Three Guidelines for Avoiding Vague Pronouns

We can suggest three specific guidelines for avoiding vague pronouns.

1. The antecedent *must* be a previous noun or pronoun.
2. Whenever possible, place the pronoun and its antecedent in the same sentence. They usually support each other best when placed in the same sentence. If necessary, the antecedent can be in the sentence immediately preceding the pronoun.
3. Avoid having any other noun or pronoun come between a pronoun and its antecedent. If it is impractical to adhere to this suggestion, make sure the intervening noun or pronoun could not logically refer to the pronoun.

Antecedents Must Be Nouns or Pronouns. The first suggestion is a rule: an antecedent *must* be a noun or pronoun. Remember that the definition of a pronoun states it is a word that takes the place of a noun or pronoun and *not* any other part of speech and certainly not an entire sentence, paragraph, etc. In this next error, *that* seems to refer to an entire sentence:

X Joanna went to the park yesterday and played with her children. That was nice.

Even if you think you understand what *that* means, the sentence is grammatically incorrect because pronouns take the place of nouns or pronouns, not sentences.

Pronouns and Antecedents Need to Be Close. The second suggestion is not a true rule. However, placing the antecedent and pronoun in the same sentence reduces the possibility that readers will be confused about the meaning of your pronoun. It is still possible to have a clear pronoun if the antecedent is in the sentence right before the pronoun. In both examples that follow, the pronoun and antecedent are sufficiently close:

Because the phone was not working, it had to be repaired.

On top of my car, someone had left a note. This was written to me.

Intervening Nouns and Pronouns Should Be Avoided. All of the correct examples provided so far also follow our third guideline, for not having any noun or pronoun placed between a pronoun and an antecedent. The problem with putting a noun or pronoun in this position is that readers might mistakenly assume it is the antecedent. In this next example, is *it* referring to *monitor* or *computer*?

X Tyrone's computer, which has a new monitor, is expensive; it is not working properly.

Based on this sentence alone, we cannot determine what the writer intended *it* to mean. Because *monitor* is the closest noun, *it*—grammatically speaking—must refer to *monitor*. Even if that meaning is indeed what the writer intended, the sentence is still poorly written because many readers will think that the computer, not the monitor, is working improperly. To correct such a problem, the sentence must be reworded so readers do not have to choose between two or more possible antecedents. Here is one possible revision:

Tyrone's expensive computer is not working properly, and he just bought a new monitor for it.

Look again at the revision. This rewrite happens to contain the pronoun *it* to refer to *computer*, which appears much earlier in the sentence. Our third guideline indicates you should avoid having other nouns or pronouns come between a pronoun and its antecedent, yet the pronoun *he* comes between *computer* and *it*. As we also indicated, you can have an intervening noun or pronoun *if* this word could not logically be an antecedent. Our revision would not make sense at all if *it* stood for *he*. Thus, this sentence illustrates how you might put a noun or pronoun between the pronoun and antecedent. It is essential, however, that there be no way the pronoun could refer to this intervening word.

Grammar Tip: *This, That,* and *It*

When precision is important, keep an eye on your uses of *this, that,* and *it* to make sure they follow the three guidelines noted earlier. These three pronouns are especially prone to being used in vague ways.

The Perils of This *and* That *as Pronouns*

As noted, the guidelines and rules covered in this section apply to all pronouns requiring an antecedent, but we have focused on *this*, *that*, and *it*. Most people are surprised when told these are the pronouns most often involved in vague pronoun errors, but these three pronouns are indeed most likely to have unclear antecedents. Certainly, you can use all three correctly, and it would be impossible to eliminate these words altogether from your speech and writing (try in particular to eradicate the use of *it*, and you will soon find the attempt futile).

We are suggesting that you closely monitor these pronouns to make sure they adhere to the three guidelines we have covered. In writing, always proofread carefully to make sure these three pronouns are used correctly and clearly.

Grammar Tip: Use *This* and *That* as Adjectives

Avoid using *this* and *that* as pronouns. Turn them into adjectives by following them immediately by a noun.

Converting This *and* That *to Adjectives*

Although using *this* and *that* as pronouns can be perfectly grammatical, you can avoid possible ambiguity by using them as adjectives instead. In this way, you do not have to worry about an antecedent at all because adjectives never require one.

Notice how these errors have been corrected by supplying a suitable noun (underlined twice) after *this* or *that* (underlined once):

X Joanna went to the park yesterday and played with her children. That was nice.

Joanna went to the park yesterday and played with her children. That outing was nice.

X Carol told me apple juice is made from just the juice of apples, while apple cider is made from fermented apples. I already knew this.

Carol told me apple juice is made from just the juice of apples, while apple cider is made from fermented apples. I already knew this distinction.

You can add more than just a noun after *this* or *that*, but there should still be a noun right after the pronoun, as seen here:

X A rock scraped the hood of my car and then hit the windshield. This ruined my day.

A rock scraped the hood of my car and then hit the windshield. This sequence of events ruined my day.

Our strategy depends on recognizing the difference between an adjective and a noun. (See Chapter 1 for more information on these parts of speech.)

Summary

- A pronoun is a word that takes the place of a noun or pronoun.
- Some pronouns require an antecedent—a previous word that supplies the meaning of the pronoun.
- The antecedent must be a noun or pronoun.
- The antecedent should appear in the same sentence as its pronoun (or in the sentence immediately preceding the pronoun).
- Avoid separating a pronoun and an antecedent with any other noun or pronoun (unless this intervening noun or pronoun could not logically be the antecedent).
- The pronouns *this, that,* and *it* are frequently used vaguely.
- If you immediately follow *this* or *that* with a suitable noun, you transform these pronouns into adjectives, meaning you do not have to worry about antecedents.

Reflexive Pronouns: Problems with "*-self*" and "*-selves*" Words

The **reflexive pronoun**—or its name anyway—is a much less known type of pronoun. Reflexive pronouns are common and useful. They include the "*-self*" pronouns, such as *myself, himself,* and *herself.* In fact, all reflexive pronouns are formed by adding *-self* or *-selves* to a particular personal pronoun, as seen in the table a little later.

A reflexive pronoun is used to "bend back" (think of the words *reflect* or *reflex*). A true reflexive pronoun allows something to do something to itself, as shown in these examples:

> Congress gave itself a raise.

> The office manager hurt himself with a stapler.

In these examples, the same people who perform the acts are also the recipients of the acts. In other words, the same people both perform and receive the actions. The reflexive pronoun allows us to state such an idea clearly and concisely. Try, in fact, to reword either sentence without using a "*-self*" word. (In more technical terms, a major function of the reflexive pronoun is to indicate that the subject of a sentence and the direct object are the same person, place, or thing.)

You can also use a reflexive pronoun in other ways, as long as the word it refers to is in the same sentence, as seen in this example:

The bird made a nest for itself.

The pronoun is referring back to *bird*, so the sentence is correct. The bird is not really doing anything to itself, but the pronoun is correctly used as the object of the preposition *for*. Even if *itself* is not a direct object, the reflexive pronoun creates an effect similar to something doing something to itself.

Be aware that there is another major function of reflexive pronouns (the so-called emphatic function). This function complicates matters a bit, so first we focus on true reflexive pronouns—those that follow the definitions just given. We will return to the emphatic function later.

PERSONAL PRONOUNS AND REFLEXIVE PRONOUNS

Personal Pronouns	**Corresponding Reflexive Pronouns**
I, me, my, mine	myself
you, your, yours	yourself, yourselves
we, us, our, ours	ourselves
he, him, his	himself
she, her, hers	herself
they, their, them, theirs	themselves
it, its	itself

What's the Problem?

Three types of problems occur with reflexive pronouns:

1. Some people use words that might *look* like reflexive pronouns but actually are not acceptable words at all.

2. A true reflexive pronoun should normally have an antecedent in the same sentence. If not, there is likely an error.

3. It is incorrect to use a reflexive pronoun as the subject of a sentence.

Avoiding the Problem: Nonexistent Reflexive Pronouns
Reflexive pronouns must take one of the forms listed in the table just given.

It is not unusual for people to think that other reflexive pronouns exist. However, there are no such words as *hisself, theirselves, themself,* or *ourself.* The first two are the most common mistakes made in this regard. In fact, we hear these "nonwords" so often that we might not even take notice, making it more likely we could commit these errors ourselves.

Thus, you simply have to memorize the correct forms. If nothing else, remember that *himself* and *themselves* are proper reflexive pronouns.

Avoiding the Problem: Reflexive Pronouns and Antecedents
Keep a reflexive pronoun and its antecedent in the same sentence.

As noted, a reflexive pronoun normally bends back to create the effect of something doing something to itself. There is a close relationship between the pronoun and the word to which it refers, and you should accordingly keep these close together in a physical sense. In short, a reflexive pronoun and its antecedent should normally be in the same sentence, with the pronoun coming second.

The word the pronoun refers to is called an **antecedent**. In this next example, the antecedent for the reflexive pronoun *herself* is *chef.* Without the antecedent, *herself* would be meaningless.

The <u>chef</u> surprised even <u>herself</u> with the delicious entree.

An error occurs in formal English when the antecedent does not precede the reflexive pronoun in the same sentence, as in these examples:

X The doctor gave a prescription to Juanita and <u>myself</u>.
X For John and <u>myself</u>, one slice of pie will be sufficient.

Yes, the sentences make sense. However, according to rules of formal English, the underlined pronouns are incorrectly used because neither has an antecedent in the same sentence (or maybe not even in whatever sentences came before). The simplest way to correct such errors is to use a personal pronoun instead of a reflexive pronoun. In these corrections, the personal pronouns are underlined:

> The doctor gave a prescription to Juanita and me.
> For John and me, one slice of pie will be sufficient.

> **Grammar Tip: Reflexive Pronouns Followed by *And***
> **When a reflexive pronoun is linked by *and* to another word, create a version of the sentence that uses only the reflexive pronoun. If the pronoun sounds odd in this new version, the original sentence probably contains an error.**

As seen in our previous examples, errors involving reflexive pronouns are most likely to occur in a compound structure (when the pronoun is linked by *and* to a noun or another pronoun). For some reason, people will create errors in this sort of structure when they would never use the reflexive pronoun incorrectly if used alone.

Thus, our tip requires you to create a test sentence to see if you are using the reflexive pronoun needlessly. Here is an example of an error along with a test sentence:

Original error: X On Friday, the lawyer contacted Barbara and myself.
Test sentence: X On Friday, the lawyer contacted myself.

Perhaps the original error would have escaped your notice, but not the one in the test sentence. Grammatically speaking, though, the two sentences have the same problem. If you would not use a reflexive pronoun in the test sentence, do not use it in the original. Following is a correct version. Notice, by the way, that you could apply a similar test to our rewrite.

Correction: On Friday, the lawyer contacted Barbara and me.

If you rewrote the test sentence by just using *me*, the sentence would sound fine. Thus, *me* is indeed correct.

You can use a reflexive pronoun in compound structures. Here is a correct example, along with a test sentence that shows the example is indeed correct:

Original: Today, Brian managed to hit Tyrone and himself with a hammer.
Test sentence: Today, Brian managed to hit himself with a hammer.

Avoiding the Problem: Something That Reflexive Pronouns Cannot Do

Never use a reflexive pronoun as the subject of a sentence.

In truth, this third problem is usually just a specific version of the second error we just examined. However, this third problem is so common and serious it deserves its own treatment.

Also, we can be even briefer and clearer about the rule: you simply should never use a reflexive pronoun as the subject of a sentence. Following are sample errors. Note how they, like most others we have covered, appear in compound structures:

X Alicia and myself are going to the mall.
X George and herself went to the mall just yesterday.

These reflexive pronouns are errors for two reasons. First, a reflexive pronoun should not be the subject of a sentence. Second, nobody is doing anything to themselves, so a regular personal pronoun—not a reflexive pronoun—is what we need. If you want to be thorough in proving these two pronouns are incorrectly used, create two test sentences:

Test sentence: X Myself is going to the mall.
Test sentence: X Herself went to the mall just yesterday.

Needless to say, these test sentences sound ridiculous, but the original sentences are committing the same error by using the incorrect type of pronoun. To correct the errors, use personal pronouns to replace the reflexive pronouns:

Alicia and I are going to the mall.
George and she went to the mall just yesterday.

If you remember that reflexive pronouns should never be subjects of a sentence, then you do not even need to apply the tip. In the original errors, *myself* and *herself* are subjects, making them erroneous. The fact that they are part of a compound subject (joined by *and* to a noun) does not change the rule: you still cannot use reflexive pronouns as grammatical subjects of a sentence.

Reflexive Pronouns and Emphasis

It would be nice to stop at this point, but the truth is reflexive pronouns have one other function: to provide emphasis. In these next correct examples, the underlined pronouns are not involved at all in "something doing something to itself." Their sole purpose is to add emphasis—to intensify a previous noun or pronoun.

I myself talked to the CEO.
Elvis himself would be proud of your singing.

It is important to understand that these pronouns do have an antecedent in the same sentence. Thus, these sentences adhere to the rule requiring the reflexive pronoun to have an antecedent in the same sentence. Their function changes, but the pronouns still must adhere to certain rules for reflexive pronouns.

This next sentence is not breaking the rule prohibiting a reflexive pronoun (underlined) from serving as a subject:

Ulysses S. Grant himself was fined for speeding while he was president, though he was driving a horse and buggy.

Ulysses S. Grant is the subject of the sentence. The pronoun *himself* is merely intensifying the subject as a participant in an action. There is *not* a compound subject (in fact, if you put *and* between *Grant* and *himself,* the sentence will not make sense).

The major difference between these **emphatic** (or **intensive**) **pronouns** and those reflexive pronouns covered earlier is this: the emphatic pronouns do not involve something doing something to itself. True reflexive pronouns are essential parts of the sentence, but the three examples immediately preceding are just adding a little "gravy"—a bit of emphasis to an existing idea.

Some grammar handbooks will even separate reflexive pronouns from emphatic pronouns. That is, some people see these as two different categories of pronouns, even if they look exactly the same and have some similarities.

Grammar Tip: Deleting the Emphatic Pronoun

A true reflexive pronoun cannot be deleted. However, the emphatic version can always be deleted; the result will always be a grammatical sentence that means exactly the same thing as the original.

Notice how we can take out *myself* and *himself* in the following correct examples. The result is a completely grammatical sentence that means exactly the same thing as the original.

I myself talked to the CEO. (Emphatic *myself.*)
I talked to the CEO.

Elvis himself would be proud of your singing. (Emphatic *himself.*)
Elvis would be proud of your singing.

In short, we can prove that these are emphatic variations of reflexive pronouns. Deleting a true reflexive pronoun will change meaning significantly and almost always result in an ungrammatical sentence, as seen in this next instance:

> The office manager hurt himself with a stapler. (Reflexive *himself.*)
>
> X The office manager hurt with a stapler. (This is ungrammatical because the reflexive pronoun is missing.)

This emphatic variation of the reflexive pronoun might seem confusing, but you can use these pronouns appropriately if you follow the same rules noted earlier. In particular, remember that the antecedent should appear in the same sentence as the pronoun—no matter if it is a true reflexive pronoun or the emphatic variation.

One final suggestion: avoid overusing this emphatic version of reflexive pronouns. Although overuse does not result in a true grammatical error, readers expect you to use emphatic pronouns only when it is worth emphasizing somebody or something. Some people are especially prone to using *myself* to needlessly call attention to themselves in a sentence.

Summary

- All reflexive pronouns are formed by adding *-self* or *-selves* to personal pronouns. Common reflexive pronouns include *myself*, *ourselves*, and *itself.*
- True reflexive pronouns involve the notion of something doing something to itself.
- In formal English, there are no such words as *hisself* or *theirselves.* Use *himself* and *themselves.*
- A reflexive pronoun should have an antecedent. The antecedent is the word that the pronoun refers to.
- The antecedent and reflexive pronoun should appear in the same sentence.
- Do *not* use a reflexive pronoun as the subject of a sentence.
- Most errors involving reflexive pronouns occur when the pronoun is connected by *and* to another word. Monitor such structures carefully to see if perhaps you should use a personal pronoun, not a reflexive pronoun.
- The "*-self*" and "*-selves*" pronouns can also be used to emphasize or intensify the antecedent. Such pronouns still must have antecedents in the same sentence.

Pronoun Agreement Errors

As noted in the earlier sections, some pronouns can (or must) have an **antecedent**—a previous word that gives meaning to the pronoun. Here, for instance, the pronoun *he* makes sense *only* if we connect it to the antecedent *lookout*:

> A lookout in the crow's nest of the *Titanic* saw an iceberg, but the warning that he gave came too late to save the doomed ship.

Although there are different types of pronouns, all must adhere to certain rules. One is that a pronoun and its antecedent must match up in a logical sense. For instance, using *they* rather than *he* in the preceding sentence would be illogical. The antecedent (*lookout*) refers to one person, so the corresponding pronoun must also refer to just one person. This concept of logically matching the pronoun with its antecedent is referred to as **agreement**. The pronoun and antecedent must grammatically "agree" on basic matters such as the number of people involved and their gender.

(The notion of agreement is also used to describe logical connections between subjects and their verbs. See Chapter 7 for more information on subject-verb agreement.)

What's the Problem?

A pronoun agreement error occurs when a pronoun and its antecedent do not agree. Often such problems are harmless, especially in casual speech. At other times, a mismatch between pronoun and antecedent can confuse people because the mismatch causes them—consciously or subconsciously—to look elsewhere for the antecedent of the pronoun. Even if there is no confusion, many readers become annoyed by the lack of a logical connection between two ideas that are supposedly the same.

To help you avoid these problems, we will consider three strategies: (1) understanding the basic rule, (2) identifying certain pronouns—certain **indefinite** pronouns—that are often connected with agreement errors, and (3) correcting agreement errors while also avoiding sexist language.

Avoiding the Problem: Basic Advice

Make sure a pronoun and its antecedent agree in terms of number and gender.

More on the Basic Rule

Pronoun agreement, as stated, means that a pronoun and its antecedent should match up in a logical way. The two most common areas of needed agreement are *number* and *gender*:

- **Number agreement** requires both the antecedent and the pronoun to be singular or both to be plural.
- **Gender agreement** requires both the antecedent and the pronoun to be female or both to be male, or a "genderless" pronoun is to be used appropriately to refer to either males or females.

In the next three examples, all pronouns are in agreement in terms of number and gender (pronouns underlined once, antecedents underlined twice):

Early typewriters were cumbersome. Some required a foot pedal to return the carriage. (Both *typewriters* and *some* are plural and genderless.)

In 1867 Christopher Sholes built the first typewriter that was considered practical. He later signed a contract with gunsmiths E. Remington and Sons to manufacture his machine. (*Christopher Sholes, he*, and *his* are all singular and male.)

I learned these facts from my grandfather and sister; they collect typewriters. (The nouns *grandfather* and *sister* are used together as a plural subject; *they* is plural. The genderless *they* can refer to either male or female.)

Checking your pronouns and antecedents in this fashion (in terms of number and gender) can help you avoid most pronoun agreement errors.

In this next example, what appears to be the antecedent does *not* agree with the pronoun *they*:

X I need to speak with the head supervisor; they never seem to help, however.

Your first step is to determine what *they* refers to (that is, find the antecedent). The writer might have something else in mind, but the only possible choice in the sentence we are given is *head supervisor*. The pronoun *they* must always have an antecedent, and *I* is certainly not it. However, *they* is plural, while *head supervisor* is singular. Thus, there is a pronoun agreement error involving number.

The error can be corrected in many ways. One approach is to change the number of either the antecedent or pronoun. Another approach is to reword the sentence so there is no pronoun or antecedent at all. Here are both correction approaches applied to the preceding error:

I need to speak with one of our head supervisors; they never seem to help, however. (Both *head supervisors* and *they* are plural and genderless.)

I need to speak with the head supervisor; this approach has never seemed to help, however. (The pronoun *they* has been deleted.)

Avoiding the Problem: The Specific Case of Indefinite Pronouns

Several indefinite pronouns might seem plural, but grammatically they are singular.

More on Indefinite Pronouns

Undoubtedly, one of the greatest sources of agreement errors arises with a handful of pronouns that belong to a category called **indefinite pronouns**. Any indefinite pronoun is general enough that it can be used to refer to various things, people, or places (hence the name *indefinite*). Here are examples of these pronouns:

Common Indefinite Pronouns

all	everyone	none
any	many	one
anyone	more	several
anything	most	some
both	much	somebody
each	neither	someone
either	no one	something
everybody		

Following are two correct examples of an indefinite pronoun agreeing with its antecedent. This first example uses an indefinite pronoun (underlined twice) as the antecedent for a later pronoun (underlined once):

indefinite pronoun

Something seems to have left its footprints in the sand.

The next sentence uses the indefinite pronoun (underlined once) serving as the "major pronoun," with a previous noun (underlined twice) as the antecedent:

indefinite pronoun

The cake was beautiful, but most of it is gone now.

Errors involving indefinite pronouns rarely deal with gender. However, these pronouns are involved in a large proportion of agreement errors involving number. The problem is that a few indefinite pronouns are always plural (such as *both* and *many*), some are always singular (such as *one* and *each*), and still others can be singular *or* plural (such as *some* and *most*) depending on how they are used in a particular sentence. Thus, memorizing every indefinite pronoun in terms of which is singular or plural is unappealing, perhaps impossible, because some can go either way depending on whether the antecedent is singular or plural.

The first strategy we suggested earlier will help you again: look carefully at the pronoun to make sure it agrees with the antecedent. However, our second strategy suggests you consider more carefully this particular type of pronoun.

Even more specifically, you should understand there are some indefinite pronouns that are most likely to be involved in agreement errors involving number. These pronouns are *always* singular, no matter how plural they might appear to you at first. This list is manageable and worth remembering. Another characteristic (one that makes it easier to memorize the list) is that these pronouns are formed by mixing and matching certain root words, as shown here:

	every-	**some-**	**any-**	**no-**
-thing	everything	something	anything	nothing
-one	everyone	someone	anyone	no one
-body	everybody	somebody	anybody	nobody

The problem is that these words certainly *seem* to be referring to more than one person or thing. Nonetheless, grammatically they are singular, as the following tip proves:

Grammar Tip: The *Are* Test for Plurals

To help determine if an indefinite pronoun can be plural, see if you can put the verb *are* right after it. If the combination seems odd, then the pronoun is always singular.

Does "everybody are" or "someone are" sound odd? Yes, so the pronouns *everybody* and *someone* are never plural. This test confirms that *everybody* and *someone* do not agree with their plural counterparts in these erroneous sentences:

singular plural

X Everybody needs to bring their grammar book tomorrow.

singular plural

X The company needs someone who is motivated. They will always have a place with us.

Avoiding the Problem: Avoiding Sexist Pronouns and Agreement Errors

Do not create an agreement error in the attempt to avoid sexist language. Do not use a masculine pronoun such as *he* to refer to both men and women. But neither should you create an agreement error in terms of number.

Sexist Language Versus Pronoun Agreement

To avoid appearing sexist, some people would prefer to commit a pronoun agreement error rather than indicate, say, that they believe only males or females are motivated (see the last example given). At one time, most people considered it acceptable to use the masculine pronoun *he*, *his*, or *him* to refer generically to anyone (male or female). However, such language is now rightfully considered sexist or demeaning.

The genderless *they* indeed allows people to avoid sexist language, but there is no reason to create a new problem by avoiding another. Indefinite pronouns are also frequently involved in this sort of dilemma, as seen in this example:

singular (Nobody) — plural (their)

X Nobody brought their book despite my request.

Assume the sentence is supposed to refer to both males and females. It would have been sexist to use *his*, but the sentence contains an agreement error because the indefinite pronoun *nobody* is always singular, while *their* is always plural.

Other types of antecedents can be involved in problems of sexist language versus number agreement. In this next example, the singular noun *dance instructor* is the antecedent for the singular personal pronoun *her*:

X A dance instructor should always care about her students.

Although the antecedent and pronoun agree in terms of number (both are singular), using *her* incorrectly indicates *only* females can be dance instructors. However, changing *her* to a genderless *their* would be incorrect as well, because then we would be again facing an agreement problem involving number. Again, do not correct one error by creating another.

Grammar Tip: Plurals to Avoid Sexist Language and Agreement Errors

Using pronouns and their antecedents in the plural form will usually help you avoid agreement errors as well as sexist language. This tip will allow you to use the genderless *they, them,* and *their* to refer to men and women alike.

Applying This Tip

If we change pronouns and antecedents to the plural form in the preceding errors, we can correctly use *their* and *they*. These are genderless, so you can use them to refer to both men and women (just be sure the antecedents are plural). As seen in the following, you might need to make a few other minor revisions (remember subject-verb agreement) as well:

plural plural

All students need to bring their grammar book tomorrow.

plural plural

The company needs employees who are motivated. They will always have a place with us.

plural plural

No students brought their book despite my request.

plural plural

Dance instructors should always care about their students.

Summary

- A pronoun is a word that takes the place of a noun. An antecedent is the word to which the pronoun refers.
- A pronoun should agree with its antecedent. They should agree in terms of gender and in terms of how many persons or things are involved.
- Indefinite pronouns are frequently involved in agreement errors involving number. Some indefinite pronouns are always plural, some are always singular, and some can be either depending on whether the antecedent is singular or plural.
- Some indefinite pronouns—such as *everyone*, *everything*, *somebody*, and *anyone*—are especially likely to be involved in agreement errors because they seem to be plural but actually are singular.
- Confirm whether an indefinite pronoun can be plural by seeing if you can put *are* right afterward. If it sounds odd (such as *everybody are*), then the pronoun is always singular, and its antecedent should also be singular.
- Avoid creating an agreement error when attempting to avoid sexist language. By using a plural pronoun such as *they*, *them*, or *their* along with a plural antecedent, you can avoid both problems.

9

Verb Problems

In this chapter, we will discuss three high-frequency verb problems: tense shifting between present and past; choosing the right tense for past-time events; and *rise* or *raise*? *sit* or *set*? *lie* or *lay*?

1. Tense shifting between present and past: The term **tense shifting** refers to a writer's switching from present tense to past tense or from past tense to present tense in the same paragraph or even in the same sentence. Sometimes tense shifting is inappropriate; sometimes it is obligatory.

Here is an example of tense shifting when it is not appropriate (verbs in italics):

X Whenever I *see* an old Monty Python episode on television, I *taped* it.

The writer has improperly shifted from present tense (*see*) to past tense (*taped*).

Here is a reverse example, of not shifting when we should:

X Last summer we *went* to a resort that *was* near Santa Barbara.

The writer has improperly failed to shift from past tense (*was*) to present tense.

The problem of shifting is rooted in not understanding the different functions of the present and past tenses.

2. Choosing the right tense for past-time events: In this section, we focus on how to decide whether we should use the **past tense**, the **present perfect tense**, or the **past perfect tense** to describe a past-time event. Each of these three past-time tenses has its own distinct meaning. A skillful writer knows which one will best suit the intended meaning.

3. *Rise* or *raise*? *sit* or *set*? *lie* or *lay*? These three pairs of verbs are often confused. Part of the reason why it is so difficult to remember which member of each pair to use is that they are related to one another in a highly unusual way. By understanding how the verbs in each of the pairs are systematically related to one another, you will be better able to use them correctly.

Tense Shifting Between Present and Past

To shift or not to shift, that is the question. The term **tense shifting** refers to a writer's switching from present tense to past tense or from past tense to present tense in the same paragraph or even in the same sentence. Here is an example of inappropriate tense shifting (verbs in italics):

X Whenever we *went* to my grandfather's house, we always *have* to eat with the TV on.

The verb in the first clause (*went*) is in the past tense, while the verb in the second clause (*have*) is in the present tense. In this example, the writer could not decide whether she was telling a story about visiting her grandfather's house (past tense) or making a statement of fact about what eating at her grandfather's house is like (present tense). Either choice is perfectly fine, but it is not fine to switch horses in midstream. The writer should commit to one alternative and stick with it.

If the writer wanted to tell a story about a visit, then she should have stayed in the past tense throughout the narrative:

Story: Whenever we *went* to my grandfather's house, we always *had* to eat with the TV on.

If the writer wanted to make a factual statement about visits to her grandfather's house, then she should have stayed in the present tense throughout her statement:

Statement of fact: Whenever we *go* to my grandfather's house, we always *have* to eat with the TV on.

The problem of shifting is rooted in not understanding the different functions of the present and past tenses. Following is a brief summary of their different functions. For more detailed information, look at the section on present and past tense use in Chapter 4.

Present Tense

The term *present* is misleading. The **present tense** is not tied to the present moment of time. The two main uses of the present tense are (1) to make statements of fact and (2) to make generalizations. Here are some examples of statements of fact and generalizations (present tense verb in italics):

Statement of fact
Chicago *is* in the Central Time Zone.
The planet Mercury *has* no atmosphere.

Generalizations
The new VW bugs *are* the cutest car on the market.
San Francisco *is* a more interesting city than New York.
John *works* on Saturdays.

Notice the last example, *John works on Saturdays.* One kind of generalization is about people's regular customs or habitual actions. The use of the present tense in this sentence tells us that it is John's regular custom to work on Saturdays.

Both statements of fact and generalizations are essentially timeless. That is, they are not limited to a particular moment of time or even to a span of time. They are universally true (statements of fact) or an assertion of one's opinion about what is true (generalizations). Nonfiction writing is typically written in the present tense. Notice, for example, that the present tense is used throughout this book—except for examples, which often depict specific, time-bounded events.

Past Tense

The **past tense**, obviously, is used to describe events that took place in past time. However, there is more to the use of the past time than this statement would imply. Because the present tense is preempted for making timeless statements of fact and generalizations, the past tense becomes the primary vehicle for all narration that deals with time-bounded events. For this reason, nearly all fiction—stories and novels—are written in the past tense.

There is one rather odd exception to the distinction between the use of the present tense for nonfiction and the use of the past tense for fiction. Sometimes stories and novels, even ones set in a past time, are written entirely in the present tense. When the present tense is used this way, it is called the **historical present**. For example, a novel written in the historical present about Queen Elizabeth I might read like this (verbs in italics):

> Elizabeth *enters* the council chambers and *sees* Lord Leicester. She *asks* him what he *thinks* about the Spanish threat.

Most writing guides strongly advise beginning writers to stay away from the historical present. It is difficult to handle and it gets very tiresome, very quickly. Interestingly, about the only place we ever encounter the historical present is in jokes, for example (verbs in italics):

> This guy *goes* into a bar and *sits* down. A few minutes later this polar bear *comes* in and *sits* down next to him and *orders* a drink. . . .

When Should We Shift Tenses?

What we have said to this point makes it sound like tense shifting is a bad thing. Certainly, shifting tenses unnecessarily is a bad thing. However, we need to shift tenses whenever we shift from narration to generalization or statement of fact—something we do quite often. Here is an example of legitimate and necessary tense shifting (verbs in italics):

> Shakespeare *wrote* Hamlet around 1600. The action of the play *is* set in Elsinore Castle in Denmark, though there *is* no evidence that

Shakespeare ever *visited* Denmark—or ever even *left* England, for that matter.

Notice that the tenses bounce back and forth from past (*wrote*) to present (*is* twice) and then back to past (*visited* and *left*). The first sentence

Shakespeare *wrote* Hamlet around 1600.

deals with an event that took place in past time, so the past tense *wrote* is perfectly appropriate. The next clause

The action of the play *is* set in Elsinore Castle in Denmark

shifts to the present tense. The present tense is appropriate here because the writer is now giving us a statement of fact about the play—a legitimate function of the present tense. If the writer had kept the clause in the past tense, it would have sounded quite odd:

? The action of the play *was* set in Elsinore Castle in Denmark

This use of the past tense implies that while Shakespeare had originally set the action of the play in Elsinore Castle, he later changed his mind and set it somewhere else.

The remaining part of the sentence

though there *is* no evidence that Shakespeare ever *visited* Denmark—or ever even *left* England, for that matter

begins in the present tense (*is*). The present tense is appropriate because the author is making a statement of fact (*there is no evidence . . .*). Then the author shifts to the past tense (*visited* and *left*) to tell us about events that took place in past time.

Probably the most common single situation in which writers fail to shift tenses when they should shift is when they embed a piece of factual information inside a past tense narrative. Here is a typical example (verbs in italics):

X We then *visited* Key West, which *was* the southernmost city in the continental United States.

The use of past tense (*visited*) for a narrative is normal and expected. However, in this case, the writer mistakenly stays in the past tense (*was*) while giving a statement of fact. The writer makes it sound as though Key West is no longer the southernmost city in the continental United States. Here, the writer should have shifted to the present tense:

We then *visited* Key West, which *is* the southernmost city in the continental United States.

Summary

The term *tense shifting* refers to shifting from present tense to past tense (or vice versa) in the same passage or sentence. Tense shifting can be either appropriate or inappropriate. The key to understanding tense shifting is understanding the different functions of the present and past tenses. The present tense (despite its name) is timeless. That is, we use it to make statements of fact or generalizations—neither of which is connected to the present moment of time. The past tense is for describing events—actions that are time-bounded. We use the past tense for all narrations. The basic rule is not to shift tenses unless there is a reason, but if there is a reason, then you must shift.

Choosing the Right Tense for Past-Time Events

In this section, we will focus on choosing the right tense for past-time events. Specifically, how do we decide when we should use the **past tense**, the **present perfect tense**, or the **past perfect tense**? We will first briefly recap how each of the three tenses is formed and then turn to a more detailed discussion of how the tenses are used.

Past Tense

The regular **past tense** is formed by adding *-ed* or *-d* to the end of the base form of the verb, for example, *talk, talked*; *wave, waved.* Many verbs have irregular past tense forms. The verbs with irregular past tenses are discussed in more detail than most people would want to know in Chapter 4.

The past tense is used to describe time-bounded events. The term *time-bounded* refers to a description of a single event that took place at one specific moment in space and time. The past tense is the normal tense for all narration. Virtually all stories and novels are written in the past tense.

Present Perfect Tense

The **present perfect tense** is formed by the present tense of the helping verb *have* followed by a second verb in the past participle form, which we can summarize as follows:

present perfect = *have/has* + past participle

We use the present perfect to describe actions that have occurred continuously or repeatedly from some time in the past right up to the present moment (sometimes with the implication that these actions will continue into the future). Here are some examples of continuous action (present perfect in italics):

Their phone *has been* busy for half an hour.
The kids *have watched* cartoons all afternoon.

Here are some examples of repeated action (present perfect in italics):

The choir *has sung* that hymn a hundred times.
It *has rained* off and on all summer long.

The fundamental difference between the present perfect and the past tense is that the present perfect emphasizes the continual or repeated nature of events across a span of time, while the past tense describes a single-event action that is now over and done with. To see the difference, compare the following sentences:

Present perfect: Elliot *has lived* in Chicago for ten years.
Past: Elliot *lived* in Chicago for ten years.

The present perfect sentence tells us two things: (1) Elliot has lived in Chicago continuously for ten years and (2) Elliot still lives in Chicago now. The sentence also implies that Elliot will continue to live in Chicago for the foreseeable future. The past tense sentence tells us that while Elliot lived in Chicago for ten years, he does not live in Chicago anymore. His presence in Chicago is over and done with.

A second use of the present perfect describes a recent past event whose impact is felt over a period of time right up until the present moment. Here are some examples:

I'm sorry, Ms. Smith *has stepped* away from her desk for a moment.
Sam *has lost* his car keys.

In both cases, an event that was begun in the past still continues in effect and very much impacts the present moment. In these examples, the present perfect emphasizes the ongoing duration of the impact of the action.

Often the choice between the past tense and the present perfect is not always a matter of right or wrong but of what the writer wants to imply. For example, compare the following questions:

Past tense: *Did* you *see* Mary?
Present perfect tense: *Have* you *seen* Mary?

The past tense question is ambiguous because it is not anchored to any specific past time. Without further specification of the time frame, the speaker could mean just now, yesterday, last week, or last year.

However, the present perfect question can only refer to the recent past. Accordingly, we cannot use the present perfect to describe an event that took place at a time even slightly removed from the present. For example, notice how strange the following present perfect sentence sounds:

X Sam *has lost* his car keys yesterday.

Past Perfect Tense

The **past perfect tense** is formed by the past tense of the helping verb *have* followed by a verb in the past participle form:

past perfect = *had* + past participle

Here are two examples of sentences with past perfect tenses:

Their phone *had been* busy for half an hour before I got through.
The choir *had* already *sung* that hymn at the beginning of the service.

We use the past perfect when we want to emphasize the fact that a particular event in the past was completed *before* a more recent past-time event took place. Here are three examples with commentary (past perfect in italics):

I *had stepped* into the shower just when the phone rang.

In this example, two things happened: (1) the speaker stepped into the shower and (2) the phone rang. The speaker is using the past perfect to emphasize the inconvenient order of the two past-time events.

When we bought the house last year, it *had been* empty for ten years.

In this example, the past perfect is used to emphasize the fact that the house had been empty for the ten-year period *before* it was bought.

They'*d had* a big fight before they broke up.

In this example, the past perfect sequences two events: (1) a big fight and (2) a breakup. Here the past perfect implies that not only did these two events happen in this order, but there is probably a cause-and-effect connection between them. That is, their big fight may have caused their subsequent breakup.

The past perfect tends to be underused in writing, possibly because it is not used much in casual conversation. The past perfect requires more advanced planning than most of us can muster in the rapid give-and-take of animated conversation. One of the cardinal differences between the spoken language and the written language is that while writing necessarily sacrifices the spontaneity of spoken language, writing gives us the opportunity to revise and edit, so that we can say exactly what we mean. For example, the following sentence is what we might say in conversation:

> After I *was* in the classroom for a week, all my theories of education *went* out the window.

Both clauses are in the past tense.

The corresponding sentence in more formal, more precise written form would be like this:

> After I *had been* in the classroom for a week, all my theories of education *went* out the window.

The use of the past perfect in the first clause tells the reader that the two clauses refer to different time periods. First, the writer went into the classroom, and then (presumably as a result of this experience) the writer's theories went out the window. In the written form, the writer is able to exploit the built-in time relationship of the past perfect to get across the meaning in a more effective manner.

Summary

The three main tenses that we use for talking about past-time events are the past tense, the present perfect tense, or the past perfect tense. Each of these three tenses has its own distinctive meaning.

The past tense is used primarily for single, unique events that are now over and done with. The past tense is used in nearly all narrations—stories and other works of fiction.

The present perfect tense is used for events that span a period of time or are repeated over time.

The past perfect tense is used for a somewhat special purpose—to emphasize that one past event occurred before a second, more recent event. Sometimes the past perfect tense is used to imply a cause-and-effect relation between the two events (i.e., the first event caused or affected the second event).

Rise or *Raise*? *Sit* or *Set*? *Lie* or *Lay*?

These three pairs of verbs—*rise* or *raise*, *sit* or *set*, and *lie* or *lay*—are often confused. Part of the reason why it is so difficult to remember which member of the pair to use is that they are related to one another in a highly unusual and confusing way. Before discussing each of the three pairs in detail, we will turn to a fourth pair of verbs that are related in exactly the same way—but that are much easier to work with.

Fall/Fell *and Causative Verbs*

The verb *fall* is an **intransitive verb** meaning, well, "to fall," for example:

Humpty Dumpty *fell* off the wall.

The verb *fell* is a **transitive verb** that means "to cut or bring something down." The most common use of *fell* is in reference to cutting down a tree, for example:

The loggers *felled* all the trees on the ridge.

The word *fell* can also be used to refer to bringing down an animal, for example:

The hunter *felled* the charging rhino with a single shot.

(There are two other, totally unrelated uses of the word *fell*: (1) a noun derived from a Latin word that means the skin of an animal, related to the word *pelt*, and (2) an adjective derived from another Latin word that means "cruel" or "terrible," related to the noun *felon*.)

It would seem obvious that the verbs *fall* and *fell* are somehow related. They are, but they are related in a special and unusual way that, to be understood, requires an excursion into the history of the English language.

In an early stage of English, there was a special ending that could be attached to nearly any verb. The ending is what linguists today would call a **causative**. When this suffix was added to a verb, it had the meaning of to "cause the action of the verb." For example, if we added this ending to the verb *sneeze*, we would create a new verb with the meaning of to "cause someone to sneeze." If we added the ending to the verb *sleep*, we would create a new verb meaning to "cause someone to sleep." If we added the ending to the verb *fall*, we would create a new verb meaning to "cause something to fall." As you can probably guess, the verb *fell* is the causative form of the verb *fall*. To *fell* a tree is to cause it to *fall*.

The example of *fall/fell* also illustrates a second characteristic of this causative suffix: when the suffix was attached to an intransitive verb (a verb that has no object), it changed the verb from intransitive to transitive. That is, the resulting new causative verb required an object. This shift from intransitive to transitive survives into Modern English. For example, the causative verb *fell* requires an overt statement of what it was that is being cut or brought down. When we *fell*, we have to fell something.

Finally, *fall/fell* illustrates the third characteristic of this causative suffix: it caused a change in the vowel of the verb it was attached to. As a consequence, the intransitive verb without the causative suffix has one vowel, and the transitive verb with the causative suffix has another vowel. (The rules governing the vowel change were extraordinarily complicated. The same rules also caused many of the irregular plurals in Modern English, for example, *man, men*; *goose, geese*; and *mouse, mice*.)

The verb *fall*, the original intransitive verb, is irregular:

Base/present tense:	fall/falls
Past tense:	fell

Past participle: fallen
Present participle: falling

The transitive causative verb *fell* is regular:

Base/present tense: fell/fells
Past tense: felled
Past participle: felled
Present participle: felling

We will now turn to the other three pairs of verbs that follow the same pattern as *fall* and *fell*.

Rise/Raise

The intransitive verb *rise* means to "go up" or "get into an upright position," for example:

The courtroom bailiff says, "All *rise*!"
If you get the yeast right, the dough will always *rise*.
The sun *rises* in the east.

Historically, the transitive causative verb *raise* meant to "cause something to rise." Its meaning has broadened over time to also mean, among other things, to "lift," to "rear" (as children or animals), or to "grow" (as plants).

Raise your glasses and join me in a toast to the bride and groom!
I had to *raise* three children on my own.
We *raise* winter wheat for export.

The verbs *rise* and *raise* follow the same basic pattern as *fall* and *fell* in that the original intransitive verb is irregular while the transitive causative verb is regular (though with a different vowel from the original intransitive verb):

Rise

Base/present tense:	rise/rises
Past tense:	rose
Past participle:	risen
Present participle:	rising

Raise

Base/present tense:	raise/raises
Past tense:	raised
Past participle:	raised
Present participle:	raising

Sit/Set

The intransitive verb *sit* means to "be seated" or to "be situated," for example:

Please *sit* down.
The house *sits* on a hill overlooking the river.

Historically, the causative transitive verb *set* meant to "cause something or someone to sit." Its meanings have also broadened over time to mean, among other things, to "place," "arrange," or "fix," for example:

He *set* the briefcase on the table.
We will *set* the table as soon as we can.
They need to *set* the date for the meeting.

Adding to the confusion of *sit* and *set* is the fact that the verb *set* can also be used as an intransitive verb, for example:

The sun rises in the east and *sets* in the west.

The verb *sit*, the original intransitive verb, is irregular:

Base/present tense:	sit/sits
Past tense:	sat

Past participle:	sat
Present participle:	sitting

The transitive causative verb *set* is one of those odd monosyllabic verbs ending in a *-t* or *-d* (like *hit* and *rid*) that uses the same form for the present, the past, and the past participle:

Base/present tense:	set/sets
Past tense:	set
Past participle:	set
Present participle:	setting

Lie/Lay

This pair of verbs is the most difficult of the gang of four. One reason is that the present tense of the transitive causative verb (*lay*) happens (by historical accident) to be identical with the past tense of the original intransitive verb (*lay*).

The original intransitive verb *lie* meant to "recline." The meaning has broadened over time to mean "spread out" or "be placed," for example:

I will *lie* down for a few minutes before dinner.
The x-ray technician had me *lie* on my right side.
The residential area of town *lies* along the west bank of the river.

Historically, the transitive causative verb *lay* meant to "cause to lie," that is, to "place," for example:

Please *lay* your briefcase and papers on the table.
I needed to *lay* my packages down.
The movers will *lay* the rugs in the living room this afternoon.

The verb *lie*, the original intransitive verb, is irregular:

Base/present tense:	lie/lies
Past tense:	lay
Past participle:	lain
Present participle:	lying

The transitive causative verb *lay* is actually regular, though the spelling somewhat disguises it—the final *y* in *lay* changes to *i* when followed by a consonant:

Base/present tense:	lay/lays
Past tense:	laid
Past participle:	laid
Present participle:	laying

Notice that the form *lay* is confusing: *lay* is both the base and present tense form of *lay* and the past tense of *lie.*

In casual conversation, there seems to be a tendency to use *lay* as an intransitive verb. If you had heard the following sentences in conversation, would you have noticed they were actually incorrect?

X Don't just *lay* there—do something!
X She got sunburned from *laying* around the pool too long.
X The kids have *laid* around the house all day.

Technically, all three of these sentences should have used some form of *lie*:

Don't just *lie* there—do something!
She got sunburned from *lying* around the pool too long.
The kids have *lain* around the house all day.

The fact that our ear has grown somewhat accustomed to using *lay* as an intransitive verb means that we have to be especially careful to monitor our use of *lay* in writing. Remember, if it doesn't have an object, *lay* is inappropriate in formal writing. If you have trouble with *lie* and *lay*, it might be worthwhile to memorize the following:

You *lie* around, but you *lay* something down.

Summary

The verbs *rise* and *raise*, *sit* and *set*, and *lie* and *lay* are often confused with each other. These pairs of verbs are modern survivors of a causative ending that changed intransitive verbs to transitive verbs. The new transitive verb meant to engage in the action of the intransitive verb. For example, the transitive verb *fell* comes from the intransitive verb *fall*. To *fell* a tree means to cause the tree to *fall*.

All three pairs of verbs are related in exactly the same way:

Intransitive Verb	**Transitive Causative Verb**
rise	raise (To cause something to *rise*.)
sit	set (To cause something to *sit*.)
lie	lay (To cause something to *lie*.)

The key to keeping the verbs straight is to remember that the causative verb requires an object. When you *raise*, you have to raise something. When you *set*, you have to set something. When you *lay*, you have to lay (down) something.

10

Modification

This chapter deals with two types of modification problems:

1. **Misplaced and squinting modifiers:** In the first section, we examine **misplaced modifiers.** Sentences containing misplaced modifiers are not ungrammatical. The problem is that misplaced modifiers make sentences say something the writers do not intend to say. Here is an example with the misplaced modifier *almost*:

Senator Blather *almost* spoke for two hours.

Now, it is (barely) possible that the sentence means exactly what the writer said, that Senator Blather was scheduled for a two-hour speech but mercifully something happened to prevent it from being given. However, it is much more likely that what the writer meant to say was this:

Senator Blather spoke for *almost* two hours.

In other words, Senator Blather did indeed speak, and the speech lasted nearly two hours.

2. **Dangling modifiers:** In the second section, we deal with dangling modifiers. A **dangling modifier** is an out-and-out grammatical error. The error results from incorrectly formed modifying participial or infinitive phrases. These modifiers are said to dangle because they are improperly attached to the rest of the sentence. Here is an example (dangling modifier in italics):

X *Having hiked all day*, my backpack was killing me.

What the writer meant to say was that as a result of his having hiked all day, his backpack was killing him. However, what the writer actually said was this:

X My backpack hiked all day and was killing me.

Misplaced and Squinting Modifiers

A **misplaced modifier** is a modifier placed in a position where it modifies something that the writer does not intend it to modify. A **squinting modifier** is an adverb that can be interpreted as modifying two completely different things. Misplaced and squinting modifiers result in writers' saying things they don't mean.

Modifier errors are much more common in ordinary conversation than in writing, but speakers and listeners rarely notice them. When we talk, most of us do not carefully plan out exactly what we are going to say. We rarely go back over what we have said and edit it, unless it is grossly wrong. (Remember in the movie *Willy Wonka and the Chocolate Factory* when Willy Wonka would get excited and say phrases backward? He would stop, make a revolving motion with his hands, and then correct himself.) Likewise, our listeners are quite tolerant of all kinds of verbal mistakes. Part of the reason is that we are primarily listening for *what* people are saying, not *how* they are saying it.

When we write, however, it is a different story. Writing, unlike conversation, is planned and corrected in private. When we show our writing to others, there is an expectation of correctness far beyond our expectations of day-to-day conversational language. Mistakes that are routinely accepted without notice in conversation are glaringly apparent in writing. Nowhere is the difference between the standards of casual speech and writing more apparent than in the correct placement and use of modifiers.

Misplaced Modifiers

Misplaced modifiers do not make sentences ungrammatical. Misplaced modifiers are wrong because they say something the writer did not intend to say. The placement of an adverb can make a world of difference in meaning. For example, the placement of the adverb *only* in the following sentences changes the meaning rather considerably:

Only I love you.
I love *only* you.

Most of the misplaced modifier errors fall into two main categories: **misplaced adverb qualifiers** and **misplaced prepositional phrases.**

Misplaced Adverb Qualifiers. Suppose you intended to comment on how much chicken your friend Portly Bob ate, and you wrote this:

Bob *nearly* ate the whole chicken.

Unfortunately, what you actually said was that Bob did not eat any chicken at all, though he did contemplate eating a whole one. The problem is the placement of the adverb modifier *nearly*. What you should have written is this:

Bob ate *nearly* the whole chicken.

The problem this writer encountered is that *nearly* is one of a group of adverbs that have the unusual property of being able to modify noun phrases (like *the whole chicken* above) in addition to their usual adverb function of modifying verbs. The mistake the writer made was to unthinkingly place the adverb in front of the verb because that is where adverbs normally go.

Here are some other adverbs like *nearly*: *almost*, *just*, and *only*. When using these adverbs, we need to be aware that they are easily misplaced. We need to check the possibility that they really modify something *following* the verb—usually, but not always, a noun phrase. Here are three more examples of misplaced adverb quantifiers:

Alice *almost* spent $200 on a new CD player.

Now, did Alice actually get a new CD player or not? If she did not, then *almost* is correctly placed. However, if she did get her new CD player, then what the writer really meant was this:

Alice spent *almost* $200 on a new CD player.

We *just* located two vendors for that product.

If the writer meant that they just now located two vendors, then the modifier is correctly placed. But if the writer meant that they were able to find only two vendors, then this is what the writer should have written:

We located *just* two vendors for that product.

The committee *only* meets on Wednesdays.

In this example, the differences are more subtle. The placement of *only* in front of the verb *meets* implies that the committee takes no action at its Wednesday meetings. Presumably, the committee takes action at some other time. However, suppose the writer really meant to say that the committee has just a single weekly meeting—on Wednesdays. In that case, the adverb needs to follow the verb:

The committee meets *only* on Wednesdays.

The moral of this presentation is the following: watch out for the adverb qualifiers *almost*, *just*, *nearly*, and *only*. Sometimes these adverbs do not modify the verb as one might expect, but rather they modify a noun phrase or another structure following the verb.

Misplaced Prepositional Phrases. Prepositional phrases can play two different roles: adjectives and adverbs. One problem with prepositional phrases at the end of a sentence is that the reader interprets the prepositional phrase as one part of speech, while the writer intended the other. Here is an example with the prepositional phrase in italics:

The runners stood ignoring the crowd *in their lanes*.

It seems as though the writer is using the prepositional phrase as an adjective modifying *crowd*. The sentence seems to say that the crowd was in the runners' lanes, a highly unlikely situation. What the writer meant was for the prepositional phrase to be used as an adverb telling us where the runners stood. Here is what the writer should have written:

> The runners stood *in their lanes* ignoring the crowd.

A second problem with prepositional phrases is that when there is more than one clause, adverb prepositional phrases can be placed so that they modify the wrong verb. Here is an example of such an adverb prepositional phrase (in italics):

> He went to a hospital where he underwent emergency surgery *in a limousine.*

On first reading, we interpret the adverb prepositional phrase *in a limousine* as modifying the nearest verb, *underwent*:

X He underwent emergency surgery *in a limousine.*

What the writer meant, of course, is for the prepositional phrase to modify the first verb, *went*:

> He went to a hospital *in a limousine.*

The best way to correct the misplacement is to move the prepositional phrase next to the verb it modifies:

> He went *in a limousine* to a hospital where he underwent emergency surgery.

The best way to monitor for misplaced prepositional phrases is to always make sure the prepositional phrase is directly attached to the word that it should modify. Pay special attention to prepositional phrases at the ends of sentences. They are the ones most likely to be misplaced.

Squinting Modifiers

Squinting modifiers are adverbs that are placed at a boundary of two clauses or phrases with the unfortunate result that the reader cannot tell which clause or phrase the adverb should go with. These modifiers are called "squinting" because they seem to look in two different directions at the same time. Following are two examples of squinting adverbs (in italics):

> The mayor promised *after her reelection* she would not raise taxes.

Here, the modifier is the adverb prepositional phrase *after her reelection.* The adverb phrase "squints" because we can interpret it in two different ways:

1. *After her reelection* modifies the preceding verb *promised.* We can paraphrase this interpretation as follows:

> After the mayor was reelected, she promised that she would not raise taxes.

That is, the mayor has already been elected.

2. *After her reelection* modifies the following verb *would raise.* We can paraphrase this interpretation as follows:

> The mayor promised that after she was reelected, she would not raise taxes.

That is, the mayor is making a promise about what she would do if and when she were reelected.

In the following example

> Students who practice writing *often* will benefit.

the modifier is the adverb *often.* The adverb "squints" because we can interpret it in two different ways:

1. *Often* modifies the preceding verb *writing*. We can paraphrase this interpretation as follows:

> Those students who often practice writing are the ones who will benefit.

2. *Often* modifies the following verb *will benefit*. We can paraphrase this interpretation as follows:

> Students will *often* benefit when they practice writing.

Sentences containing squinting modifiers are not ungrammatical per se. The problem is that the squinting modifier creates an unintended and undesired ambiguity. Once the writer realizes the confusion, the ambiguity is easily resolved one way or another. The problem, of course, is that the writer sees only the intended meaning, not the unintended one.

There is no simple solution or test for squinting adverbs. Nonetheless, it is helpful for writers to be aware of the condition in which squinting adverbs can occur. Squinting adverbs occur at the boundary between two clauses or phrases. Once writers are aware that this boundary is a squinting adverb danger zone, they can take the extra second to consciously check to see if adverbs at the boundaries can be interpreted in more than one way.

Summary

Misplaced and squinting modifiers are difficult problems for all of us because *we* know what we meant. It is really hard to train our eyes to see not just what we meant but what we actually said.

Misplaced modifiers are modifiers put in the wrong place so they modify something we do not intend for them to modify. The most likely culprits are the adverb qualifiers *almost*, *just*, *nearly*, and *only* because they can modify both verbs (as we would expect) and also noun phrases. Other common misplaced modifiers are adverb prepositional phrases at the end of sentences that can be interpreted as modifying the nearest verb rather than the more remote intended verb.

Squinting modifiers are modifiers that are used at the boundary of two clauses or phrases. The result is that the reader cannot tell which clause or phrase the modifier should go with.

The only real defense against misplaced and squinting modifiers is to be aware of the kinds of modifiers that are likely to be misused and the places that modifier mistakes are most likely to occur. Forewarned is forearmed.

Even the most experienced writers never outgrow the need to consciously check high-risk modifiers and places for unintended meanings.

Dangling Modifiers

A **dangling modifier** is said to dangle because it looks like it might fall off the sentence it is attached to. Dangling modifiers are adverbial phrases of various sorts, **participial** and **infinitive phrases** being the most common. Here are some examples with the dangling modifier underlined (and some questions that suggest why the modifier is dangling):

X <u>Regretfully declining the dessert menu</u>, the waiter brought us our bill. (Who declined the dessert menu? It sounds like the waiter did.)

X <u>Worried about being late</u>, a taxi seemed like a good idea. (Was the taxi really worried about being late?)

X <u>After getting a new job</u>, my commuting costs have doubled. (Did my commuting costs get a new job?)

X <u>To recover from the surgery</u>, the doctor recommended bed rest. (How's the doctor feeling now?)

The problem is that these modifiers break a basic rule of grammar that we will call *"the man who wasn't there" principle*. You may know this poem:

As I was going up the stair
I met a man who wasn't there.
He wasn't there again today.
I wish, I wish he'd stay away.

—*"Antigonish" (1899), Hughes Mearns*

"The man who wasn't there" principle of grammar means that it is OK to not be there as long as you don't go away. In other words, we can drop something out of a part of a sentence *if* we can get it back from somewhere else in the rest of the sentence.

Here is an example of a modifier (underlined) that correctly obeys "the man who wasn't there" principle:

Turning the key in the lock, Holmes quietly slipped into the room.

In this sentence, the subject of the verb *turning* has been dropped. But in this example, we can find out who did the turning by looking at the subject in the main part of the sentence. It was Holmes: Holmes turned the key in the lock. In other words, we can legitimately drop the subject *Holmes* from the modifier because we can get it back from the main sentence.

We can find out if the modifier is dangling or not by a simple two-step process that tests to see if the subject in the modifier has been legitimately dropped:

1. Move a copy of the subject of the main sentence into the subject position of the modifier:

   [Holmes] Turning the key in the lock, Holmes quietly slipped into the room.

2. Change the verb in the modifier so that it agrees with the restored subject:

   Holmes turned the key in the lock.

Now ask yourself this question: does this new sentence make sense? If the answer is no, then it is a dangling modifier. If the answer is yes, then the modifier is correct. In this case, the answer is yes, so we know that the modifier is not dangling.

Now we can see what is wrong with the first four examples: the subject of the main sentence does not make sense when it is used as the understood subject of the modifier, and therefore it was not legitimate to have dropped the subject from the modifier in the first place. To see that this is the case, let's go through the two-step process:

X Reluctantly declining the dessert menu, the waiter brought us our bill.

1. Move a copy of the subject to the modifier:

   [the waiter] Reluctantly declining the dessert menu, the waiter brought us our bill.

2. Change the verb in the modifier to agree with the subject:

   X The waiter reluctantly declined the dessert menu.

This doesn't make sense because it was the customers who declined dessert. Therefore, the modifier is dangling, and either the modifier or the main sentence must be rewritten.

X Worried about being late, a taxi seemed like a good idea.

1. Move a copy of the subject to the modifier:

   [a taxi] Worried about being late, a taxi seemed like a good idea.

2. Change the verb in the modifier to agree with the subject:

   X A taxi worried about being late.

This doesn't make sense. Therefore, the modifier is dangling, and either the modifier or the main sentence must be rewritten.

X After getting a new job, my commuting costs have doubled.

1. Move a copy of the subject to the modifier:

   After [my commuting costs] getting a new job, my commuting costs have doubled.

2. Change the verb in the modifier to agree with the subject:

   X After my commuting costs got a new job, my commuting costs have doubled.

This doesn't make sense. Therefore, the modifier is dangling, and either the modifier or the main sentence must be rewritten.

X To recover from the surgery, the doctor recommended bed rest.

1. Move a copy of the subject to the modifier:

   [the doctor] To recover from the surgery, the doctor recommended bed rest.

2. Change the verb in the modifier to agree with the subject:

   X The doctor recovered from the surgery.

This doesn't make any sense. The doctor did not undergo surgery—the patient did. Therefore, the modifier is dangling, and either the modifier or the main sentence must be rewritten.

You can do one of two things to correct a dangling modifier:

1. Change the modifier to make it compatible with the main part of the sentence.
2. Change the main part of the sentence to make it compatible with the modifier.

You should explore both possibilities to decide which one you like the best. For example, let's go back to the first example and explore both options:

X Reluctantly declining the dessert menu, the waiter brought us our bill.

1. Change the modifier to make it compatible with the main part of the sentence:

   Collecting the dessert menus, the waiter brought us our bill.

2. Change the main part of the sentence to make it compatible with the modifier:

   Reluctantly declining the dessert menu, we asked for our bill.

Obviously, there are many other ways to rewrite the original sentence with the dangling modifier corrected, but these two revisions illustrate the main alternatives. Both revisions are now grammatical, but which alternative is best is a stylistic question that you will have to decide for yourself. Often the choice hinges on what you want to emphasize. In version 1, the emphasis is on the waiter. In version 2, the emphasis is on the people eating. If the focus of the whole passage is on the waiter, then version 1 is probably better. If your focus is on the people, then version 2 is probably better.

Summary

A dangling modifier is typically some kind of adverbial phrase at the beginning of a sentence. The phrase dangles because the implied subject of the verb in the adverbial phrase is not the same as the subject of the sentence it modifies.

The way to check for dangling modifiers is to see if the subject of the main sentence makes sense as the understood subject of the verb in the adverbial phrase. If it does not, then the adverbial phrase is dangling, and either the adverbial phrase or the sentence must be rewritten.

11

Commas

This chapter covers the varied uses of commas—and the errors associated with this punctuation mark. In fact, commas seem to account for a huge proportion of most people's questions and concerns regarding correct grammar, punctuation, and usage.

1. Commas with *and*, *but*, and *or* (and other coordinating conjunctions): A **coordinating conjunction** is a word used to connect other words. The most common coordinating conjunctions are *and*, *but*, and *or*.

A coordinating conjunction can combine various words and groups of words. One of the most common problems involves using a comma right before a coordinating conjunction in what is—or what only appears to be—a **compound sentence**. A compound sentence is a single sentence that is composed of what could be two separate sentences. Here is an example that is correctly punctuated, with the coordinating conjunction underlined:

I want to read the classics, but I have a short attention span.

In this section, we discuss two related problems. The first involves failing to put a comma before the coordinating conjunction in a compound sentence. The second involves mistakenly putting a comma before a coordinating conjunction because the sentence appears to be (but is not) a compound sentence. We also provide one tip for avoiding both errors.

2. Commas with introductory elements: An **introductory element** is a general term used to refer to a word or group of words placed at the front of the sentence—before the subject and verb. Following are two examples:

According to some sources, Benjamin Franklin roasted a turkey on a rotating electric spit in 1749.

In the 1950s, a Texas town named Lolita almost changed its name to avoid being associated with a controversial novel with the same name.

People often have strong preferences as to whether some introductory elements can, must, or must not have a comma afterward. Most general handbooks indicate a comma should be used, but some professions and organizations indicate otherwise.

As we discuss in this section, certain types of introductory elements are less debatable in terms of punctuation. We also explain why we suggest putting a comma after every type of introductory element, unless the writer knows the readers expect otherwise.

3. Commas with adjective clauses: An **adjective clause** is a group of words that together describe a person, place, or thing. Adjective clauses often begin with *who*, *whom*, *whose*, *which*, or *that*. Sometimes an adjective clause is separated from the rest of a sentence by a comma. At other times, it would be an error to set off the clause with commas. Following are correct examples (adjective clauses underlined):

Outdoor scenes in the movie *Oklahoma*, which was a huge hit in 1955, were actually filmed in Arizona.

I know a mechanic who can help you.

The decision regarding using a comma is a complex one. As we describe in this section, the matter rests on whether the word being described by the adjective clause is sufficiently clear and specific *without* the clause. If so, the clause is nonessential, and commas are required, as seen in the example about the movie *Oklahoma*.

4. Commas with adverb clauses: An **adverb clause** is a group of words that act together. As its name suggests, the adverb clause functions as an adverb. In this section, we focus on commas used when the adverb clause functions to modify a verb.

Some adverb clauses must have commas separating them from the rest of a sentence. With other adverb clauses, there should not be any such commas. And in still other situations, using commas is optional. Following are examples of correctly punctuated adverb clauses (underlined):

> While I was in England visiting friends, I was told that the game of darts started in the Middle Ages as a way to train archers.
>
> The numbering system on a dart board is a bit of a mystery because nobody knows its origins.

This section discusses the rules that most grammar experts agree on in terms of punctuating adverb clauses. This section also offers suggestions on how to deal with some of the situations when there is not such widespread agreement.

5. Commas with appositives: An appositive is a word (or group of words) with no other function except to rename a previous noun or pronoun. Contrary to what many people assume, appositives are not necessarily set off with commas. If an appositive is not really necessary, it is set off with commas, but appositives that readers need in order to understand the sentence are *not* set off with commas.

Here are two examples of appositives (underlined), the first of which requires commas because the appositive is not necessary:

> A month before being shot in his car by law officers, Clyde Barrow, a notorious criminal, wrote a letter to Henry Ford praising him for the "dandy" automobile he made.
>
> In 1885 the Apache chief Geronimo was outnumbered by 150 to 1 yet managed to hold off the U.S. Army for half a year.

In this section, we discuss when you should and should not use commas with appositives.

6. Commas with adjectives: Adjectives are words that modify nouns, and it is common for writers to have two or more adjectives in a row before the noun they modify. Some people mistakenly assume all such adjectives are separated by commas from one another. Sometimes commas are required, but sometimes not, as seen here (adjectives underlined):

We bought a large, expensive computer.
Terrie is wearing a red cotton skirt.

Commas are needed when adjectives are "coordinate"—when they belong to the same basic class of adjectives. When the adjectives belong to different classes, commas should not be used. This matter might seem confusing because few people are aware of the different categories of adjectives. We offer two commonsense tips for helping people see the distinctions and punctuate adjectives correctly.

Commas with *and*, *but*, and *or* (and Other Coordinating Conjunctions)

A **coordinating conjunction** is a word used to combine words, phrases, or entire sentences. When combining sentences, use a comma immediately before the coordinating conjunction. Coordinating conjunctions are words that have little meaning by themselves; their primary purpose is to connect other words that do have important meaning. In this section, we focus on coordinating conjunctions used to combine entire sentences. To a lesser extent, this section covers guidelines for combining verbs that share the same subject.

The most common coordinating conjunctions are *and*, *but*, and *or*. As noted earlier, a good way to remember all the coordinating conjunctions is using the acronym FANBOYS:

For
And
Nor
But
Or
Yet
So

These three sentences correctly use a comma along with a coordinating conjunction (underlined) to combine sentences:

> Guion Bluford was the first African American to fly in space, <u>and</u> he was a decorated Air Force veteran.
>
> I asked for cream in my coffee, <u>but</u> the waiter did not give me any.
>
> You can submit the report on time, <u>or</u> we can all work until midnight to get the work done.

Commas have many functions, and many errors occur simply because people cannot keep up with the varied ways in which a comma should be used—or not used. One of the most common uses (and misuses) is when a comma is used to combine entire sentences. Actually, there are two types of errors connected with this use of a comma. Although both types are relatively common, neither is particularly serious in the eyes of most readers—certainly not as serious or annoying as a fragment or a comma splice. In fact, neither type of error has a name that people agree on (which is why the title of this section is unusually long). Before considering these two types of errors, remember the following rule to avoid the problem altogether:

Avoiding the Problem: Commas and Complete Sentences

Place a comma before a coordinating conjunction that is used to combine two sentences. Do not use a comma when what comes after is not a complete sentence. In other words, keep this pattern in mind:

sentence #1 + comma + coordinating conjunction + sentence #2

Think of it this way: the comma in this situation is like a weak period. The comma is taking the place of what could be a period, as shown here:

Somebody ordered ten filing cabinets, but they have not arrived.

or

Somebody ordered ten filing cabinets. But they have not arrived.

Many readers regard starting a sentence with *but* or another coordinating conjunction to be too informal. However, technically you can do so. The important point is that you should combine two sentences by using a comma plus a coordinating conjunction.

Let's discuss the first type of error connected with this sort of sentence. A common mistake people make is that they leave out the comma, as illustrated in these two incorrect sentences:

X We will reimburse you for expenses but you should be careful about how much you spend.

X Ants might not seem very intelligent yet their brains are larger than those of most other insects their size.

The problem is that the comma is supposed to be a subtle clue. It indicates that what comes afterward is an idea that, even if related to the first part of the sentence, is going in a new direction. Grammatically speaking, the comma prepares readers for a new subject and a new verb. This creates a **compound sentence**—a sentence composed of what could be two sentences (see Chapter 6). Another way of putting it is that a compound sentence is made of at least two independent clauses. By far, the most common means of connecting the two parts of a compound sentence is a comma, although using a semicolon is another option (see Chapter 13).

Applying the rule easily corrects these problems. Place a comma where you could place a period (immediately before the coordinating conjunction):

We will reimburse you for expenses, but you should be careful about how much you spend.

Ants might not seem very intelligent, yet their brains are larger than those of most other insects their size.

There is a second type of error connected with a coordinating conjunction and what *appears* to be a compound sentence: some people mistakenly use a comma before a coordinating conjunction. That is, sometimes a person will take the aforementioned rule too far and unnecessarily use a comma, as in these two examples:

X The band is playing too loudly, and wearing obnoxious clothes.
X Widgets Incorporated recalled this computer, but has not informed us how to replace it.

What comes after each comma cannot stand on its own as a complete sentence. Put another way, you cannot replace these two commas with periods:

The band is playing too loudly.	X And wearing obnoxious clothes.
Widgets Incorporated recalled this computer.	X But has not informed us how to replace it.

Because the second halves cannot stand alone, the original sentences were not true compound sentences. Thus, a comma is not needed before the conjunction.

Again, consider the rule: use a comma before a coordinating conjunction used to combine what could be two sentences. This rule also means that you should *not* use a comma when what comes afterward relies on the first part of the sentence. Grammatically speaking, these last two sentences are not compound sentences. Rather, they involve compound verbs. In each sentence, the subject is doing two actions:

The band → is playing too loudly.
The band → is wearing obnoxious clothes.

Widgets Incorporated → recalled this computer.
Widgets Incorporated → has not informed us how to replace it.

In each of these examples, putting a comma between the two actions interrupts the way in which the two verbs go back to a single subject. To fix the problem, leave out the commas:

> The band is playing too loudly and is wearing obnoxious clothes.
> Widgets Incorporated recalled this computer but has not informed us how to replace it.

As noted, neither of these errors (leaving out the comma or putting it in needlessly) is considered to be very serious by most readers. In fact, this is one of those gray areas of punctuation. Many grammar handbooks state that you have the option of omitting the comma in a compound sentence *if* the first part of the sentence is fewer than five words, as in *I drove home but nobody was there.* Also, some people—especially if they are trying to be emphatic or simulate the way people pause when speaking—will use a comma to separate two verbs, as in *I want you to leave, and never return.* These are the exceptions, and the prudent approach is to not break the rules lightly.

Summary

To figure out if you need a comma before a coordinating conjunction (such as *and*, *but*, or *or*), you should determine if what comes after the coordinating conjunction could potentially be a complete sentence. If yes, the comma is needed before the conjunction. If no, no comma is needed before the conjunction.

Commas with Introductory Elements

Sentences normally begin with a subject followed by a verb. An **introductory element** refers to other types of words that are not part of the subject but are still placed at the beginning of a sentence, as shown in these two examples (introductory elements underlined):

> When I was sixteen, my father gave me a sailboat.
> However, the boat sank after I had it only a week.

A comma is useful because it is a marker indicating where the "real" sentence begins—with the subject and its verb. In fact, a handy way to detect an introductory element is to see if it can be moved around so that the sentence can begin another way.

Grammar Tip: Moving Introductory Elements

If a word or group of words coming at the beginning of a sentence can be moved around, then it is probably an introductory element.

Applying this tip reveals that the two examples just given indeed have introductory elements:

My father gave me a sailboat when I was sixteen.
The boat, however, sank after I had it only a week.

As you can see, commas might or might not be needed if you move an introductory element to some other place in a sentence, but this issue is not important because you are just toying with the original sentence. The point is that you can move *when I was sixteen* and *however* around, indicating that indeed they are introductory elements.

What's the Problem?

The problem is that writers must decide if a comma is needed after an introductory element once they know a sentence has such an introductory element. The bigger problem, though, is that not all readers or grammar handbooks are in agreement about using a comma after an introductory element, largely because the term *introductory element* is a catchall term that covers several types of structures. See the table that follows for additional information, though it is not necessary to remember all of these structures. (Introductory elements are underlined.)

MAJOR TYPES OF INTRODUCTORY ELEMENTS

Adverb clauses*	Although 124 midgets appeared in *The Wizard of Oz*, few people remember any of the actors' names.
Appositives placed in front of the word they rename	A true friend, Tess took over my duties while I was sick.
Conjunctive adverbs*	However, she did not do a good job.
Direct address	Brian, please remove your hat.
Interjection	Hey, do you have a dollar I can borrow?
Prepositional phrases*	In a fit of rage, Max smashed the glass.
Single-word adverbs that modify a verb*	Yesterday, the firm filed a lawsuit.
Single-word adverbs that modify the sentence	Yes, you can leave work early.
Verbals or verbal phrases	Hearing her name called, Kisha went to the receptionist's desk.

Almost every handbook agrees that some types of elements (such as direct address) *must* have commas. Most handbooks also agree that there are times when the comma is optional, especially if the element is short (as with short prepositional phrases). However, there are different definitions about what is short or long (most handbooks define a long introductory element as one that is five words or more). To compound the problem, there are certain readers, businesses, or professions that—no matter what the handbooks or English teachers say—have strong preferences about requiring or banning the use of commas after introductory elements.

*Particularly common types found in formal writing.

Avoiding the Problem: Playing It Safe

First, if possible, determine the preferences of your readers. Accept the fact that this is a gray area of grammar and there is disagreement about whether commas after introductory elements are optional, required, or undesirable.

If it is not possible to make this determination, the safest approach is to use a comma after *all* introductory elements.

Most handbooks that—like this one—are written for people in diverse situations state that commas are required for certain types of introductory elements. These handbooks also indicate there are some instances when commas are optional. However, almost no general-use handbook states that it is wrong to put a comma after an introductory element. Thus, the safe approach seems to be that, if in doubt, you should use a comma after an introductory element because doing so is almost never wrong according to the great majority of grammar handbooks aimed at a general audience.

Keep in mind, though, the following exceptions to our suggestion of using a comma after all introductory elements:

- One informal type of introductory element is the coordinating conjunction (see Chapter 1) and normally a comma should *not* be used in this situation, as shown here (coordinating conjunctions underlined):

  Paulette was asked to call us immediately. <u>But</u> she must have decided otherwise.
  You can leave now. <u>Or</u> we will have to call the authorities.

- In certain professions (such as journalism), commas are usually left out after introductory elements, unless doing so would clearly make the sentence difficult to understand.
- Although preferences in this matter are difficult to measure, there seems to be an increasing number of organizations and businesses that

prefer commas to be omitted after short introductory elements. In time, the safe approach we have described might not be so safe!

Other Areas of Agreement

Again, it is unlikely that you would break a widely accepted rule if you put a comma after every introductory element. Here are other guidelines that are widely accepted:

1. You must use a comma if leaving it out could cause serious misreading of a sentence. If you leave out the comma, there are times when the reader cannot tell if a word is the last part of the introductory element or if it is the subject of the whole sentence:

X When eating the cat purrs loudly.
X While Ann was bathing the telephone rang.

In the first sentence, you might think somebody ate the cat, and in the second, it might seem that Ann gave her phone a bath. Although both of the elements are short, commas are needed to prevent misreading:

When eating, the cat purrs loudly.
While Ann was bathing, the telephone rang.

2. Even people who prefer that commas be used sparingly tend to agree that long introductory elements require commas. As noted earlier, there is no standard definition of what is long, but clearly sentences such as the following need a comma to let readers know where the main part of the sentence begins:

Although Mark Twain wrote several lengthy novels during his distinguished career, he was granted a patent for a book that contained no words at all (entitled *Self-Pasting Scrapbook*).

Having been taught to use a comma after most introductory elements in a sentence, Jerome rarely had to consult a grammar book on the issue.

Summary

When deciding if you should use a comma after an introductory element, consider the following:

- An introductory element can be easily recognized because they can almost always be moved to another position in the sentence.
- Most grammar handbooks written for general purposes state that it is never wrong to use a comma after an introductory element. Nonetheless, some people assume otherwise, so it is wise to determine the preferences of your readers, business, or organization.
- If in doubt, use commas after introductory elements of all types.
- Definitely use a comma when it is needed to prevent confusion or when the element is long (five words or more).
- It is optional to use a comma after short introductory clauses and prepositional phrases, but again it is simpler and more consistent to use commas after every introductory element.

Commas with Adjective Clauses

An **adjective clause** is a group of words used together to describe a person, place, or thing. Adjective clauses often begin with *who*, *whom*, *whose*, *which*, or *that*. As seen in the fourth example that follows, sometimes these words can be deleted, though they are understood to be there.

> We need a photocopier <u>that will not break down twice a week.</u>
>
> Edwin Booth, <u>who was the brother of the man who shot Abraham Lincoln</u>, once saved one of Lincoln's sons from being run over by a train.
>
> I saw a woman <u>whom I once dated.</u>
>
> I saw a woman <u>I once dated.</u>

In each of the four sentences, the underlined clause describes a noun (a photocopier, Edwin Booth, or a woman). Thus, each clause is a single unit that functions as an adjective. (Adjective clauses are sometimes called **relative clauses**; the two terms mean exactly the same thing.)

What's the Problem?

As illustrated in the preceding examples, some adjective clauses are separated from the rest of a sentence with commas, while others are not. This is a complicated issue because it rests on the specific nature of each sentence and what the writer assumes is essential in order for readers to understand the sentence. The punctuation decision seems particularly subjective because ultimately it comes down to what the writer and reader consider to be essential information.

> **Avoiding the Problem**
>
> Use a comma to set off an adjective clause only when it does not contain information that helps to identify the person, place, or thing being described. If the noun or pronoun being described by the clause is specific, then usually the clause does not contain important information. Use a comma when this noun or pronoun being described is already specific and clear.

Using Commas with Adjective Clauses

Normally, the punctuation decision is not difficult if you keep the preceding tip in mind. Just look at the noun or pronoun being described by the clause. (This noun or pronoun will usually appear immediately before the adjective clause.) If this noun or pronoun has already been made specific for readers, then the clause is merely giving a little additional information. Adjective clauses are underlined in the following:

My mother, <u>who lives in Seattle</u>, calls me every day.
I drove to Ralph's Hardware Store, <u>which is open on Sundays</u>.

In the first sentence, the word *mother* is already made specific because of the adjective *my*, so you do not need the underlined clause. You know whose mother is involved, and the fact that she lives in Seattle is some additional tidbit. If we can assume that there is only one Ralph's Hardware Store, then similarly the adjective clause in the second example is not needed in order to know which store the writer has in mind. In short, a nonessential adjective clause is set off from the "meat" of the sentence. It is nonessential if the reader does not need it to determine which person, place, or thing the writer has in mind.

An error would occur if commas were not used to set off a nonessential adjective clause, as in this example:

X Dr. Dolittle who has been my physician for years has asked me not to come back.

The clause modifies a term (*Dr. Dolittle*) that is already specific and clear. Such an error can be easily corrected by inserting commas:

Dr. Dolittle, who has been my physician for years, has asked me not to come back.

This example, noted already, might seem more difficult to punctuate:

Edwin Booth, who was the brother of the man who shot Abraham Lincoln, once saved one of Lincoln's sons from being run over by a train.

The adjective clause is describing Edwin Booth and does include important information in the sense that most people do not know who Edwin Booth is. Even though the clause seems vital, the noun *Edwin Booth* is still so specific that the adjective clause is not essential. An adjective clause might contain important facts or details, but the key is usually whether the noun or pronoun is already specific. Such is the case with this sentence, so the writer must use commas.

Adjective Clauses That Do Not Need Commas

As stated, do not use a comma when the clause is essential for helping readers identify the noun or pronoun being described. Again, consider whether the person, place, or thing being modified has already been sufficiently identified. Is the noun or pronoun general enough to require additional identifying information? If so, the adjective clause is too important to separate from the word it describes.

> We hired a lawyer whose firm specializes in mass litigation. (Which lawyer?)
> I have something that I need to discuss with you. (What something?)

Errors occur when the writer uses commas with adjective clauses that are essential for identifying the noun or pronoun being modified:

X The person, who has borrowed the company van, needs to return the vehicle at once.

The term *person* is much too vague without the clause. It's not just *any* person who must return the vehicle but the one who borrowed it. Use commas to set off adjective clauses *only* if the word being described is sufficiently specific and clear. As you can see, correcting this error is simple—just leave out the commas:

> The person who has borrowed the company van needs to return the vehicle at once.

Sometimes It Just Depends

Every now and then, the word being modified by the adjective clause could be sufficiently specific by itself—or not. The matter depends on the larger situation beyond the sentence.

Consider this sentence:

> My son who is a stamp collector is at a convention in Tulsa.

Are commas needed? It depends on how many sons the writer has. If there is only one, the term *my son* is already specific, for it could only mean one thing. Accordingly, the sentence would need commas to separate the nonessential adjective clause from the rest of the sentence:

My son, who is a stamp collector, is at a convention in Tulsa. (If there is only one son.)

But if the writer has more than one son, then *my son* is not clear. Thus, the adjective clause is now essential for us to understand which son the writer has in mind. Leave out commas when a clause is this essential:

My son who is a stamp collector is at a convention in Tulsa. (If there are two or more sons.)

The tip discussed earlier still tells you whether to use commas or not: use a comma with an adjective clause only if the clause is not essential for identifying the person, place, or thing being described. With some sentences, though, you must consider the larger context and intention to determine how clear the noun or pronoun is.

Summary

• An adjective clause is a group of words that act together to describe a previous noun or pronoun.
• Use commas with adjective clauses only when this noun or pronoun is sufficiently specific and clear.

Commas with Adverb Clauses

It might be easier to consider a few examples of **adverb clauses** before reading the complex definition (adverb clauses underlined):

I must leave before the party ends.
When Nora wants to sing, we hide.
The movie *E.T.* was banned in Sweden because it showed parents acting hostilely toward their children.
We decided to travel by car to Idaho, even though it will be a ten-hour drive.

As these examples show, an adverb clause has the following characteristics:

1. It is a group of words that must include a subject and verb, even though the adverb clause cannot stand by itself as a complete sentence.
2. An adverb clause begins with a subordinating conjunction, such as *before, when, because, even though, although,* or *since.*
3. The group of words work together as a single adverb that modifies a verb, an adjective, or another adverb.

The best-known function of an adverb clause is modifying a verb, and it is this type of adverb clause that is sometimes confusing in terms of punctuation. Thus, we focus on this function of an adverb clause.

What's the Problem?

Adverb clauses by themselves pose few problems; they come easily to most people and frequently appear in speech and writing. The problem is whether to use a comma to separate the adverb clause from the rest of the sentence. Two of the preceding examples use commas in this way, while the other two do not.

Avoiding the Problem: Consider Where the Clause Appears
In general, use a comma after an adverb clause that comes at the beginning of the sentence. Only rarely is a comma needed before an adverb clause.

This hint will serve you well most of the time, but read the following to understand the exceptions, which do occur fairly often.

Adverb Clauses at the Beginning of a Sentence

Most adverb clauses can be placed in different positions in a sentence, and putting an adverb clause at the beginning of a sentence is common. Indeed, the resulting structure is simply one type of an introductory element. The same concept applies again: in general, use a comma to set off the introductory element, whether it is an adverb clause or some other type of introductory element.

> While I was reading a fascinating book on grammar, the electricity went out.
>
> Since our company was founded in 1902, the president has held an annual picnic for all employees.

At one time, most grammar handbooks urged putting a comma after all adverb clauses that come at the beginning of a sentence. However, the trend now is that a writer can leave out a comma after a short adverb clause (fewer than five words, or so most handbooks suggest).

> When Jane arrived Tarzan was in the backyard.
>
> If Neill calls we should not talk to him.

In fact, you might find that some readers, especially in the business sector, prefer that you not use a comma after an introductory adverb clause unless the clause is long. This trend is growing, but most handbooks still indicate a preference for using a comma after introductory adverb clauses. Thus, we suggest you keep it simple whenever possible and put a comma after all introductory adverb clauses (short or long)—unless you encounter readers who insist on leaving commas out.

Adverb Clauses at the End of a Sentence

In general, do not use a comma before an adverb clause. Some people mistakenly use a comma in such situations simply because they "feel" a pause. This is especially the case with adverb clauses that begin with *because.*

X I incorrectly want to use a comma, because I sense a pause in the sentence.

X Beefalo is what you get, when you cross buffalo with cattle.

X Aluminum is cheap, since it is the most common metal in the earth's crust.

To correct these errors, you merely need to omit the commas:

I incorrectly want to use a comma because I sense a pause in the sentence.
Beefalo is what you get when you cross buffalo with cattle.
Aluminum is cheap since it is the most common metal in the earth's crust.

Why do we set off adverb clauses that appear at the beginning but not at the end of a sentence? A comma is used to set off an introductory clause so readers will have a clear sign as to where the "real" sentence begins. There is usually no other reason to set off an adverb clause, so avoid using a comma with adverb clauses that appear anywhere else.

But the hint noted earlier indicates that there is an exception, and here it is: use a comma before the sentence-ending adverb clause when it deals with a strong sense of contrast. Such clauses usually begin with *even though*, *while*, *although*, or *though*.

She was ready to leave the party immediately, while her husband wanted to stay all night.
I remember that the Lone Ranger's horse is named Silver, though I keep forgetting that Tonto's horse is named Scout.

It is not altogether clear why the rule evolved this way. Most likely, the comma helps readers see that the last part of the sentence will involve a strong contradiction or contrast with what came before. This structure is not rare in speech or writing, and overgeneralizing this situation causes many people to err by putting a comma before other types of adverb clauses. Again, the norm is that a comma should not set off a sentence-ending adverb clause. As with any rule, it can be broken when writers feel they want to emphasize an idea or achieve some other effect, but you should avoid intentionally breaking the rule in formal writing unless you are certain of a positive effect.

Summary

- Use a comma after an adverb clause that comes at the beginning of a sentence.
- You have the option of omitting the comma if the introductory clause is fewer than five words.
- Rarely should you use a comma before an adverb clause that comes at the end of a sentence.
- However, use a comma before the adverb clause if it involves a strong sense of contrast and begins with words such as *even though* or *although.*

Commas with Appositives

An **appositive** is a noun or pronoun that renames another noun or pronoun. Most commonly, the appositive is a noun appearing almost immediately after another noun. Notice how the appositive seems to bend back to rename a previous noun (appositives underlined):

> My dog, Pearl, is a husky.
> Shari talked to her lawyer, Perry Mason.

An **appositive phrase** includes not only a noun but words describing it. In this next example, *president* is the appositive, but it is described by *the twenty-ninth* and *of the United States.* All these words together are bending back to rename *Woodrow Wilson.*

> Woodrow Wilson, the twenty-ninth president of the United States, said that automobiles symbolized "the arrogance of wealth."

Grammar Tip: Rewriting the Sentence

To confirm an appositive, see if you can rewrite the sentence using only the appositive. If the rewrite is grammatical, you've confirmed the appositive. The example

> My dog, Pearl, is a husky.

could be written as

> Pearl is a husky.

What's the Problem?

As you have seen, appositives are frequently set off by commas. However, this is not always the case, as evidenced in these examples:

> My friend Nicole helped write this report.
> Shakespeare's play *The Tempest* was the inspiration for a 1956 movie called *Forbidden Planet.*

Avoiding the Problem: Is the Appositive Essential?

Set off an appositive with commas *unless* the appositive is essential for identifying the word being renamed.

Appositives with Commas

Nonessential information is often set off by commas. This basic guideline applies to other types of grammatical structures as well (for instance, see Commas with Adjective Clauses in this chapter). Although all appositives add clarity and detail, most are not crucial. Here, for example, the appositive (underlined) clarifies exactly who the doctor is:

> I contacted our family physician, Dr. Stout.

Assuming the writer has only one family physician, you could leave out the appositive and not confuse readers. Sure, they would not know the name of the doctor, but the appositive is not essential because the writer has only one family physician.

The safest approach is to assume that an appositive needs commas, for usually the rest of whatever you are writing makes the appositive nonessential.

Appositives Without Commas

In general, do *not* use commas to set off words that are essential to the overall meaning of a sentence. The problem is sometimes it seems every word is important. However, as discussed, the key with appositives is to look at the words they rename and consider how confused readers would be without the appositive. An appositive is essential when readers must have it to understand *which* person, place, or thing you have in mind. In such cases, you must leave out the commas.

X My friend, Jewel, needs a ride. (Confusion: *Which* friend? We assume you have more than one.)
My friend Jewel needs a ride.

X You need to read the book, *The Color Purple*. (Confusion: *Which* book? There must be millions of books available.)
You need to read the book *The Color Purple*.

Here are more examples of appositives that correctly omit the commas. Note how each appositive eliminates confusion by reducing the various ways readers could interpret each sentence.

The children's song "Ring Around the Rosie" originated during the bubonic plague.
The country Denmark has had the same national flag longer than any other nation in history.
The French ruler Napoleon Bonaparte knowingly financed his Russian invasion with counterfeit money.

Sometimes It Can Go Either Way

On a few occasions, an appositive might be essential or not depending on what readers already know about the word being renamed. Consider again this sentence. It is fine as written *if* it could only be referring to one dog.

My dog, Pearl, is a husky. (OK if the writer has only one dog.)

But what if the writer has more than one dog? The appositive is essential because we are not sure which dog the writer has in mind. In this case, the appositive should not be set off by commas.

My dog Pearl is a husky. (OK if the writer has more than one dog.)

As you can see, the matter is usually settled by what the writer stated in previous sentences or by what the reader knew even earlier.

Summary

• An appositive is a noun or pronoun that renames a previous noun or pronoun.
• In general, use commas to set off appositives.
• Leave out the commas, however, when the appositive is needed in order to prevent confusion.

Commas with Adjectives

An **adjective** is a word that describes a noun or a pronoun. That is, an adjective describes the characteristics of a person, place, or thing. As seen in these examples, most words that are adjectives appear immediately before the word being described (adjectives underlined):

big tree several people recent invoice
almost everyone ten reasons

As will be explained, there are different types or categories of adjectives. The term **coordinate adjective** refers to adjectives that are in the same category.

What's the Problem?

Most people know that adjectives can be strung together before a noun, as in *a big, lazy, ugly cat*. However, many people mistakenly believe that such adjectives must be separated by commas. The truth is that not all adjectives are separated by commas. Compounding the problem is that, even though most of us know what an adjective is, the punctuation decision depends on the lesser-known fact that there are different categories of adjectives.

Avoiding the Problem: Use Commas with Coordinate Adjectives

Use commas to separate coordinate adjectives (those that belong to the same category of adjectives). Do not use a comma between adjectives that fall into different categories of adjectives.

As seen in the table that follows, there are different categories of adjectives depending on the type of description they give. For example, some adjectives deal with amounts, while others deal with age. Again, only adjectives that fall within the same category are set off by commas. Coordinate adjectives are adjectives that fall into the same basic category.

MAJOR CATEGORIES OF ADJECTIVES

Determiner	General	Age	Color	Origin/Location
the	big	old	red	American*
a (an)	short	young	blue	Swiss
two	attractive	new	pastel	Dutch
fifteen	silly	aged	blond	Southern
these	perfect	mature	pink	European
that	special	immature	dark	Japanese
some	tall	ancient	brunette	African
Mary's	expensive	newborn	pale	French

Fortunately, it is not necessary for you to memorize all these categories, although knowing the rule can help you explain the truth to people who mistakenly believe all adjectives are separated by commas. The following tip will make it easier to punctuate consecutive adjectives:

*It is unlikely you would string together so many noncoordinate adjectives, but notice how they would sound best in the order presented here: determiner, general, age, color, origin/location. The scheme is reliable, but there are exceptions because it is a matter of intuition, not science. For instance, *dark* might refer to a color or to a mood (in the latter case, it would be a general adjective).

Grammar Tip: Coordinate Adjectives Can Be Switched
Coordinate adjectives can be switched around. That is, if adjectives can trade places and still create a natural-sounding sentence, the adjectives are coordinate. Use a comma between adjectives that can be moved around. Otherwise, do not use a comma between adjectives.

Using Commas Between Adjectives

All the following examples are correctly punctuated because the adjectives can be put in a different order:

the huge, wretched beast	*also*	the wretched, huge beast
dull, slow, and tall people	*also*	slow, tall, and dull people
a strange, mysterious sight	*also*	a mysterious, strange sight

Your intuition—though not always the best basis for punctuation—should tell you that each of these versions sounds natural. Thus, use a comma between the coordinate adjectives.

Think of it this way. The word *coordinate* basically means "equal in status." Things that are truly equal can be switched around, as with coordinate adjectives. Or you can simply not think about the term *coordinate adjective* at all, and just remember that adjectives that can trade places with one another must be separated by commas.

If in doubt and all else fails, we suggest putting a comma between adjectives. Most adjectives fall into one category (general), so chances are that the adjectives you might string together are in this class, meaning they are coordinate and require commas. Again, play the odds only if you cannot make a better determination.

Omitting Commas Between Adjectives

Do not use a comma between adjectives from different categories. Or put more simply, if the adjectives *cannot* be switched around, do *not* use a comma. Keeping the *not's* in mind can help you remember this rule: *cannot* switch, do *not* use a comma.

Notice how awkward these adjectives sound when they change places, meaning they should not be separated by commas.

shiny Chinese coin	X Chinese shiny coin
some new employees	X new some employees
red cotton shirt	X cotton red shirt
Amy's big U.S. flag	X Amy's U.S. big flag
	X big U.S. Amy's flag

Grammar Tip: Placing *and* Between Coordinate Adjectives
You can also place *and* between coordinate adjectives. Thus, use a comma when you could use *and* between adjectives.

A Quick Look at the and *Tip*

Notice how you can also use *and* between the coordinate adjectives covered earlier:

the huge, wretched beast	*also*	the huge and wretched beast
dull, slow, and tall people	*also*	dull and slow and tall people

However, trying to put *and* between other adjectives proves that you should use commas:

shiny Chinese coin	X shiny and Chinese coin
some new employees	X some and new employees

Summary

- Commas sometimes go between adjectives in a series, and sometimes they do not.
- Use a comma between coordinate adjectives (adjectives that can be switched with one another).
- Do not use a comma between adjectives that fall into different categories (adjectives that cannot trade places with one another).

12

Apostrophes

If you thought commas were a handful, meet the apostrophe—one of the more misused of our punctuation symbols. In this chapter you'll discover—or rediscover—that they are not just for indicating possession.

1. Apostrophes indicating possession: In this section, we examine the peculiar origin of the **possessive apostrophe**. Understanding how the possessive apostrophe came about helps make sense out of how it works today. The key to understanding the possessive apostrophe is to think of the two possessive apostrophe forms (*-'s* and *-s'*) as having these meanings:

-'s This means possessive only. Do not think of *-'s* as meaning the singular possessive. Instead, think of *-'s* as meaning the possessive form of *whatever* noun the *-'s* is attached to. This makes sense of the possessive apostrophe for both regular *and* irregular nouns.

-s' This means both plural *and* possessive.

The next component deals with two topics:

- How to spell possessives, especially possessives of names that end in *-s*
- How to treat compound possessives

The final component of this section gives two tests for recognizing possessives:

- The *of* test, which uses an *of* paraphrase to identify possessives
- The possessive pronoun test, which uses possessive pronouns to recognize possessive nouns

2. Apostrophes in contractions and the problem of *it's* and *its*: The most common **contractions** are of personal pronouns plus helping verbs (for example, *I'm*, *you've*, *we'll*) and helping verbs plus *not* (*aren't*, *can't*, *won't*). While actual mistakes with these contractions are rare, the biggest problem is overuse. In formal, nonfiction writing, contractions are marginally acceptable at best. If you have any doubts about the appropriateness of contractions in what you are writing, then do not use them.

The second main topic of this section is the problem of choosing between *it's* and *its*. *It's* is the contracted form of *it is*. *Its* is the possessive form of the personal pronoun *it*. A highly useful test is to see if you can replace *it's* or *its* with the noncontracted form *it is*. If you can, then *it's* is correct. If you cannot, then *its* is correct.

3. Other uses of the apostrophe: In this section, we examine three other uses of the apostrophe:

• **Apostrophes in expressions of time, value, and measure:** The term *possessive* is somewhat misleading because apostrophes are used for more than showing possession. Apostrophes are also used to show relations of time, value, and measure, for example:

Time:	an *hour's* delay
Value:	the *dollar's* decline
Distance:	a *hand's* width

The *of/for* paraphrase test for apostrophes with expressions of time, value, and measure is a reliable way to confirm that a time, value, or measure expression requires an apostrophe. For example, the fact that we can paraphrase *a night's sleep* as *sleep of* (or *for*) *a night* is confirmation that we need to use an apostrophe.

• **Apostrophes to indicate the subjects of gerund phrases: Gerund phrases** are noun phrases headed by gerunds, for example:

Orville hated Wilbur's *flying* all those stupid kites.

Gerund phrases are really reduced sentences. When we retain the subject underlying the verb in the gerund, that retained subject *must* be made possessive (*Wilbur's* in the example just cited).

A helpful test for identifying the subjects of gerund phrases is the possessive pronoun test. If you can replace the noun with a possessive pronoun, then the noun requires a possessive as the subject of a gerund. For example, we can replace *Wilbur's* in the example with *his*, confirming that *Wilbur's* is the subject of a gerund phrase.

• **Apostrophes for plurals of certain letters, abbreviations, and words used as topics:** Apostrophes are used to indicate plurals of lowercase letters and abbreviations in order to prevent confusion, for example:

I got two *a's*. X I got two *as*.

Likewise, when writing about the use of words, we would use the apostrophe to indicate where the word ends and the plural begins, for example:

There are four *but's* in the first page. X There are four *buts* . . .

Apostrophes Indicating Possession

Our use of the apostrophe to indicate possession does not go back much beyond Shakespeare's time. We will begin the discussion of the possessive apostrophe with an account of the strange origin of the possessive apostrophe. Only by understanding how this use of the apostrophe came about can we make sense of how it is used.

The Origin of the Possessive Apostrophe—or How Did We Get in This Mess?

The origin of the Modern English use of the **apostrophe** to indicate possession is a curious tale. In older forms of English, the apostrophe had only a single use: to indicate missing letters. If you were a sign painter in Chaucer's time and had to write a long word on a small sign, you would probably use apostrophes to show your readers that you had deliberately left out some letters in order to fit the words into the space available. For example, if you did not have enough room to write "Established 1385," you might write this: "Est'blish'd 1385."

The story of the apostrophe now takes a strange twist. In the sixteenth century, when literacy was just becoming widespread in England, publishers saw a market for books that purported to teach newly literate people how to write properly. (Some things never change!) Some of these books popularized the notion that the *-s* marker in possessive nouns was really a contraction of *his*. For example, the phrase *John's book* was thought to be a contraction of the phrase *John, his book*. Because the *his* is contracted to *-s*, it was argued, the possessive should properly be written with an apostrophe to show the missing letters. As a result, instead of the older form *Johns book* (without an apostrophe), we then got *John's book* (with an apostrophe).

Now, from a historical standpoint, this is complete nonsense. The *-s* ending on nouns is as old as time and has absolutely nothing to do with the English possessive pronoun *his*. To see how dopey the idea is, imagine how hard it would be to explain how *Jane, her book* could possibly have morphed into *Jane's book*. Despite the fact that there is absolutely no historical or linguistic basis for writing the possessive with an apostrophe, it has become part of the standards of Modern English. Deal with it.

Over time, the idea that the apostrophe in possessive phrases represents a contraction has been forgotten. People have come to think of the apostrophe as a marker of the possessive—a way to distinguish a possessive *-s* from a plural *-s*, for example:

Noun	Possessive	Plural
dog	dog's	dogs
cat	cat's	cats
horse	horse's	horses

The strange story of the apostrophe now takes its final twist. Once the idea has been established that the apostrophe is a marker representing the idea of "possession," then we are free to move the apostrophe marker after the *-s* to indicate that the *-s* is both plural *and* possessive, for example:

Noun	Possessive	Plural	Plural Possessive
dog	dog's	dogs	dogs'
cat	cat's	cats	cats'
horse	horse's	horses	horses'

Making Sense out of the Possessive Apostrophe

Here is the best way to think of the possessive apostrophe. There are three *-s* endings for nouns. We use the apostrophe to distinguish them from one another:

-'s This *-s* is possessive only.
-s This *-s* is plural only.
-s' This *-s* is both plural *and* possessive.

The key idea here is to think of the *-'s* as meaning only possessive, *not* singular possessive. The reason for this is the possessive forms of irregular nouns. Many irregular nouns form their plural not by adding an *-s* but by changing the vowel. Here are three common irregular nouns with this type of plural:

Noun	Singular Possessive	Plural	Plural Possessive
man	man's	men	men's
woman	woman's	women	women's
child	child's	children	children's

Notice that both the singular possessive *and* the plural possessive are formed the same way: with -*'s*. If we think of -*'s* as inherently meaning singular possessive, then the -*'s* with the plural possessive forms *men's*, *women's*, and *children's* makes no sense.

Instead, if we think of -*'s* as meaning the possessive form of *whatever* noun the -*'s* is attached to, then everything makes sense.

When -*'s* is attached to a regular singular noun, it means that the singular noun is now in its possessive form, for example:

cat + -*'s* = cat's (The possessive form of the singular noun *cat*.)

When -*'s* is attached to an irregular plural noun, it means that the plural noun is now in its possessive form, for example:

men + -*'s* = men's (The possessive form of the plural noun *men*.)
women + -*'s* = women's (The possessive form of the plural noun *women*.)
children + -*'s* = children's (The possessive form of the plural noun *children*.)

The Spelling and Use of Possessives

We will now get down to the fine print about spelling and using apostrophes.

Spelling the Possessive Form of Names Ending in -*s*. For the most part, the possessive of names (proper nouns) is exactly what you would expect: add -*'s*, for example, *Uncle George's car*, *Mrs. Smith's address*, and *Argentina's foreign policy*. The problem is that some polysyllabic names end with an -*s* or *s*-like sibilant sound, in which case you can break the rule and spell the singular possessive with just an apostrophe. For example, besides the expected -*'s* spelling of names like these:

Dickens's novels
Ted Williams's hitting streak
Dylan Thomas's poetry

you will see possessive spellings like the following:

Dickens' novels
Ted Williams' hitting streak
Dylan Thomas' poetry

Most (but not all) reference books recommend just using the *-'s* spelling for the possessive of all names, whether they end in an *-s* or not. There are, however, two genuine exceptions: *Jesus* and *Moses*. The possessive of these two names is conventionally spelled with just an apostrophe:

In *Jesus'* name
Moses' Commandments

The Possessive Form of Compound Names. Most of the time, compounded names imply joint ownership. In that case, only the last noun uses *-'s*, for example:

Aunt Sarah and *Uncle Bill's* house
Laurel and *Hardy's* comedies
San Francisco and *Oakland's* METRO system
Charles and *Diana's* marriage

If the compound does not imply joint ownership, then both nouns use *-'s*, for example:

John's and *Ruth's offices* are on opposite sides of the building.
The president's and *the treasurer's* duties are both given in the charter.
The Democrats' ideas and the *Republicans' ideas* completely clashed.

Testing for Possessives

There are two useful tests for identifying possessive nouns.

The *of* Test

You can paraphrase many possessive nouns by using the word *of*. An additional benefit of the *of* test is that the paraphrase helps the user decide whether the possessive noun is singular or plural. Here are some examples:

X the *judges* decision

***of* paraphrase:** (a) the decision of the judge, or (b) the decision of the judges

At this point, you, the writer, have to decide whether you are talking about one judge or multiple judges. If there is one judge, the correct answer is *the judge's decision*. If there are multiple judges, the correct answer is *the judges' decision*.

X a *teachers* pet

***of* paraphrase:** (a) the pet of a teacher, or (b) the pet of the teachers

If (a) is correct, then the answer is *a teacher's pet*. If (b) is correct, then the answer is *a teachers' pet*.

The Possessive Pronoun Test

Noun phrases containing possessive nouns can be replaced by the appropriate possessive pronoun: *his, her, its*, or *their*. For example:

X The court ordered the *suspects* release.

In this sentence, we can confirm that *suspects* is a possessive because we can replace it (and whatever adjectives happen to modify it) with an appropriate possessive pronoun:

X The court ordered the suspects release.

The court ordered his/her [or their] release.

The fact that a possessive pronoun can replace *suspects* confirms that *suspects* is a possessive and should be used with a possessive apostrophe:

The court ordered the *suspect's* [or *suspects'*] release.

Here is a second example:

X The children played the *queens* helpers.

We can replace *the queens* with *her* (or *their*, in the case of more than one queen):

X The children played the queens helpers.

The children played her [or their] helpers.

The fact that we can replace *queens* with *her* (or *their*) tells us that *queens* is a singular (or plural) possessive noun:

The children played the *queen's* [or *queens'*] helpers.

Summary

Apostrophes are used to signal when an *-s* is used as a possessive:

An *-'s* ending signals that the noun is possessive.
An *-s'* ending signals that the noun is both plural *and* possessive.

Two helpful tests for identifying possessive nouns are the *of* test and the possessive pronoun test. Both tests also help you determine whether the possessive noun is singular or plural.

Apostrophes in Contractions and the Problem of *It's* and *Its*

The tradition of using an apostrophe to indicate missing letters has come down through the ages largely unchanged. We still use apostrophes to show missing letters in notes and other quickly written messages. However, we most often use apostrophes in our writing today to indicate the missing letters in the contracted pronunciation of words.

Apostrophes in Contractions

The most commonly used contracted words are combinations of personal pronouns plus helping verbs, especially the helping verbs *be*, *have*, and *will*.

Here are some examples (the contracted letters are in bold):

Be

I + **am** =	I'm
you + **are** =	you're
he + **is** =	he's
it + **is** =	it's (More about this later.)

Have

I + **ha**ve =	I've
you + **ha**ve =	you've
I + **had** =	I'd
they + **had** =	they'd

Will

I + **will** =	I'll
we + **will** =	we'll

The other common group of contractions is a helping verb plus *not*, for example:

are + **not** =	aren't
was + **not** =	wasn't

were + **not** =	weren't
has + **not** =	hasn't
had + **not** =	hadn't
can + **not** =	can't
will + **not** =	won't

The last example, *won't,* is the oddest contraction. The reason is historical. In the Middle Ages, there was no standard form of English. There were often substantial differences in dialect, even from village to village. Sometimes different dialect forms of the same word have both survived into Modern English. That is the case with *will* and *won't.* We got *will* from one dialect and the historically related word *won't* from another dialect. (Trivia time: another example of related words from different dialects is *fox* and *vixen.* A *vixen* is a female *fox. Vixen* is from a dialect area in which *f* changed to *v.*)

While errors in writing contractions do occur, they are infrequent. Here are the two most common contraction errors:

X are'nt
X does'nt

Examine them closely, and see if you can recognize a pattern to the mistakes.

What these two errors seem to show is that the writers are using the apostrophe to divide words by meaning, not to indicate missing letters. That is, the apostrophes are used to separate the verb (*are, does*) from the attached negative (*not*). It is like the writers are using the contraction apostrophe the way they might use a hyphen to separate compound words.

The biggest problem with contractions is not that they are misspelled but that they are used where they should not be. Contractions are perfectly normal in fiction, especially in dialogue, where the writer is attempting to convey something of the sound of actual spoken language.

In formal, nonfiction writing, however, contractions are only marginally acceptable. In more formal writing, the best bet would be to avoid contractions completely. There is a tendency to let contractions slip back in when we are composing. When we are in the process of writing, most of us actually "hear" in our minds the words as we write them. The fact that we hear the words leads us into writing down on paper what seems natural to our ear. This is a mistake. We need to edit our writing with the cold eye of a hostile lawyer, focusing only on what is actually written on the page.

The Problem of It's *and* Its

Of all the errors involving apostrophes, by far the most common is the confusion of *it's* and *its*. *It's* is the contracted form of *it is*. *Its* is the possessive form of the personal pronoun *it*. To talk about these similar constructions, we will call *it's* the **contracted *it's***, and we will call *its* the **possessive *its***. Compare the following sentences:

Contracted *it's*: We will go, even if *it's* raining.
Possessive *its*: I hated the place. *Its* constant rain drove me crazy.

One reason for the confusion is the fact that we tend to associate the apostrophe with possession, as in *John's book* and *Mary's bicycle*. This association causes us to think of the apostrophe in *it's* as a possessive apostrophe. By the same token, the fact that *its* does *not* have an apostrophe makes us forget that *its* really is a possessive.

Let us begin by looking at all the personal pronouns:

Subject	**Object**	**Possessive**
I	me	my
you	you	your
he	him	his
it	it	its
she	her	her
we	us	our
they	them	their

As you can see, none of the possessive personal pronouns uses an apostrophe. (Remember, possessive nouns did not use apostrophes either until the sixteenth century, and then it was only by mistake.)

The apostrophe in *it's* is not a possessive marker. The apostrophe is used to indicate a missing letter in the contraction of *it is*.

Intellectually, then, it is easy to see the difference between *it's* and *its*. What we need, though, is a simple, practical way that we can use to decide whether to use *it's* or *its*. Fortunately, there is such a test.

The *It Is* Test

Anytime you see *it's* or *its*, stop and see if you can replace the *it's* or *its* with the uncontracted expression *it is*. If *it is* sounds fine, then use the contracted *it's*. If *it is* sounds truly weird (a technical linguistic term), then use the possessive *its*.

Here are some examples of the *it is* test in action:

X *Its* time to get going.
it is* test:** ***It is time to get going.

This sounds fine, so we need to use the contracted *it's*:

It's time to get going.

I couldn't believe that report! X *It's* conclusion is absurd!
it is* test:** X ***It is conclusion is absurd!

"It is conclusion" sounds terrible. Therefore, we need to use the possessive *its*:

I couldn't believe that report! *Its* conclusion is absurd!

X The committee announced *it's* cancellation of the meeting.
it is* test:** X The committee announced ***it is cancellation of the meeting.

"It is cancellation" sounds terrible. We need to use the possessive *its*:

The committee announced *its* cancellation of the meeting.

X The committee announced *its* canceling the meeting.
it is* test:** The committee announced ***it is canceling the meeting.

"It is canceling" sounds fine. We need to use the contracted *it's*:

The committee announced *it's* canceling the meeting.

Summary

An important use of apostrophes is to indicate missing letters in contractions. Contractions should be used sparingly in formal, nonfiction writing.

The most common error involving contractions is the confusion over whether *it's* is the contracted form of *it is* or the possessive personal pronoun *its*. A highly useful test is to see if you can replace *it's* or *its* with the noncontracted form *it is*. If you can, then the contracted *it's* is correct. If you cannot, then use the possessive pronoun *its*.

Other Uses of the Apostrophe

So far, we have seen in this chapter on apostrophes that there are two main uses of the apostrophe:

1. To indicate possession
2. To mark missing letters in contractions

In this section, we examine three other uses of the apostrophe: to express relations of time, value, and measure; to signal the subjects of gerund phrases; and to indicate the plurals of lowercase letters, abbreviations, and words used as topics.

Apostrophes in Expressions of Time, Value, and Measure

What we call the possessive is something of a misnomer. To see why this is so, we need to take another excursion into history. In earlier forms of

English, nouns and pronouns had a set of distinctive endings called **cases.** There was a **subject case**, two **object cases** (one for the direct objects of verbs, the other for the objects of prepositions and for the indirect objects of verbs), and a **genitive case** (the ancestor of the possessive in Modern English). The personal pronouns of Modern English have preserved most of this older case system. For example, *I* is a subject pronoun, *me* is an object pronoun, and *my* is historically a genitive pronoun.

The genitive case was used for a variety of functions. By far the most common and important of these functions was to show possession or ownership. That function, of course, is why we call it the possessive in Modern English. The next most common function for the genitive was for expressions of time, value, and measure. People counted in the genitive case. (Trivia time: Modern English preserves odd bits of the old genitive counting system. For example, when we say "a ten-foot ladder," the word *foot* is actually plural—a plural genitive, that is.)

Today, the use of the possessive (nee genitive case) is alive and well for expressions of time and for certain expressions of value and measure. Here are some examples:

Time:	a *night's* sleep, a *day's* work, a *month's* vacation
Value:	a *nickel's* worth, the *dollar's* value, the *euro's* rise
Measure:	a *stone's* throw, at a *snail's* pace, at *arm's* length

As you can see, all of the expressions require the use of an apostrophe. Omitting the apostrophe with this construction is a relatively common error. Undoubtedly, the main reason for the error is that writers so strongly associate the apostrophe with the meaning of *possession* that they do not see the need to use the apostrophe with these nonpossessive expressions. Just to take the first example of *a night's sleep*, it is indeed impossible to see a possessive relationship. A *night* does not own or possess *sleep* in any ordinary sense of the words *own* or *possess*. To take another example, in *a stone's throw*, it is hard to see how a *stone* can own or possess a *throw*.

The first step in correcting this error is to simply be alert to the need for apostrophes in expressions of time, value, and measure. The second step is to use the following test to confirm the need for an apostrophe:

The *of/for* Paraphrase Test

See if you can paraphrase expressions of time, value, and measure by reversing the words and adding *of* or *for*. If you can, then you need to use an apostrophe with the words expressing time, value, or measure. If the test does not yield a meaningful result, you probably do not need to add an apostrophe.

Here are a number of examples using the *of/for* paraphrase test:

X Sleep is a problem in *todays* fast-paced society.
***of/for* test:** Sleep is a problem in the *fast-paced society of today*.
Sleep is a problem in *today's* fast-paced society.

X We are still debating this *years* budget.
***of/for* test:** We are still debating *the budget for this year*.
We are still debating this *year's* budget.

X After an *hours* nap, I went back to work.
***of/for* test:** After *the nap of an hour*, I went back to work.
After an *hour's* nap, I went back to work.

X It is a long *days* drive from here to Cleveland.
***of/for* test:** It is *the drive of a long day* from here to Cleveland.
It is a long *day's* drive from here to Cleveland.

Apostrophes to Indicate the Subjects of Gerund Phrases

Gerund phrases are noun phrases headed by gerunds. Gerunds are the *-ing* forms of verbs used as nouns. Here are several examples of gerund phrases (gerund phrases underlined, gerunds in italics):

<u>*Seeing*</u> is <u>*believing*</u>.
<u>*Being* tired</u> is no excuse for <u>*being* late</u>.
Orville hated <u>*flying* all those stupid kites</u>.

Gerund phrases are (relatively) easy to recognize because they can always be replaced by *it*, for example:

Orville hated *flying* all those stupid kites.
Orville hated it. (*it* = flying all those stupid kites)

Gerund phrases are really reduced sentences. When we retain the subject underlying the verb in the gerund, that retained subject *must* be made possessive. Going back to our example about Orville, suppose that what Orville really hated was that his brother flew the kites. *Wilbur* is the subject of the gerund *flying* and, as such, must now be used in the possessive form:

Orville hated **Wilbur's** *flying* all those stupid kites.

When you are unsure whether the *-s* on a noun in front of an *-ing* verb indicates that the noun is the subject of a gerund, here is a useful technique:

The Possessive Pronoun Test for Subjects of Gerund Phrases

See if you can replace the noun phrase with an appropriate possessive pronoun. If you can, then the noun is the subject of a gerund phrase and should be made possessive. If you cannot, then the noun is not the subject of a gerund phrase, and no apostrophe should be used.

Here are some examples of the possessive pronoun test:

X The schools offering soccer is something new.
Possessive pronoun test: Its [or Their] offering soccer is something new.
The *school's* [or *schools'*] offering soccer is something new.

X The lights coming through the open window woke us up.

Possessive pronoun test: Its [or Their] coming through the open window woke us up.

The *light's* [or *lights'*] coming through the open window woke us up.

X We encouraged the boys taking judo.

Possessive pronoun test: We encouraged his [or their] taking judo.

We encouraged the *boy's* [or *boys'*] taking judo.

Apostrophes for Plurals of Certain Letters, Abbreviations, and Words Used as Topics

The final use of apostrophes that we will examine is quite different from all the others. In certain circumstances, apostrophes are used to indicate plurals. The apostrophes are necessary to prevent confusion. For example, when we write about lowercase letters (*a*, *b*, *c*, etc.), there is a problem about making them plural. Suppose we were to write about lowercase letters without using apostrophes for plurals. This is what would happen:

X How many *ps* are there in *Mississippi*?
X There are two *ps*.

The *ps* looks like we are talking about a tire going flat. We use the apostrophe so the reader can tell where the letters end and the plural begins:

How many *p's* are there in *Mississippi*?
There are two *p's*.

The general rule is to use -*'s* to indicate the plural of all lowercase letters and abbreviations. Here are some more examples:

The engine smokes at high *rpm's*.
He's just learning his *abc's*.
The new car has doubled my *mpg's*.

The same rule holds for the plural of words that are being talked about as terms, for example:

Never mind the *why's* and *wherefore's.*
I counted seventeen *maybe's* in his talk.

It is also conventional to use an apostrophe with the plural of any abbreviation that ends with a period, for example:

The number of *M.D.'s* is increasing.
Don't use too many *etc.'s* in your writing.
They award *M.A.'s* and *Ph.D.'s.*

Finally, there is the reverse problem of putting in unnecessary apostrophes for numbers and uppercase letters, for example:

That was popular in the *1920s.* (Not *1920's.*)
We got two *8s* and four *9s.* (Not *8's* and *9's.*)
Three *SUVs* were in the parking lot. (Not *SUV's.*)
We got more *RSVPs* in the mail. (Not *RSVP's.*)
We do not take *IOUs.* (Not *IOU's.*)

Summary

Apostrophes serve three other functions besides possession and contraction. The most important additional function is in expressions of time, value, and measure. A helpful test in monitoring for this use of the apostrophe is the *of/for* paraphrase test. If you can paraphrase a time, value, or measure expression with *of* or *for,* then the expression requires an apostrophe.

The second additional use of the apostrophe is to mark the subject of gerund phrases. A useful test here is the possessive pronoun test. If you can replace the noun in question with a possessive pronoun, then the noun is the subject of a gerund phrase and requires an apostrophe.

The third additional use of the apostrophe is to avoid confusion in writing the plurals of lowercase letters, of abbreviations, and of words that are being talked about.

13

Semicolons and Colons

This brief chapter focuses on two punctuation marks that are both notably similar and profoundly different: the semicolon (;) and the colon (:). On one hand, they certainly appear similar, and both can—under special circumstances—be used when writers are creating lists. On the other hand, it is actually relatively rare for semicolons and colons to be used in the same sentence; semicolons are usually not needed at all in a list, while a colon is used only with certain types of sentence structures.

In this chapter, we clarify the purposes of these punctuation marks and show how they are easier to use than many writers believe.

1. Semicolons: A **semicolon** has two basic functions, yet only one of these is truly important for the vast majority of writing most people do. And this one function—separating two parts of a compound sentence—is much easier to achieve than many people believe. Following is an example:

> On average, a coffee tree produces a pound of coffee beans per year; it takes many such trees to satisfy the increasing demand for coffee.

In this section, we focus on this important and straightforward use of the semicolon. In doing so, we discuss how **transitional terms** can (but do not have to) appear with semicolons.

In addition, we point out the lesser-used function that can be useful at times: using semicolons in complex or lengthy lists.

2. Colons: A **colon** has several functions, yet only one function confuses most people: using the colon to amplify an idea. (This function includes, but is not limited to, using a colon to introduce certain types of lists.) Following are examples:

> To counteract the pain caused by hot peppers, the human brain releases certain chemicals: morphinelike endorphins.
>
> My daughter prefers several peppers that are not hot at all: bell peppers, paprika, and pimientos.
>
> According to many experts, only one thing helps get rid of the burning sensation of peppers: eating sour cream.

In this section, we discuss how to use the colon to create such structures. We give special attention to the common misconception that all lists are preceded by colons.

Semicolons

A **semicolon** (;) has two major functions in formal English. By far, the most common is to separate two independent clauses in a compound sentence. An **independent clause** is a group of words that could stand alone as a complete sentence. When you combine two independent clauses into a single sentence, the result is a compound sentence such as the following:

> Podunk is the real name of a city; it is near Worcester in Massachusetts.

What's the Problem?

Although most correctly used semicolons involve compound sentences, some people misuse semicolons in surprisingly diverse ways. Some confuse semicolons with colons, while other people mistakenly use semicolons to set off phrases or even individual words. Once again, there are really only two ways to use a semicolon in formal writing, and one of these accounts for the vast majority of semicolons that are correctly used.

Avoiding the Problem: Semicolons and Periods

In general, use a semicolon *only* if you could replace it with a period to create two separate sentences. In other words, if you can use a period, you can use a semicolon.

The Major Use of Semicolons: Separating Independent Clauses

As already noted, the most common use of a semicolon is to separate what could be two separate sentences. Here are examples that properly use semicolons.

Correct Semicolons		**Two Sentences**
My car would not start this morning; the battery was dead.	=	My car would not start this morning. The battery was dead.
Jewelers have rankings for the quality of diamonds; the highest rating is D-flawless.	=	Jewelers have rankings for the quality of diamonds. The highest rating is D-flawless.
Europe does not have a true desert; it is the only continent without one.	=	Europe does not have a true desert. It is the only continent without one.

Keep in mind that this hint rests on your recognizing a sentence that is grammatically complete. You might think several of the second parts of the preceding sentences cannot stand alone because each needs the first part to make much sense or be clear. However, each part—the first and second part alike—can indeed stand on its own as a grammatically complete sentence having a subject and a verb. (See Chapter 6 for information on recognizing complete sentences.)

Shortly, we will note some ways to fine-tune our basic tip for using a semicolon. But if you follow this simple pattern, you should have few, if any, outright errors involving a semicolon:

sentence #1 + semicolon + sentence #2

My favorite movie is *Alien*; I have seen it fourteen times.

Saving the Semicolon for Closely Related Ideas

You might wonder why most compound sentences do not use semicolons. Even though the major use of semicolons is to create a compound sentence, most people use semicolons sparingly, if at all. Actually, the most common way to create a compound sentence is to use a comma plus a coordinating conjunction (see Chapter 11).

Semicolons are used when the two parts of a compound sentence—the two independent clauses—are very closely related. That is, writers use this relatively rare approach when they want to emphasize the connections between what could be two separate sentences. That is why you do not often see semicolons. If they were more common, semicolons would be ordinary and thus lose the effect of showing a special relationship between two ideas.

Even though technically you can combine two independent clauses, most readers will expect that you do so *only* when the clauses are very closely related. You might, in fact, have encountered a teacher who marked a semicolon as "incorrect" even though you used it according to the pattern noted earlier. Most readers are not quite that picky. But whether the picky readers are right or wrong isn't our point. The point is you can be technically correct in using the semicolon but still not make the best choice. Save your semicolons for emphasizing a close relationship between two clauses.

Semicolons and Transitional Terms

As a matter of fact, the relationship between the two parts of a compound sentence might be so strong that you might want to emphasize their connection in other ways. Many writers use not only a semicolon but a **transitional term**—a word or words that spell out the relationship between the two independent clauses. Some common transitional terms include *however*, *thus*, and *therefore*. (See the table a little later for a list of other transitional terms and the type of relationship for which they stand.)

Grammar Tip: Deleting or Moving a Transitional Term
A transitional term can *always* be deleted or moved elsewhere in a sentence. The result will be a completely grammatical sentence. If you cannot delete the term or move it around, the term is something other than a transitional term.

The pattern noted earlier, though perfectly correct, can be modified to include transitional terms:

sentence #1 + semicolon + (optional transitional term) + sentence #2

My favorite movie is *Alien*; consequently, I have seen it fourteen times.

The sentence is correct with or without the transitional term (sometimes called **conjunctive adverb**). As the grammar tip explains, you can also move the transitional term around in the second part of the sentence (as in *I have consequently seen it fourteen times*). The term is simply making it clear that the second idea (seeing the movie fourteen times) is a result of the first (liking the movie). Following are more examples of semicolons correctly used with transitional terms (underlined):

This book states that I should not overuse semicolons; therefore, I will not use them often.

The town of Hershey, Pennsylvania, has long been associated with a famous candy maker; consequently, the streetlights there resemble Hershey's Chocolate Kisses.

Some forms of vegetation provide more than one spice; for example, the nutmeg tree provides both nutmeg and mace.

Commas with Transitional Terms

As you can see, the general preference is that transitional terms used with a semicolon are followed by a comma. Some people, in fact, consider it a rule to use commas with transitional terms, especially when they begin an independent clause. In truth, transitional terms are much like introductory elements that begin sentences, because an independent clause could in fact be a separate sentence. (See Chapter 11 for more on using commas with introductory elements.)

The table that follows includes common transitional terms (conjunctive adverbs) and the type of relationship they help create between two ideas. Note that these terms can be used with or without semicolons, and some might have other functions depending on how they are used.

Types of Transitional Terms

Example	for instance, for example, in fact, namely
Similarity	likewise, similarly, again, also, furthermore
Contrast	however, in contrast, on the other hand, instead, otherwise, nevertheless, still
Cause/effect	consequently, therefore, thus, accordingly, subsequently
Emphasis	indeed, in fact, certainly, undoubtedly
Sequence	subsequently, finally, then, next, now

The Less Common Function: Separating Complex Items

If all you remember about a semicolon is that it is used to separate what could be two sentences, you will encounter few problems with semicolons. In fact, it is the second use of semicolons that sometimes confuses people so much that they cannot correctly use a semicolon at all. Therefore, read this last part of the section only if you feel you have an excellent understanding of everything said up to this point.

The other major legitimate use of a semicolon involves *both* of the following:

1. A list or series (of words, phrases, or clauses) introduced by a colon

2. A complex list (because of the length of or punctuation found within the list)

Despite what some people assume, you should *not* use a semicolon to separate items in every list or series. (And for heaven's sake, never use a semicolon to introduce such a list!) As explained later in this chapter, a colon is used to introduce some, but not all, lists. Normally, you should use a comma to separate the words within a list, as shown here:

> We visited three states: Alabama, Louisiana, and Mississippi.

Use a semicolon *only* when the list is complex. The semicolon is a useful way to make it easier for readers to pick out the different items in a complex list. By *complex*, we mean one or both of the following:

- A list in which at least one of the items is very long (perhaps ten words or more, though your definition of *long* depends on what you are writing and for whom)
- A list in which at least one of the items has commas of its own, as with commas used to separate adjectives

Note how the following examples use semicolons to make it easier for readers to understand a list that would be confusing or intimidating otherwise. Notice also that, once you use even one semicolon in a list, you must separate all items with semicolons:

> Remember these three rules: you must clock in by 8:00 A.M.; no smoking is allowed except in the areas designated in the courtyard and receiving dock; you must contact your supervisor three weeks in advance of taking any time off for vacation or personal business.
>
> Gary has several hobbies: swimming; finding, fixing, and selling old computers; cooking; and collecting stamps made during wars.

How often do most people write sentences such as these? Not often. This use of the semicolon is rare but certainly can be useful when it is necessary to have complex lists.

With the growing use of word processing, more and more people are using bulleted lists or other formatting tools to avoid such difficult lists. The rules governing semicolons in bulleted or indented lists are not standardized for most professions, so you might encounter different perspectives on whether to use semicolons with specially formatted lists. In general, though, following the two guidelines just noted will work for all lists, specially formatted or not.

Summary

- Semicolons have only two major functions in formal American English.
- Undoubtedly, the most common function is to separate two independent clauses in a compound sentence.
- Although not a requirement, many semicolons in a compound sentence are followed by a transitional term (such as *nonetheless* or *therefore*). Use a comma after the transitional term.
- A rarer use of the semicolon is to separate items in certain types of lists that start with a colon, but use semicolons in the list *only* if the list is complex and hard to read without the semicolons.

Colons

A **colon** (:) has several functions, and few cause problems in most people's writing. Such functions include using the colon to

- Separate hours from minutes (10:30 A.M.)
- End a salutation in formal letters (Dear Dr. Houston:)
- Separate a title from a subtitle ("Star Trek: The Next Generation")
- Begin a direct quotation (George stated: "The time to act is now.") (Note: Commas also introduce quotations and actually are preferred by most readers, except in particularly formal writing.)
- Set off subheadings (Introduction:)
- Separate various types of information on a bibliography for a research paper (New York: Greensworth, 2004)

One function, however, is more complex and problematic. This section focuses on one major use of the colon: using colons to amplify an idea.

What's the Problem?

The most complex use of the colon is to amplify (to elaborate or explain) a specific concept preceding the colon. Here is an application of this basic rule:

> At the zoo, we saw something frightening: a cobra killing a mouse.

That might seem to be a simple sentence and an equally simple matter, but the problem with the general rule governing the example is threefold.

First, this rule is very general so that it can be applied in various types of sentences. The result of this generality, though, is that the rule is so vague it can be difficult to understand fully. In fact, learning this use of the colon usually involves intuition along with hit-and-miss practice and feedback from someone who can let the writer know when he or she is using the colon correctly.

Second, many people significantly misapply the aforementioned rule and create both major and minor errors. One of the most serious misapplications is this: some writers mistakenly use a colon to introduce *any* sort of list. Later, we'll return to this major type of error.

Third, as a result of the vagueness of this rule and the errors associated with colons, many people simply avoid using the colon except for the most menial of grammatical tasks. Yet the colon, when used correctly, can help people write more clearly, concisely, and emphatically.

Avoiding the Problem: Is There a Complete Sentence?

Make sure that what comes before the colon could be a complete sentence. Use the colon to amplify a word appearing before the colon.

This is a more specific version of the general rule noted earlier. Our more specific tip will include almost every type of sentence that the general rule covers and will help you avoid the most common misuses of the colon. However, you must understand both parts of our tip. (Keep in mind that we are not discussing the minor uses of colons.)

Use the Colon After an Independent Clause

Let's start with the easier part of our tip. Make sure that what comes *before* the colon could be a complete sentence, otherwise known as an **independent clause.** In other words, you must first see if a period could replace the colon. Is what comes before the period a complete sentence? If yes, your sentence passed the first test. Otherwise, do not use a colon.

When you apply our test, you should have something left after the period (or colon). This leftover could be a complete sentence or not. It does not matter as long as what comes *before* is a complete sentence, as seen here:

Correct Colon		**Complete Sentence + Leftover**
At the zoo, we saw a frightening sight: a cobra killing a mouse.	=	At the zoo, we saw a frightening sight. + a cobra killing a mouse
In the planning stages of "Star Trek," the *Enterprise* went by a different name: the *U.S.S. Yorktown.*	=	In the planning stages of "Star Trek," the *Enterprise* went by a different name. + the *U.S.S. Yorktown*
Psychologist William Moulton Marston is best known for two things he created: the lie detector and the comic book character Wonder Woman.	=	Psychologist William Moulton Marston is best known for two things he created. + the lie detector and the comic book character Wonder Woman

Our tip depends on your being able to recognize a complete sentence. (See Chapter 6 if you are not certain you can distinguish a complete sentence from a fragment.)

Amplifying a Previous Word

Now moving ahead in our tip, see if what comes *after* the colon is playing off a previous noun (or pronoun) in the independent clause. Because of the way the clause is worded, readers should have an expectation (a "pregnant pause," as some people put it) that you will explain this noun. That is, readers expect you to amplify, explain, or elaborate on this one word. In the following, this "expectant word" is underlined; notice how what comes after the colon bends back to amplify this word:

> At the zoo, we saw a frightening sight: a cobra killing a mouse.
>
> On an old telephone dial, there are two letters you will never find: Q and Z.

The wording of each independent clause creates suspense. Curious readers will want to know something as a result: what "frightening sight" or which "two letters." What comes after the colon fulfills the expectation created in the first part of the sentence. Think of it this way: if you left out the second part of the sentence, you would be a tease. That is, you set up readers to expect clarification of a particular idea, yet you did not deliver. If your sentence does not create this clear sense of expectation or suspense, you probably should not use a colon.

Although not a requirement, the noun or pronoun being amplified often appears toward the end of the independent clause—a position that helps create the expectation that this word will be explained further.

Here, then, is a pattern to assist you in creating this useful type of sentence:

> independent clause (having an "expectant" noun or pronoun) + colon + amplification

As you can see in the previous examples, what comes after the colon can be a single word or a group of words. In fact, you might even follow the colon with an entire independent clause (a group of words that could conceivably be a separate sentence).

Grammar Tip: Capitalizing After Colons

If an independent clause does follow the colon, most grammar textbooks indicate you have the option of capitalizing or not capitalizing the first word after the colon. The most common approach is not capitalizing in such instances.

Colons and Lists

As noted already, one type of structure associated with the colon involves a list, usually a list of nouns. This type of sentence involves the same two elements previously discussed: (1) an independent clause and (2) amplification of a noun or pronoun in this clause. Here are three more examples (with each amplified noun underlined):

> When you go to the store, remember to buy the following <u>items</u>: milk, bread, and wine.
>
> Four <u>states</u> in the United States have active volcanoes: Alaska, California, Hawaii, and Washington.
>
> The cartoon character Popeye has four <u>nephews</u>: Pipeye, Peepeye, Pupeye, and Poopeye.

Thus, using a colon to introduce a list is just a specific variation of the type of sentence we have discussed in this section. What comes before the colon creates suspense and expectation; what comes after delivers. If you left out the list, readers would be notably disappointed, peeved, or confused.

Grammar Tip: Separating Items in a List

When using a colon with a list, you normally separate each item in the list with a comma. There are rare occasions (see earlier in this chapter) when you would use semicolons to separate the items, but never use a semicolon to introduce a list.

Incorrectly Using Colons with Lists

Some people overgeneralize this notion of using colons to introduce a list. In other words, some writers use colons in front of *any* sort of list and forget that what comes before the colon must be a complete sentence. Here are two examples of this error:

X For my birthday, I want: another car, a more powerful computer, and a good book.

X Pam has several hobbies, such as: playing video games, working with clay, and writing poetry.

Why are these errors? In each, the colon is in the middle of an independent clause, not after it. You could not replace the colon with a period, as seen here:

X For my birthday, I want.

X Pam has several hobbies, such as.

In more technical terms, the original errors separated a direct object or the object of a preposition from the rest of the sentence. More simply put, each colon is incorrectly separating words that depend on one another grammatically. In these examples, first, the verb *want* must have the words that come afterward, and next, *such as* must be followed by its list. These two examples go beyond merely creating suspense, as with the correct examples. Instead, you are using words that depend on each other to create complete sentences.

To correct such errors, you usually just need to delete the colon:

For my birthday, I want another car, a more powerful computer, and a good book.

Pam has several hobbies, such as playing video games, working with clay, and writing poetry.

Alternatively, you could add a noun or pronoun before the colon so that what comes before the colon would be a complete sentence (added noun or pronoun underlined):

For my birthday, I want several items: another car, a more powerful computer, and a good book.

Pam has several hobbies, such as these: playing video games, working with clay, and writing poetry.

In the last example, the pronoun *these* does indeed create a complete sentence, even though the meaning does not seem complete.

Why You Should Not Neglect the Colon

Some of the problems associated with colons lead many people to take the easy approach: never using the colon except for relatively simple matters, such as in designating times. You would be able to get by without using colons in more sophisticated ways, but you would also miss out on two major benefits: emphasis and conciseness.

Because the colon is used to create a little suspense, readers normally pay attention to what comes after it. When used appropriately, this psychological trick can work to pull in a writer's readers. As you might have noticed, we have used the colon in this book fairly often, not just to set off examples but to emphasize certain ideas.

The colon can also allow you to be more concise. If you do not use the colon, you would usually have to repeat words to avoid creating a fragment, as shown here:

With Colon	**Without Colon**
She made a fascinating discovery: the slot machine was broken.	She made a fascinating discovery. She discovered that the slot machine was broken.
Juan visited several cities: Pittsburgh, Philadelphia, Detroit, and Chicago.	Juan visited several cities. These cities are Pittsburgh, Philadelphia, Detroit, and Chicago.

Thus, don't neglect the colon merely because it is not the easiest piece of punctuation to use.

Colons with Special Formatting

The increasing use of word processing is leading to more and more people using special features to set off lists or ideas. In particular, people are frequently indenting bulleted lists that might not need colons if the lists were integrated normally into a sentence. In fact, some people do not blink at all when a colon is used to set off any list that has been indented and bulleted.

The bottom line is that grammar purists want you to use the colon correctly, whether you are using an indented, bulleted list or not. But for better or worse, the rules we have discussed in this section were not developed for such special formatting.

There seems to be a trend toward relaxing the rules for lists that are indented and bulleted. In particular, some professional writers will use the colon even when it does not come at the end of an independent clause. We suggest you follow the safe approach (abiding by our tips and rules, summarized in the following) unless you know your readers prefer otherwise.

Summary

- Colons have several functions, such as ending salutations or separating hours from minutes when designating time.
- The function that most confuses people is using a colon to amplify or explain an idea.
- When using a colon correctly in this type of sentence, make sure that (1) what comes before the colon could be a complete sentence and (2) what comes afterward satisfies an expectation triggered by a noun or pronoun that comes before the colon.
- Do not use a colon to introduce every list. When using colons with lists, the sentence should meet both of the requirements just noted.

14

Quotation Marks

Quotation marks are the Rodney Dangerfield of punctuation. This piece of punctuation seems to get little respect.

Some people do not even think of quotation marks as punctuation at all, perhaps because in a sentence quotation marks seem to hang in the air rather than join commas and other punctuation on the line of a page. As we discuss in this chapter, one rule for quotation marks, while admittedly arbitrary, is frequently ignored by professional writers and editors. You might also note how quotation marks seem to be the only form of punctuation that a speaker might sometimes try to "draw" visually in the air (by using two fingers on each hand). But also notice how, when this happens, the speaker almost seems to be mocking the use of the quotation marks, as if using them is a bit of a joke.

In addition, quotation marks are used in highly unusual ways. Increasingly, it seems people are using them for no clear reason at all, though it might be that quotation marks are being confused with boldfacing or other ways of emphasizing words.

In this chapter, we describe two specific issues related to quotation marks, while noting a few other but less important issues as well.

1. **Quotation marks with direct quotations and paraphrase:** First, after touching on various functions of quotation marks, we focus on how writers can most effectively indicate that they are directly quoting someone else or just paraphrasing them. Quotation marks are used to indicate writers are quoting someone word for word (a **direct quote**). In contrast, a **paraphrase** means writers are changing somebody's words while keeping the original ideas intact. A true paraphrase does not utilize quotation

marks. These basics are simple, yet we explain the finer points of these rules so that writers can avoid certain errors and use quotation marks more effectively.

2. Quotation marks with other punctuation: Second, we describe one of the most common (though maybe least significant) errors in American English: misplacing periods and commas when they appear with quotation marks. Here is an example of this problem:

X The city of Magnesia is the source of the word "magnet".

According to grammar and style guides meant to be used in various American professions and schools, a period or comma should always be placed inside the quotation marks. We discuss the problems of this rule and how it is not universally followed. This section also describes how to use quotation marks with other types of punctuation: colons, semicolons, question marks, and exclamation points.

Quotation Marks with Direct Quotations and Paraphrase

Quotation marks have assorted functions, including the following:

- To quote somebody else, using his or her exact wording. (Sharon said, "I quit!")
- To indicate sarcasm, irony, or mockery. (Your painting is indeed "quaint.")
- To indicate titles of short works, such as short stories. (Have you read "The Yellow Wallpaper"?)
- To use a word as a word. (I never use the word "whereas" unless forced to.) You can also use underlining or italicizing to achieve this purpose.

The first function listed—to directly quote someone—is the best-known function of quotation marks and the source of the name given this punctuation. Quotation marks were relatively slow to make their way into widespread acceptance. Hundreds of years ago, printers used several different ways to indicate words or sentences that were taken from another source. For instance, some printers used a unique typeset for quoted material, while others used various symbols (including pointing fingers) placed in the margins near the quoted material. Eventually, quotation marks became the standard practice.

Grammar Tip: Needless Quotation Marks

For some strange reason, people seem to be increasingly using quotation marks needlessly. In particular, some people mistakenly use them to emphasize a word or two, which is not a function of quotation marks. Use boldfacing, underlining, or italics—not quotation marks—if you want to emphasize certain words.

The term **direct quotation** means only one thing: using somebody else's language, word for word. In contrast, **paraphrase** (also known as an **indirect quotation**) means you are putting somebody else's ideas into your own words, keeping the original meaning the same inasmuch as possible.

What's the Problem?

This section focuses on three relatively common issues involving quotation marks:

1. People do not always make it clear that they are quoting material directly because of the way they use the word *that* to introduce the quote.
2. To set off direct quotations you should follow certain conventions: using a comma (or colon) and capitalizing the first word of the quotation.
3. You have the option of something that seems to be both a direct and an indirect quotation, but you must be accurate in what you are claiming to be your own words.

Avoiding the Problem: Use *That* with Indirect Quotations
Avoid using the word *that* immediately in front of a direct quotation. On the other hand, it is perfectly normal to begin a paraphrase with *that*, though not a firm requirement.

The word *that* is frequently used to set off paraphrases, as shown here:

The secretary said *that* the photocopier is still broken.
Carl said *that* you should not worry so much about things beyond your control.

In speech, quotation marks are nonexistent (unless you use your fingers to form imaginary quotation marks in the air). Thus, people need other cues to know if something is a direct quotation or paraphrase. The word *that* is one such cue and indicates you are about to hear (or read) a paraphrase, as shown in the preceding examples.

It is conceivable that you might use *that* immediately before a direct quotation as well, but such instances are rare. Even when correct, placing *that* in front of a direct quotation can confuse people because of the mixed message. Thus, we suggest that you not use *that* in front of a direct quotation.

Avoiding the Problem:
Capitalize and Punctuate Direct Quotations
The first word in a direct quotation should be capitalized. Most direct quotations are set off with a comma or colon (a colon is considered the more formal option).

No matter where the direct quotation appears in a sentence, the first word of the quote should be capitalized, as long as there is no paraphrasing at all.

Davy Crockett once said: "My love was so hot as mighty night to burst my boilers."

According to Otto Kerner, "Our nation is moving toward two societies, one black, one white—separate and unequal."

Notice also how these quotations are set off by a comma or colon. This punctuation is required no matter where the quotation appears. Most writers prefer to introduce a direct quotation with a **tag** (the part that identifies the source of the quotation). However, you can place the tag after the direct quotation. In this next example, a comma (not a colon) must be used to set off the direct quotation from the tag (underlined) that appears at the end of the sentence:

"Every murderer is probably somebody's old friend," as writer Agatha Christie once wrote.

If you are writing an extensive dialogue, you do not have to use a tag each time somebody speaks. The convention, though, is to begin a new paragraph each time a different person is speaking.

Avoiding the Problem: Use Quotation Marks as Needed

In a paraphrase that also includes some parts of the original quotation, make it clear which parts are direct and which are paraphrased. Err on the side of caution when deciding whether to use quotation marks around "some parts" of the language in question.

Sometimes you want to use certain words exactly as somebody else used them, but you also want to change other words (perhaps to be clearer or more concise). This is a perfectly legitimate option, allowing you to create something that is part direct quotation and part paraphrase. Here are two examples:

The floor manager said that we should be "judicious when having close relationships" with other employees.

According to one expert, the nation should expect "medium to light" unemployment during the next fiscal year.

This sort of hybrid is primarily a paraphrase but with some features of a direct quotation. You must still use quotation marks around those parts of the sentence that are distinctly related to the source. You would not capitalize the words that are being directly quoted, unless they are a proper noun that always should be capitalized (see Chapter 15).

The problem is that, when paraphrasing, people commonly use at least a couple of words that are also in the original. Does this mean every little word (such as *the*) needs to be set off with quotation marks? Obviously not. However, there are times when using even one word from the original requires quotation marks. The general rule is this: use quotation marks around any words that would jump out at readers as being taken directly from this particular person, if readers had access to the original source. If the original source used a word or phrase that you usually do not use or would not normally use to describe the basic topic being covered, even that one word or phrase should be put in quotation marks, as shown in this example:

The company president described our progress as "awe-inspiring."

You can also set off words or phrases in a paraphrase to make it clear you *really* do not want to be identified with a particular word choice, as here:

Ralph said that you seemed a bit "plump."

If in doubt about whether to use quotation marks for certain parts, err on the safe side by using quotation marks. People might think you are plagiarizing or being dishonest if you fail to change words sufficiently in what you claim to be your own words.

Contrary to popular myth, there is no rule on how many words must be changed in order to create a paraphrase—a source of frustration for writers, especially students writing research papers. If you are not sure if the words require quotation marks or not, use quotation marks around the parts that appear in the original sources. Few readers will be bothered when you err on the side of caution, unless you go too far and use quotation marks excessively around trivial words.

Grammar Tip: Block Quotations

If you have a lengthy direct quotation (for example, three lines), you can use a **block quotation**: set off the entire quotation by indenting it, without using quotation marks. The specifics of block quotations vary, but usually you set off the block quote by ten spaces, on the left side only.

Summary

- Direct quotations capture somebody else's words exactly.
- A paraphrase (or an indirect quotation) makes significant changes in the original material, putting the ideas into different words.
- Avoid using the word *that* immediately before a direct quotation. A paraphrase, though, frequently begins with *that.*
- The first word of a direct quotation should be capitalized, no matter where the quotation is placed in a sentence.
- Most direct quotations are set off from the rest of the sentence by a comma or colon.
- You can use some parts of the original material in a paraphrase, but use quotation marks around words or phrases clearly taken from the original.

Quotation Marks with Other Punctuation

One of the most common questions asked about quotation marks arises when the second set of quotation marks is right next to a period, a comma, or another piece of punctuation. For instance, is this sentence correct or not?

Rob said, "You have to leave now."

What's the Problem?

Does the period, comma, colon, etc., go inside or outside the quotation marks? With periods and commas, the answer rests with one of the most arbitrary rules ever devised for punctuation. With other pieces of punctuation, the rules are more logical, though not always as easy to apply.

In the following, we provide three rules, each based on the type of punctuation in question (periods and commas, semicolons and colons, and exclamation points and question marks).

> **Avoiding the Problem: Periods and Commas**
> Periods and commas should always go *inside* the quotation marks.

Quotation Marks with Periods and Commas

The common rule is very simple: a period and comma go inside the quotation marks—no matter why the quotation marks appear. Thus, this earlier example is correct:

Rob said, "You have to leave now."

Also correct are these sentences, which use quotation marks in various ways:

General George Patton once said, "Wars may be fought with weapons, but they are won by men."
I know you hate the word "got," but it is accepted in formal English.
While studying, Shari listened to a tune entitled "Morning Song."
My husband's mother is coming for a "short visit," so maybe I will leave town for a few days.

The rule is simple but problematic. For one thing, this is the American rule. The British rule, which much of the English-speaking world abides by, is completely the opposite. In the British system, the period and comma go *outside* the quotation marks. Because most Americans read materials that adhere to British rules, we receive mixed messages about where to place the comma or period. In addition, even in the United States, it is common for publishers to place the comma and period outside the quotation marks. Indeed, this seems to be the standard practice with many newspapers and popular magazines.

Nonetheless, you should follow the rule of placing commas or periods inside quotation marks unless you are writing in an occupation or organization that has adopted a different set of rules. Again, this rule should be applied to *any* use of quotation marks, not just to quotation marks used for direct quotes.

This first rule covers the great majority of situations when quotation marks appear right next to another type of punctuation. The next two rules cover less frequent—but often confusing—situations.

Avoiding the Problem: Semicolons and Colons

Semicolons and colons should always go *outside* the quotation marks.

Quotation Marks with Semicolons and Colons

This rule is also simple: colons and semicolons always go outside the quotation marks, no matter why the quotation marks appear, as shown in the following:

> Joseph Stalin supposedly said, "You cannot make a revolution with silk gloves"; even if he did not actually say this, he would have agreed.
>
> I know one place where you can find the poem "The New Colossus": on the pedestal of the Statue of Liberty.
>
> Here is the meaning of the word "zoonosis": it is a type of animal disease communicable to humans.

Fortunately, the American and British systems (and most people's intuition) agree this time: the colons and semicolons belong outside the quotation marks, if for no other reason than that they just look odd placed inside the quotation marks.

In fact, the only reason people might be confused about the matter is that most of us rarely face the question of where to put the colon or semicolon. As we noted in Chapter 13, colons and semicolons are not common pieces of punctuation, and it is even rarer for them to appear right next to quotation marks.

Quotation Marks with Question Marks and Exclamation Points

The third rule is also standard to both the American and British systems, but the problem now is that the decision depends on the wording of each specific sentence in question.

However, you can punctuate correctly if you just think about the matter logically. If the material inside the quotation marks is a question, then shouldn't the question mark go with this material rather than being placed outside the quotation marks? The sensible answer is yes, the question mark should be placed with the question. (The same is true for an exclamatory sentence: an exclamation point should be placed with it, inside the quotation marks.)

In the following examples, the words inside the quotation marks are either questions or exclamations. Thus, the punctuation is placed inside the quotation marks.

Becky asked, "Can we leave yet?"
The poem begins with "To whom can I speak today?"
The officer yelled, "Halt!"

Avoiding the Problem: Question Marks and Exclamation Points

Question marks and exclamation points go inside the quotation marks *if* the material inside is a question or an exclamation. Otherwise, they go outside.

In these next examples, though, the entire sentence is a question or an exclamation. Accordingly, the punctuation is placed outside the quotation marks in order to show that the punctuation is covering the *entire* sentence.

Do you know the meaning of the word "triolet"?
What famous composer said, "I want to seize fate by the throat"?

In rare situations, both the sentence *and* the language inside the quotation marks are questions or exclamations. Do not use two sets of punctuation. Instead, just follow the third rule and place the question mark or exclamation point inside the quotation marks.

Who asked, "Are we almost there yet?"
When did she write the story "Can You See Me Now?"

Grammar Tip: Ignore Everything Outside the Quotation Marks

When using quotation marks with question marks or exclamation points, it might help to strip away everything except the quoted material. In other words, ignore everything else and decide if the quoted material would, by itself, need a question mark or an exclamation point. If so, put the question mark or exclamation point inside the quotation marks.

Summary

- While this rule is not universally accepted, periods and commas go inside the quotation marks.
- Semicolons and colons always go outside the quotation marks.
- If the language inside the quotation marks is a question or an exclamation, then the question mark or exclamation point goes inside the quotation marks. Otherwise, put the punctuation outside the quotation marks.

15

Capitalization

Capitalization is simple in principle but messy in practice. We will divide the chapter into two main parts:

1. Capitalizing proper nouns
2. Other uses of capitalization

Capitalizing Proper Nouns

The general rule for capitalizing nouns is quite simple: capitalize **proper nouns.** Proper nouns are the names of specific, individual persons, places, and things as opposed to **common nouns**, which are generic names for categories of persons, places, and things. In general, the distinction between proper and common nouns is clear enough, as is seen in the following table, which gives somewhat analogous proper and common nouns:

	Proper Noun	**Common Noun**
Persons	Leo X	pope
	Popeye	sailor
	Rocky	boxer
	Madonna	singer
	Stephen Hawking	astronomer
Places	Florida	state
	Canada	country
	Mississippi	river

	Mt. Lassen	mountain
	Atlantic	ocean
Things	Spanish	language
	the Constitution	law
	League of Women Voters	association
	Restoration	period
	Yale	university

However, the devil is always in the details. It turns out that determining what counts as a proper noun is not always straightforward. In the following section, we examine the categories of **person**, **place**, and **thing** in greater depth to sort out the conventions of capitalization.

Capitalization of Persons

The names and initials of persons are always capitalized, as are all other parts of their names (unless an individual chooses otherwise, as with k.d. lang and bell hooks):

John F. Kennedy
C. S. Lewis
George III
Martin Luther King Jr.

Parts of names of foreign origin follow the conventions of the native country and do not capitalize articles like *al-*, *de*, *du*, *la*, *van*, *von*, etc.:

Harun al-Rashid
Daphne du Maurier
Walter de la Mare
Charles de Gaulle
Ludwig an Beethoven

When civil, military, religious, and professional titles precede a name and are used as part of the name, they are capitalized:

President Johnson
Pope Pius X
Cardinal Newman
General Bradley
Professor Smith

If the title is used in place of a name in speaking directly to a person, it is capitalized:

Please come in, *Senator*.

However, if the title is used when referring to a person, it is not capitalized:

Ask the *senator* to come in.

Even if a noun refers to only one person, the noun is an uncapitalized common noun unless the noun is used as a title in speaking to the person. For example, compare these two uses of the noun *mother*:

Proper noun:	Call me when you get home, *Mother*.
Common noun:	My *mother* called me when she got home.

In the first sentence, *Mother* is used as a title in directly addressing the person and is thus considered to be a proper noun. In the second sentence, however, *mother* is used to refer to a third person. Even though the person uttering the second sentence only has one mother, the noun is still a common noun because it is not used as a title in direct address.

If a title is used *following* a name, the title is not capitalized, for example:

Chief Justice Warren Burger
Warren Burger, *the chief justice* of the United States

Governor Arnold Schwarzenegger
Arnold Schwarzenegger, *governor* of California

Archbishop Frederick Temple
Frederick Temple, the *archbishop* of Canterbury

Professor William Smith
William Smith, *professor* and chair of the Economics Department

The names of groups of people (racial, linguistic, tribal, religious, etc.) are normally capitalized:

Afro-American
Latino
Catholic
Chinese

Capitalization of Places

Names of specific countries, cities, streets, buildings, rivers, lakes, mountains, oceans, etc., are capitalized:

Russia
Rome
Elm Street
Empire State Building
the Mississippi River
Lake Erie
Mt. Hood
the Pacific Ocean

Regions are usually (but not always) capitalized:

the Upper Peninsula (of Michigan)
North Pole
Southeast Asia
the Southwest (of the United States)
the Continent (Europe)
the Arctic

Particularly common regional names, at least in the United States, are *North*, *South*, *East*, and *West*. When these words are used to describe a place and/or a regional culture associated with the place, they are capitalized. It is easy to tell these four words apart from the same words used as directional words because the regional names are nouns and can be replaced by the pronoun *it*. Compare the following:

Proper noun: The West has always captured popular imagination.
It has always captured popular imagination.

In this next example, if we try to replace the directional words with *it*, the result will be ungrammatical:

Directional word: Denver lies to the west of here.
X Denver lies to it of here.

Popular names of places are usually capitalized (and not enclosed in quotation marks):

Bay Area (San Francisco Bay and surrounding area)
Badlands (South Dakota)
Eastern Shore (Chesapeake Bay)
Fertile Crescent
Sunbelt
the Village (New York)

Normally, generic topographical terms such as *lake*, *river*, and *valley* are capitalized if they are part of a standard place name:

Bering Strait
Great Barrier Reef
the Red River
Rocky Mountains
Silver Lake
South China Sea

Walden Pond
the West Coast

However, when topographical terms are used descriptively rather than as part of the name, then the topographical terms are treated as common nouns and are not capitalized:

The Arizona *desert* covers most of the state.
The Mississippi *valley* is the country's biggest drainage system.
The Italian *coast* south of Naples is world famous.
The Sierra Nevada *mountains* contain many active volcanoes.

Words derived from geographical names are not capitalized when they are used with a nongeographical meaning:

china (tableware)
french fries
scotch whisky
venetian blinds

Capitalization of Things

The complete names of private and public organizations of all kinds are capitalized:

United Nations
United States Coast Guard
Bureau of the Census
California Supreme Court
Xerox Corporation
Green Bay Packers
Cheney High School
Los Angeles *Times*
New York Philharmonic

The names of historical, political, and economic events are generally capitalized:

Boston Tea Party
Great Depression
Prohibition
Reformation
New Deal
War on Poverty
World War II

The names of acts, treaties, laws, and government programs are generally capitalized:

Declaration of Independence
Treaty of Paris
Monroe Doctrine
Marshall Plan
Federal Housing Act
Social Security

The one area that does not seem to fit the general pattern of capitalization is the names of cultural movements, such as schools of philosophy and styles of art and culture. (Cultural movements derived from proper nouns are an exception to the exception, for example, *Gothic*, *Romanesque*, and *Victorian*.) Even when the names refer to what seem to be specific, even unique, cultural movements, they are not capitalized:

baroque art
classical philosophy
cubism
jazz
naturalism
romanticism
transcendentalism

Summary

Proper nouns are the names of specific, individual persons, places, and things as opposed to common nouns, which are generic names for categories of persons, places, and things. The general rule is simple: capitalize all proper nouns. However, it is not always easy to identify proper nouns, and even then, there are a surprising number of special conventions that govern the capitalization of persons, places, and things.

• **Capitalization of persons.** The names, initials, and all parts of names are capitalized. The major exception is when a title follows the name. A following title is not capitalized. Compare the capitalization of the word *governor* in the examples below:

Governor Arnold Schwarzenegger
Arnold Schwarzenegger, *governor* of California

• **Capitalization of places.** Names of specific countries, cities, streets, buildings, rivers, lakes, mountains, oceans, etc., are capitalized. Names of regions are usually capitalized, for example: the West Coast and Southeast Asia.

Popular names of places are usually capitalized, for example: the Loop (Chicago) and the Valley (California).

Normally generic topographical terms such as *lake, river,* or *valley* are capitalized if they are part of a standard place name, for example: Golden Pond and Indian Ocean.

• **Capitalization of things.** The full names of private and public organizations of all kinds are capitalized, for example: Microsoft and the Chamber of Commerce.

The names of historical, political, and economic events are generally capitalized, for example: Cold War and Civil Rights Movement.

The names of acts, treaties, laws, and government programs are generally capitalized, for example: Equal Rights Amendment and Social Security.

Other Uses of Capitalization

There are a number of other places in writing that require the use of capitalization.

Capitalization at the Beginnings of Sentences

The beginnings of sentences are always capitalized.

Capitalization of Titles

The titles of works of literature, music, film, and art have their own special conventions of capitalization. The first and last word of all titles are capitalized. All nouns, verbs, adjectives, and adverbs in the title are capitalized. It is actually easier to identify what is *not* capitalized in titles (unless, of course, they are the first or last word in the title): articles (*a/an, the*), prepositions, conjunctions, and the *to* in infinitives are not capitalized. Everything else is capitalized (though some style books recommend that prepositional phrases longer than four letters be capitalized):

The Portrait of a Lady
"Lovely to Look At"
In the Line of Fire

The same rules hold for the chapter titles and other major divisions of a work.

Capitalization of Quotations

Capitalize the first word of a directly quoted sentence (also see Chapter 14's section "Quotation Marks with Direct Quotations and Paraphrase"):

Churchill said, "Never have so many owed so much to so few."

First words of quoted fragments are not usually capitalized:

The future is always uncertain. It is "that unknown land."

Capitalization After Colons

When an independent clause follows a colon, the independent clause can begin with a capital letter (though this is a little uncommon):

We simply could not reach a decision about the proposal: *We* [or *we*] couldn't agree on the criteria for evaluating it.

Never use a capital after a colon when what follows the colon is not a complete sentence:

I made a list of what we would need: computers, office furniture, and telephones.

Capitalization in Poetry

The first word of each line of poetry is normally capitalized, even if the first word does not begin a sentence:

Gather ye rosebuds while ye may,
Old Time is still a-flying:
And this same flower that smiles to-day
To-morrow will be dying.

—"*To the Virgins, to make much of Time,*" *Robert Herrick*

In contemporary poetry, however, this rule may not hold.

Summary

There are several other, highly conventionalized uses of captitalization.

The titles of works of literature, music, film, and art are capitalized according to the following rules: the first and last words are always capitalized, as are all nouns, verbs, adjectives, adverbs, and pronouns in the title. Articles, prepositions, and conjunctions are not capitalized.

The first words of directly quoted sentences are capitalized, but first words of quoted fragments are usually not capitalized.

Words or parts of a sentence following a colon are never capitalized. It is possible (though unusual) to capitalize the beginning of an independent clause that follows a colon.

In poetry, the general convention is to capitalize the first word of each line, even if the first word does not begin a sentence.

16

Parallelism

When we use a coordinating conjunction to join two or more elements of the same type, those elements are said to be **parallel** with each other. The elements that are made parallel by the coordinating conjunction can be nearly anything: words, phrases, or clauses. But there is a huge catch: the parallel elements must all be of exactly the same grammatical category.

When we join two or more elements together with a coordinating conjunction but the elements are *not* of the same grammatical category, then we made an error called **faulty parallelism**. Here is an example of a sentence with faulty parallelism:

X Donald loves eating pizza *and* to watch reruns of "Baywatch."

The problem with this sentence is that the coordinating conjunction *and* is used to join phrases that are not the same type: *eating pizza* is a gerund phrase, while *to watch reruns of "Baywatch"* is an infinitive phrase. What is tricky is that they are both noun phrases being used as the object of *loves*. That is not enough; they have to be the same *type* of noun phrase. To eliminate the faulty parallelism, we can do either of two things:

1. We can use parallel gerund phrases:

   Donald loves eating pizza *and* watching reruns of "Baywatch."

2. We can use parallel infinitive phrases:

   Donald loves to eat pizza *and* to watch reruns of "Baywatch."

The best way to monitor for faulty parallelism is to make sure that the grammatical structure on the right-hand side of the coordinating conjunction is matched by an identical structure (or structures) on the left-hand side of the coordinating conjunction. A good way to ensure that the elements joined by the coordinating conjunction are actually the same is to arrange the elements in what we might call a "parallelism stack." In a parallelism stack, the parallel elements are placed in a column so that it is easy to see whether or not the elements have exactly the same form. Here are parallelism stacks for the two legitimate examples just given:

Donald loves	eating pizza *and*
	watching reruns of "Baywatch."
Donald loves	to eat pizza *and*
	to watch reruns of "Baywatch."

When we use a parallelism stack with elements that are not actually parallel, the error is easy for our eyes to spot:

X Donald loves	eating pizza *and*
	to watch reruns of "Baywatch."

Another important feature of a parallelism stack is that it helps us determine what is actually being made parallel. Compare the following sentences:

Donald loves to eat pizza and to watch reruns of "Baywatch."
Donald loves to eat pizza and watch reruns of "Baywatch."

When we compare the parallelism stacks for these two sentences, we can s at a glance what is parallel to what:

Donald loves	to eat pizza *and*
	to watch reruns of "Baywatch."
Donald loves to	eat pizza *and*
	watch reruns of "Baywatch."

In the first example, the parallel elements are infinitive phrases beginning with *to*. In the second example, the parallel elements are verb phrases without the *to*. Either way is perfectly grammatical.

Probably the single most common situation in which faulty parallelism occurs is when there are supposedly three (or more) parallel infinitives, for example:

X Mickey needed to go outside, check the mail, and to bring in the paper.

The parallelism stack shows that the three elements are not actually parallel:

X Mickey needed to go outside,
check the mail, *and*
to bring in the paper.

In this sentence, the writer was not consistent about what was being made parallel. The first two elements are parallel verb phrases (*go* and *check*), but the third is an infinitive (*to bring*). We can have a set of three parallel verb phrases or a set of three parallel infinitives, but we cannot have a mixture. Here are the two correct ways of handling the parallelism:

1. Make three parallel verb phrases:

   Mickey needed to go outside,
   check the mail, *and*
   bring in the paper.

2. Make three parallel infinitives:

   Mickey needed to go outside,
   to check the mail, *and*
   to bring in the paper.

Predicate adjectives and predicate nominatives are a common source of faulty parallelism, for example:

X Young Snow White was belligerent and a bit of a rebel.

Here, the writer has made an adjective (*belligerent*) parallel to a noun phrase (*a bit of a rebel*):

X Young Snow White was belligerent *and*
a bit of a rebel.

The easiest solution would be to make them both predicate adjectives:

Young Snow White was belligerent *and*
a bit rebellious.

A common source of faulty parallelism involves correlative conjunctions in which the first element is misplaced so that the intended parallelism is derailed, for example:

X Bruce would *either* campaign for the president *or* the governor.

The parallelism stack shows the problem:

X Bruce would *either* campaign for the president *or*
the governor.

The writer has inadvertently tried to make a verb phrase (*campaign for the president*) parallel to a noun phrase (*the governor*). The solution is to move *either* so that it is adjacent to the element that the writer wants to make parallel:

Bruce would campaign for *either* the president *or*
the governor.

The writer could also have repeated the *for* to make parallel prepositional phrases:

Bruce would campaign *either* for the president *or*
for the governor.

When a writer begins a sentence with a correlative conjunction, the writer is then committed to comparing two whole clauses, not a clause with just a piece of a clause, for example:

X Not only did Goldilocks eat their porridge, but made a mess as well.

The parallelism stack shows us the problem:

X Not only did Goldilocks eat their porridge, *but*
made a mess as well.

The first element is a whole clause, but the second element is only a verb phrase—a piece of a clause. The simplest solution is to make both elements complete clauses:

Not only did Goldilocks eat their porridge, *but*
she made a mess as well.

Sometimes what counts as faulty parallelism is surprising. When we use a string of three or more noun phrases, the first two noun phrases establish a pattern of modification. If the pattern is then broken, it is faulty parallelism, for example:

X Minnie always takes her briefcase, her cell phone, and BlackBerry to the office.

Here is the parallelism stack for this sentence:

X Minnie always takes her briefcase,
her cell phone, *and*
BlackBerry to the office.

We need to make the third noun phrase follow the same pattern of modification as the first two noun phrases:

Minnie always takes her briefcase,
her cell phone, *and*
her BlackBerry to the office.

The other possibility would be to strip the modifiers so that the parallel items are all bare nouns:

Minnie always takes her briefcase,
cell phone, *and*
BlackBerry to the office.

Summary

Parallelism is surprisingly finicky. Anytime you use a coordinating conjunction, you should look at the element after the coordinating conjunction and then work backward through the sentence, making sure that any other parallel elements have exactly the same form. The parallelism stack is a handy way of working through more complicated examples of parallelism.

Glossary of Terms

Examples are in *italics*.
Examples of the term being defined are both in *italics* and underlined.
References to important grammatical terms are in **bold**.
Ungrammatical phrases or sentences are indicated by an X.

Abstract noun: Abstract nouns are nouns that are not normally used in the plural or with a definite article. For example, the abstract noun *honesty* cannot be easily used in the plural (X *Honesties are the best policy*) or with *the* (X *The honesty is the best policy*).

Action verb: All verbs except **linking verbs** and **helping verbs** are **action verbs.** Typically, the subject of an action verb is the doer of the action. For example, in the sentence *Roberta sang at the Met*, the subject *Roberta* is the doer of the action of singing.

Active voice: The term **active** or **active voice** refers to the vast majority of sentences with **action verbs** in which the subject is the doer of the action—as opposed to **passive voice** sentences in which the subject is the recipient of the action. For example, in the active voice sentence *Tom saw Jerry*, the subject *Tom* is doing the seeing. In the corresponding passive voice sentence *Jerry was seen by Tom*, the subject *Jerry* is not doing the seeing; rather, he is the person (or cat) being seen.

Adjective: Adjectives play two different roles: (1) adjectives modify the nouns that they precede (*large trucks*; *disappointed lovers*), and (2) adjectives are used after **linking verbs** (such as *be*, *seem*, and *become*) to describe the subject. When adjectives are used in the second way, they are also called **predicate adjectives**. In the following sentence, the predicate adjective *blue* describes the subject *sky*: *The sky is blue.*

Adjective clause: Adjective clauses (also called **relative clauses**) always modify the nouns they follow. In the sentence *The answer that we received was not very satisfactory*, the adjective clause *that we received* modifies the noun *answer*.

Adjective object complement: Some verbs take an adjective as a second **complement** following an object—for example, *The committee believed Senator Blather capable.* The adjective *capable* is a complement to the object *Senator Blather.*

Adjective prepositional phrase: Adjective prepositional phrases are prepositional phrases functioning as adjectives to modify nouns. For example, in the sentence *The car in the driveway belongs to my aunt*, the adjective prepositional phrase *in the driveway* modifies the noun *car.*

Adverb: Adverbs can modify verbs, adjectives, or other adverbs. In the sentence *Sally spoke rapidly*, the adverb *rapidly* modifies the verb *spoke.* In the sentence *A rapidly rising tide flooded the path*, the adverb *rapidly* modifies the adjective *rising.* In the sentence *The flood rose pretty rapidly*, the adverb *pretty* modifies the adverb *rapidly.*

Adverb clause: Adverb clauses modify verbs, giving *where*, *why*, or *how* information. For example, in the sentence *I will call you after I get back*, the adverb clause *after I get back* modifies the verb *call.* The adverb clause tells *when* the speaker will call.

Adverb of place complement: Adverb of place complements are adverbs or adverb prepositional phrases functioning as verb complements. Adverb of place complements occur in two places: (1) As complements of **linking verbs.** For example, in the sentence *The milk is on the table*, the adverb prepositional phrase *on the table* is an adverb of place complement of the linking verb *is.* (2) As second complements of certain action verbs. For example, in the sentence *Justin put the milk on the table*, the adverb prepositional phrase *on the table* is an adverb of place functioning as the second complement of *put.*

Adverb prepositional phrase: Adverb prepositional phrases are prepositional phrases functioning as adverbs, typically used to modify verbs. For example, in the sentence *We finished the project after the office closed*, the prepositional phrase *after the office closed* modifies the verb *finished.*

Adverb quantifier: Adverb quantifiers are a small group of adverbs (*almost, just, nearly*, and *only*) that can modify noun phrases in addition to verbs. Adverb quantifiers are often misplaced in front of the verb when they actually modify a noun phrase following the verb. For example, in the sentence X *Bob nearly ate the whole chicken*, *nearly* actually modifies the noun phrase and should be placed after the verb (*Bob ate nearly the whole chicken*).

Adverbial: Adverbial is a generic term for any kind of structure (adverb, adverb prepositional phrase, and adverb clause) that functions as an adverb.

Agent: The term **agent** refers to the doer of the action of a sentence. In an **active voice** sentence, the subject is the agent. For example, in the sentence *John saw Mary*, the subject *John* is an agent. In the corresponding **passive voice** sentence *Mary was seen by John*, *John* is still the agent, but poor *John* is no longer the subject. *John* is the object of the preposition *by.*

Agreement: Agreement refers to certain grammatically connected words. There are two main forms of agreement: (1) **Subject-verb agreement**, in which verbs must agree with their subjects in number. For example, in the sentence *She sells seashells*, the verb *sells* is in its third-person singular form in agreement with its subject *she.* (2) **Pronoun-antecedent agreement**, in which pronouns must agree in number and gender with their **antecedents.** For example, in the sentence *Sally saw herself in the mirror*, the reflexive pronoun *herself* is singular and feminine in agreement with its antecedent *Sally.*

Antecedent: Both **third-person pronouns** and **reflexive pronouns** get their meaning from some previously mentioned noun. That previously mentioned noun is the **antecedent** of the pronoun. For example, in the sentences *Ralph got an urgent call. He returned the call immediately*, the antecedent of the third-person pronoun *he* is *Ralph*. Also see **agreement**.

Appositive: Appositives are the heads of **appositive phrases**.

Appositive phrase: Appositive phrases are noun phrases that rename or further identify preceding nouns. For example, in the sentence *Dancer, one of Santa's reindeer, has a weight problem*, the noun phrase *one of Santa's reindeer* is an appositive phrase identifying who *Dancer* is. See also **essential appositive phrase** and **nonessential appositive phrase**.

Article: Articles are a special set of adjectives that precede **descriptive adjectives**. There are two types of articles: **definite article** (*the*) and **indefinite article** (*a/an*).

Base form of a verb: The **base form of a verb** is the form of a verb that is used as the entry in the dictionary. For example, *be* and *go* are the base forms for those verbs. The base form is also the same as the infinitive form, only without the *to*.

Base-form predicate adjective: Adjectives can occur in one of three forms: a **base** (or uninflected) form, a **comparative** form, and a **superlative** form. For example, the adjective *tall* has the base form *tall*, the comparative form *taller*, and the superlative form *tallest*. Here is an example of a sentence with a **base-form predicate adjective**: *The answer was clear.*

Base verb phrase complement: Some verbs—for example, *make*—can have a complement that consists of a direct object followed by a verb phrase headed by a base verb (hence the term **base verb phrase complement**). For example, in the sentence *Santa made the reindeer pull the sleigh*, there is a two-part complement: the noun phrase *the reindeer* followed by the verb phrase *pull the sleigh*. The verb phrase is headed by the base-form verb *pull*; *pull the sleigh* is thus a base verb phrase complement.

Cardinal number: The **cardinal numbers** are *one*, *two*, *three*, *four*, etc. The other kind of numbers (*first*, *second*, *third*, etc.) are called **ordinal numbers.**

Case: The term **case** refers to the grammatical role and form of nouns and pronouns. There are three cases: a subject (or nominative) case, an object case, and a possessive (or genitive) case. In older forms of English, nouns (and the adjectives that modified them) and pronouns were overtly marked with distinctive case endings. In modern English, some of the older case system markings are preserved in the personal pronouns. For example, the first-person pronouns are marked for case: *I* is in the subject, or nominative, case; *me* is in the object case; *my* is in the possessive, or genitive, case.

Causative verb: In this book, we have used the term **causative verb** to refer to a small group of **transitive** verbs with causative meanings (*raise*, *lay*, *set*) that are historically derived from corresponding **intransitive verbs** (*rise*, *lie*, *sit*).

Clause: Clauses consist of at least one **subject** and one **tensed**, or **finite**, verb linked together in **subject-verb agreement**. If a clause can stand alone, it is called an **independent clause**. If a clause cannot stand alone, it is called a **dependent clause**.

Colon: Colons (:) have a variety of uses: to introduce a list (like this); to introduce a quote; and to join two clauses when the second clause explains or elaborates on the first—for example, *John is not a very good driver: he is always getting tickets*.

Comma: Commas (,) have three main functions: to separate coordinate elements, to set off introductory elements, and to set off interrupting elements. See Chapter 11 for a detailed discussion of the various comma uses.

Comma splice: Comma splices are the incorrect use of a comma to join two independent clauses. The following sentence contains a comma splice: X *Martha was very upset, she had just received some bad news.*

Common noun: Common nouns are nouns used for categories of people, places, and things, as opposed to **proper nouns**, which refer to specific individuals. For example, *city* is a common noun; *Chicago* is a proper noun. Common nouns are not capitalized; proper nouns are.

Comparative adjective: Comparative adjectives are the forms of adjectives ending in *-er* or preceded by *more*. The underlined adjectives in the following sentences are in the comparative form: *Donald was richer than ever. Donald became even more famous.*

Complement: Complements are grammatical elements required by a verb or preposition. For example, the verb *love* requires a noun phrase complement: *John loves ice cream*. We cannot say just X *John loves*. When someone *loves*, they have to love *something*. In traditional grammar, complements can only be nouns (and noun substitutes, like pronouns, noun clauses, gerunds, and infinitives) and predicate adjectives. In modern grammar, the term **complement** is broadened to include any grammatical element required by a verb. For example, in the sentence *John put the book on the desk*, the adverb of place *on the desk* is considered a complement because the sentence is ungrammatical if it is deleted: X *John put the book*. When you *put* something, you have to put it *somewhere*.

Complement of a preposition: Complements of prepositions are the noun phrases that follow prepositions. Prepositions and their complements make up **prepositional phrases**. For example, in the sentence *Louise saw Thelma at the bookstore*, the noun phrase *the bookstore* is the complement of the preposition *at*. Together, they form the adverbial prepositional phrase *at the bookstore*. The **complement of a preposition** is also called the **object of a preposition**.

Complete predicate: Complete predicates are everything that is not part of the subject. In other words, the complete predicate is the verb (also called the **simple predicate**) plus its complements and modifiers, all taken as a unit. For example, in the sentence *Prancer saw Rudolph reading a road map behind the barn*, the complete predicate is the verb *saw*, its complements are *Rudolph* and *reading a road map*, and the adverbial modifier is *behind the barn*. In modern grammar, the complete predicate would be called a **verb phrase**.

Complete subject: Complete subjects are everything in a sentence that is not part of the **complete predicate**. Complete subjects consist of **simple subjects** together with all their modifiers. For example, in the sentence *The tall young man in the yellow sweater ordering a double latte is my brother*, the complete subject is everything before the verb *is*.

Complex sentence: The term **complex sentence** does not mean a difficult sentence. Complex sentences contain an **independent clause** and at least one **dependent clause**. For example, the sentence *I watched a little TV before I went to bed* is a complex sentence because it consists of an independent clause (*I watched a little TV*) and a dependent clause (*before I went to bed*).

Compound: In grammar terminology, the term **compound** has two different meanings. **Compound** can refer to any two grammatical elements of the same type joined by a coordinating conjunction (typically, *and*). For example, in the sentence *Martha and George went shopping*, *Martha* and *George* are compound nouns as well as compound subjects. In the sentence *He turned and ran*, *turned* and *ran* are compound verbs as well as compound predicates. In the sentence *I went up the stairs and through the door*, *up the stairs* and *through the door* are compound prepositional phrases. The term **compound** can also refer to certain types of word combinations, such as **compound prepositions** and **compound verbs**. Here are some examples of compound prepositions: *as soon as*, *because of*, *in spite of*, and *on account of*. Here are some examples of compound verbs: *grow apart*, *pass out*, *shut up*, and *turn over*.

Compound-complex sentence: A **compound-complex sentence** is a giant combo of a **compound sentence** and a **complex sentence**. That is, it contains at least two independent clauses and at least one dependent clause, for example, *John got the pizza* [independent clause], *but Mary brought a salad* [independent clause] *because she was on a low-carb diet* [dependent clause].

Compound sentence: Compound sentences consist of two (or more) independent clauses but no dependent clauses. The following sentence is a compound sentence: *This little piggy had roast beef, but this one had none.*

Conjunction: Conjunctions are words used to join grammatical elements. There are two types of conjunctions: (1) **coordinating conjunctions**, words such as *and*, *but*, and *or* that are used to join words, phrases, or clauses as equals, and (2) **subordinating conjunctions**, words such as *when*, *since*, and *if* that begin dependent adverb clauses.

Conjunctive adverb: Conjunctive adverbs show how the meaning of the second of two independent clauses is related to the meaning of the first. For example, in the sentence *We were going to meet this afternoon; however, I had to cancel*, the two independent clauses are linked by the conjunctive adverb *however*. The *however* signals that the second independent clause is going to contradict in some way the meaning of the first clause.

Coordinate adjective: Coordinate adjectives are two or more adjectives of the same descriptive category used together. Coordinate adjectives must always be separated by commas. For example, in the sentence *The tired, defeated day trader slumped before his computer*, *tired* and *defeated* are coordinate adjectives.

Coordinating conjunction: Coordinating conjunctions join grammatical units of the same type, creating **compounds**. There are seven coordinating conjunctions. They can be remembered by the acronym FANBOYS:

For
And
Nor
But
Or
Yet
So

Correlative conjunction: Correlative conjunctions are two-part **coordinating conjunctions**, for example, *either . . . or*, *both . . . and*, and *neither . . . nor*.

Dangling modifier: Dangling modifiers are noun modifiers, usually **participial phrases**, that do not actually modify the nouns they were meant to modify. For example, in the sentence X *Damaged beyond repair, Ruth had to trash her hard drive*, the modifier *damaged beyond repair* actually modifies *Ruth*, not the intended noun *hard drive*.

Declarative sentence: Declarative sentences are **statements** (as opposed to **commands**, **questions**, or **exclamations**). Declarative sentences are always punctuated with periods. *This is a declarative sentence.*

Definite article: The term **definite article** is probably the only term in English grammar that refers to a single word: *the*. See also **indefinite article**.

Degree: The term **degree** refers to the fact that most **descriptive adjectives** can be used in three different forms: a **base** form (for example, *tall, beautiful*), a **comparative** form (for example, *taller, more beautiful*), and a **superlative** form (for example, *tallest, most beautiful*).

Demonstrative pronoun: The **demonstrative pronouns** are *this, that, these*, and *those*. Demonstrative pronouns are true pronouns that function as subjects and objects. For example, in the sentence *That is mine, that* is a pronoun functioning as the subject. The same four words can also be used as adjectives. For example, in the sentence *That book is mine, that* is not a pronoun. It is an adjective modifying the noun *book*.

Dependent clause: Dependent clauses are clauses that cannot stand alone. They are always attached to **independent clauses**. For example, in the sentence *Dependent clauses are clauses that cannot stand alone, that cannot stand alone* is a dependent clause. There are three types of dependent clauses: **adjective clauses**, **adverb clauses**, and **noun clauses**. Dependent clauses are also called **subordinate clauses**.

Descriptive adjective: Descriptive adjectives are a class of adjectives that have **comparative** and **superlative** forms and can be used as **predicate adjectives**. For example, the adjective *angry* is a descriptive adjective because it has the comparative form *angrier* and the superlative form *angriest*, and it can be used as a predicate adjective: *Popeye was very angry.*

Adjectives that are not members of the class of descriptive adjectives are called **determiners.**

Determiner: Determiners are adjectives that do not have **comparative** and **superlative** forms and cannot be used as **predicate adjectives.** Some common determiners are **articles** (*the, a/an*) and numbers, for example, *the book, a book, two books,* and *the first book.*

Direct address: The term **direct address** refers to including the actual person you are speaking or writing to as a part of the sentence. For example, in the sentence *It is my pleasure, ladies and gentlemen, to introduce our next speaker*, the words *ladies* and *gentlemen* are in direct address. Words in direct address are always set off from the rest of the sentence by commas.

Direct object: Direct objects are noun phrases required as the **complements** of certain verbs. For example, in the sentence *Harry will meet Sally in the park*, the noun phrase *Sally* is the direct object of the verb *meet.* The verb *meet* requires a noun phrase direct object. When we *meet*, we have to meet *someone.*

Direct quotation: Direct quotations are the actual, exact words that someone used. Direct quotations are always indicated by quotation marks (" "). For example, in the sentence *George said, "I cannot tell a lie,"* the words enclosed in quotation marks are a direct quote. The opposite of direct quotation is **indirect quotation**, which is the writer's paraphrase of someone's words. Indirect quotation does not use quotation marks.

Emphatic pronoun: Emphatic pronouns are **reflexive pronouns** used for emphasis. Emphatic pronouns are not objects and, in fact, play no grammatical role in the sentence. For example, in the sentence *I wouldn't kiss Miss Piggy, myself, myself* is an emphatic pronoun. Emphatic pronouns, like **interjections**, can be deleted from their sentences without damaging the grammar of the sentence. For example, we can delete *myself* from the example sentence without ill effect: *I wouldn't kiss Miss Piggy.* Emphatic pronouns are also called **intensive pronouns.**

Essential appositive and **appositive phrase: Appositives** and **appositive phrases** rename a preceding noun. If the appositive or appositive phrase serves to uniquely identify the noun, then the appositive or appositive phrase is said to be **essential**. For example, in the sentence *Shakespeare's play* Hamlet *is one of his most complex works, Hamlet* is an appositive to the noun *play*. The appositive *Hamlet* is an essential appositive because if we were to delete it, the reader would have no way of knowing *which* of Shakespeare's plays was being described. Essential appositives and appositive phrases are never set off with commas. See also **nonessential appositive** and **appositive phrase.**

Exclamatory sentence: Exclamatory sentences are statements punctuated with an exclamation point. For example, *I don't get it!* is an exclamatory sentence.

Existential sentence: Existential sentences point out the existence of something. In English, existential sentences are formed with *there* plus a linking verb (usually some form of *be*). For example, *There's a problem with the car* is an existential sentence.

FANBOYS: FANBOYS is a made-up mnemonic word for remembering the seven coordinating conjunctions:

For
And
Nor
But
Or
Yet
So

Faulty parallelism: The term **faulty parallelism** refers to a series of two or more grammatical elements joined by a coordinating conjunction that should be in the same grammatical form but are not. For example, in the sentence **X** *Senator Blather is pompous and a fool*, the adjective *pompous* is not parallel with the noun phrase *a fool.* One solution would be to make parallel adjectives: *Senator Blather is pompous and foolish.*

Finite verb: Finite verb is a term used in modern grammar for the **present form** or **past form** verb that enters into subject-verb agreement with the subject. See the synonymous term **tensed verb** for a more detailed discussion.

First-person pronoun: The **first-person pronouns** are *I* (singular subject), *me* (singular object), *we* (plural subject), *us* (plural object), *my*, *mine* (singular possessive), and *our*, *ours* (plural possessive).

Flag word: The term **flag word** is used in this book as a collective term for the introductory words that signal the beginning of **dependent clauses.** The **relative pronouns** that begin adjective clauses, the **subordinating conjunctions** that begin adverb clauses, and the ***wh-* words** that begin noun clauses are all examples of flag words.

Fragment: Fragments are parts of sentences that have been incorrectly punctuated as though they were complete sentences. Typically, fragments are pieces cut off from preceding sentences. For example, *My computer crashed and I lost my project.* X *Which I have been working on for weeks. Which I have been working on for weeks* is a fragment incorrectly detached from the preceding sentence.

Fused participle: The term **fused participle** is a rather technical term used to describe a special kind of apostrophe error involving **gerund phrases.** Gerund phrases are reduced sentences used as nouns. If the original subject of the sentence is retained in the gerund phrase, that subject (also known as the **subject of the gerund**) must be in the possessive form. For example, the sentence X *Dancer telling Santa Claus jokes amused all the elves* contains a **fused participle** because *Dancer*, the subject of the gerund, should be in the possessive form. The sentence should be rewritten as this: *Dancer's telling Santa Claus jokes amused all the elves.*

Fused sentence: Fused sentences are two **independent clauses** incorrectly joined together without any punctuation at all. For example, the following is a fused sentence: X *Popeye brought the beer Bluto got the pizza. Popeye brought the beer* is one independent clause. *Bluto got the pizza* is a second independent clause.

Future perfect tense: Future perfect tenses use the helping verbs *will have* followed by a verb in the **past participle** form. For example, the sentence *Sally will have been with the company for a year now* is in the future perfect tense.

Future progressive: Future progressives use the helping verbs *will be* followed by a verb in the **present participle** form. For example, the sentence *Sally will be working in the accounting department* is in the future progressive.

Future tense: Future tenses use the helping verb *will* followed by a verb in the **base form**. For example, the sentence *Sally will start tomorrow* is in the future tense.

Gerund: Gerunds are **present participle** forms of verbs used as nouns. For example, in the sentence *Reading is my favorite activity, reading* is a gerund. Gerunds are the heads of **gerund phrases.**

Gerund Phrase: Gerund phrases are **gerunds** together with their subjects, complements, and modifiers (in any or all combinations). For example, in the sentence *His reading of history gave him a good understanding of current events, his reading of history* is a gerund phrase.

Head: In modern grammar, **heads** are the key grammatical elements that determine the nature of their phrases. For example, nouns are the heads of noun phrases. Verbs are the heads of verb phrases. Prepositions are the heads of prepositional phrases.

Helping verb: Helping verbs are verbs used before other verbs to form multiple-verb constructions. The helping verbs are the **modals** (*can, may, must, shall,* and *will*), *have*, and *be*. The modals are followed by **base forms,** for example, *Rob can take notes. Have* is followed by the **past participle** to form the various **perfect** tenses, for example, *Rob has recorded the meet-*

ing. The helping verb *be* has two functions. When *be* is followed by the **present participle**, it creates the various **progressives**, for example, *Rob is taking notes*. When *be* is followed by a **past participle**, it creates the **passive**, for example, *Notes were taken by Rob*.

Historical present: The term **historical present** refers to the use of the present tense for stories and other narrations, which are normally presented in the past tense. We often use the historical present for jokes, for example, *This guy goes into a bar and sees a polar bear drinking a Cosmopolitan. . . .*

Imperative sentence: Imperative sentences must have an understood *you* as the subject. For example, the sentence *Close the door* has an understood *you* as its subject. Imperative sentences can be punctuated with either periods or exclamation points: *Close the door. Close the door!*

Indefinite article: The **indefinite articles** are *a* and *an*. The indefinite article *an* is used before words beginning with a vowel or vowel sound. For example, we say *an honor*, not X *a honor*, because the letter *h* is not pronounced. The indefinite article *a* is used before words beginning with a consonant or consonant sound. For example, we say *a uniform*, not X *an uniform*, because the word *uniform* begins with a *y* sound, not a vowel sound. Also see **definite article.**

Indefinite pronoun: Indefinite pronouns are pronouns that refer to unspecified persons, things, or groups. For example, in the sentence *Many are called, but few are chosen*, *many* and *few* are indefinite pronouns. Other common indefinite pronouns are *all*, *any*, *each*, *every*, *much*, *one*, and *some*.

Independent clause: Independent clauses can stand alone as complete sentences. They consist of at least one **subject** and one **tensed**, or **finite**, verb linked together in **subject-verb agreement**. The opposite of independent clause is **dependent clause.**

Indirect object: Indirect objects are **complements** of certain verbs that take not one, but two objects—a **direct object** and an **indirect object**. When a verb has two objects, the indirect object always comes before the direct object. For example, in the sentence *Donald gave Melania a present*,

Melania is the indirect object and *a present* is the direct object. The indirect object can usually be paraphrased with *to* or *for*: *Donald gave a present to Melania.*

Indirect quotation: Indirect quotations are paraphrases of what someone actually said. Indirect quotations are never used with quotation marks. Typically, indirect quotations are introduced with *that*. For example, in the sentence *The reporter said that she would call back tomorrow*, the indirect quotation is *she would call back tomorrow*.

Infinitive: Infinitives consist of *to* plus the **base form** of a verb. Here are some examples of infinitives: *to act*, *to be*, *to run*, and *to sleep*. Infinitives are also the **heads** of **infinitive phrases.**

Infinitive phrase: Infinitive phrases are phrases headed by **infinitives**. Infinitive phrases are used as nouns, adjectives, and adverbs. (1) Nouns: In the sentence *George wanted to tell the truth*, the infinitive phrase *to tell the truth* functions as a noun, the object of the verb *wanted*. (2) Adjectives: In the sentence *George is the man to see about a loan*, the infinitive phrase *to see about a loan* functions as a modifier of the noun *man*. (3) Adverbs: In the sentence *You must practice, practice, practice to get to Carnegie Hall*, the infinitive phrase *to get to Carnegie Hall* functions as a modifier of the verb *practice*.

Intensifier: Intensifiers are a small (but frequently used) group of adverbs that are used to intensify the meaning of verbs. For example, in the sentence *Mary Poppins was very upset with the children*, *very* is an intensifier modifying the verb *upset*.

Intensive pronoun: Intensive pronouns are **reflexive pronouns** used for emphasis. For a detailed explanation, see **emphatic pronoun**.

Interjection: Interjections are exclamations inserted into sentences for emphasis. For example, in the sentence *Man, it is really hot in here*, *man* is an interjection. Interjections, unlike adverbs, play no grammatical role inside their sentences.

Interrogative pronoun: Interrogative pronouns are a group of special pronouns used for asking questions. For example, the question *Where are you going?* begins with the interrogative pronoun *where*. The most important interrogative pronouns are *who*, *whom*, *what*, *where*, *when*, *why*, and *how*.

Interrogative sentence: Interrogative sentences are questions. Interrogative sentences must always be punctuated with question marks. For example, *Where are you going?* is an interrogative sentence.

Intransitive verb: Intransitive verbs are **action verbs** that do not require **complements**. Intransitive verbs may be followed by any number of optional adverbial modifiers. For example, in the sentence *The phone rang in the middle of the night*, the verb *rang* is intransitive because the adverb prepositional phrase *in the middle of the night* is not a complement required by the verb to make a grammatical sentence. Modern grammar and traditional grammar differ on what constitutes a complement—thereby also differing on what constitutes an intransitive verb. For example, the sentence *The train was on Track 5* would be considered in modern grammar to contain a transitive verb because the sentence becomes meaningless if the complement is deleted: X *The train was*. In traditional grammar, however, prepositional phrases cannot be complements. And thus, by definition, the sentence *The train was on Track 5* has to contain an intransitive verb.

Introductory element: Introductory elements are any kind of words or phrases placed in front of the subject noun phrase. Adverbs and adverb prepositional phrases are typical introductory elements. For example, in the sentence *In the afternoon, we went for a walk*, the adverb prepositional phrase *in the afternoon* is an introductory element. Introductory elements are normally set off with commas.

Inverted appositive: Inverted appositives are **appositives** or **appositive phrases** that have been moved from their normal positions after their **antecedents** to a position in front of the antecedent. Inverted appositives are most common with subject noun phrases. Here is an example of a sentence containing an appositive phrase in its normal position: *Rudolph, the only reindeer with his own press agent, hit the talk shows.* In this sentence, the appositive phrase *the only reindeer with his own press agent* is in its normal position following its antecedent, *Rudolph.* We can put more emphasis on the appositive by inverting it and putting it in the most prominent part of the sentence—the beginning: *The only reindeer with his own press agent, Rudolph hit the talk shows.*

Irregular verb: Irregular verbs are verbs with one or more unpredictable forms. In particular, irregular verbs do not use *-ed* for both their **past form** and their **past participle form**. For example, *run* is irregular because neither its past nor its past participle forms (*ran* and *run*, respectively) use -*ed*. Likewise, *hit* is irregular because neither its past nor its part participle forms (both *hit*) use *-ed*.

Linking verb: Linking verbs are a small (but highly important) group of verbs that can take **predicate adjectives** as their complements. In the following examples, the linking verbs are underlined and the predicate adjectives are in bold: *Fred was* ***frantic***; *Louise looked* **lonely**; *Sam seemed* **sad**. The most common linking verb is *be*, for example, *Al was* ***angry***. The other linking verbs are verbs of sense perception (*appear*, *look*, *smell*, *taste*) or verbs that describe the condition of their subjects, for example, *The cook got very angry*; *They became accountants.* Linking verbs are called *linking* because they "link" their complements back to their subjects. In other words, linking verbs help describe the nature of their subjects. For instance, in all the examples given, the complements describe their subjects. **Action verbs** do not take predicate adjectives as their complements.

Main clause: See **independent clause.**

Main verb: Multiple-verb constructions consist of two parts: **main verbs** and **helping verbs**. Main verbs are the **heads** of **verb phrases**. Main verbs have **complements** like direct and indirect objects or predicate adjectives; helping verbs do not. Helping verbs are only followed by other verbs. Helping verbs can be deleted without affecting the basic grammar of their sentences. Main verbs can never be deleted without destroying their sentences.

For example, in the sentence *I have been working on the year-end report*, *working* is the main verb and *have* and *been* are helping verbs. We can rewrite the sentence to eliminate the helping verbs without wrecking the sentence: *I worked on the year-end report.* However, if we delete the main verb, the sentence either is ungrammatical or becomes a totally different sentence: X *I have been on the report.* In any string of verbs, the main verb is *always* the final verb on the right.

Misplaced modifier: Misplaced modifiers are modifiers that have been placed so far away from the words they were meant to modify that they seem to modify the wrong thing. For example, in the sentence *I saw my neighbor's car at the station with a flat tire*, the modifier *with a flat tire* appears to modify the nearest noun, *station*, making it sound like the station had a flat tire. What the writer meant, of course, was that the neighbor's car had a flat tire. The problem is solved by moving the modifier next to the word it modifies: *I saw my neighbor's car with a flat tire at the station.*

Modal verb: The term **modal verb** is used in modern grammar to describe an important group of helping verbs: *can, may, must, shall*, and *will.* Modal verbs are always followed by a verb in the **base form**. In the examples that follow, modal verbs are underlined and base form verbs are in bold: *You can* ***go***; *Susan must* ***finish*** *her homework*; *We will* ***see***. For historical reasons, traditional grammar recognized only *will*, which was considered to be the best English equivalent of the future tense in Latin. In traditional grammar, the other modals remained nameless and unloved.

Nearest noun agreement error: The term **nearest noun agreement error** is used to describe a particularly common form of **subject-verb agreement** error in which the verb incorrectly agrees with the nearest noun, rather than with the more remote actual subject. For example, in the sentence X *Uncertainty about the terms of the settlements have thrown the case into the courts*, the verb *have* incorrectly agrees with the nearest noun *settlements*, rather than with the more distant subject *uncertainty.*

Nonessential appositive and **appositive phrase: Appositives** and **appositive phrases** rename a preceding noun. If the appositive or appositive phrase does *not* serve to uniquely identify the noun, then the appositive or appositive phrase is said to be nonessential. For example, in the sentence *Shakespeare's play* Hamlet, *one of his most complex works, remains amazingly popular even today, one of his most complex works* is a nonessential appositive phrase. Even though the information in the appositive phrase is important to the meaning of the sentence, the appositive phrase does not serve to identify the noun it follows. The fact that *Hamlet* is a complex play does not serve to further identify what play the sentence is talking about. *Hamlet* would still be *Hamlet* even if we did not know anything about how complex it was. Nonessential appositives and appositive phrases are always set off with commas. See also **essential appositive** and **appositive phrase.**

Nonrestrictive adjective clause: Adjective clauses modify nouns, but different types of adjective clauses have different relationships with the nouns they modify. **Nonrestrictive adjective clauses** do not define or significantly alter the identity of the nouns they modify. Instead, nonrestrictive adjective clauses, like appositives, give additional (but nondefining) information about the nouns they modify. For example, in the sentence *My father, who was born in Ireland, came to the United States as a child*, the adjective clause *who was born in Ireland* is nonrestrictive because my father would still be my father no matter where he came from. Nonrestrictive adjective clauses are always set off with commas. See also **restrictive adjective clause.**

Nonrestrictive participial phrase: Participial phrases are **participles** along with their complements and modifiers. Participial phrases modify nouns, but different types of participial phrases have different relationships with the nouns they modify. **Nonrestrictive participial phrases** do not define or significantly alter the identity of the nouns they modify. Instead, nonrestrictive participial phrases, like **appositives**, give additional (but nondefining) information about the nouns they modify. For example, in the sentence *My father, being an immigrant, was always very conscious of his accent*, the participial phrase *being an immigrant* is nonrestrictive because my father would still be my father even if he were not an immigrant. Nonrestrictive participial phrases are always set off with commas. See also **restrictive participial phrases.**

Noun: Nouns are names of people, places, things, and ideas. Most nouns can be used following the article *the* (*the book*, *the subway*, *the conclusion*) and can be made plural (*the books*, *the subways*, *the conclusions*). Nouns are the heads of **noun phrases**.

Noun clause: Noun clauses are **clauses** that function as nouns (or, more accurately, **noun phrases**). Noun clauses play the noun roles of subject, verb, object, and predicate nominative. For example, in the sentence *What you see is what you get*, the first noun clause *what you see* functions as the subject of the sentence. The second noun clause *what you get* functions as a predicate nominative.

Noun phrase: The term **noun phrase** is widely used in modern grammar as a collective term for any grammatical structure that plays a noun role. Most noun phrases are headed by nouns (with or without modifiers). For example, in the sentence *A tall young woman in a raincoat entered briskly*, *a tall young woman in a raincoat* is a noun phrase playing the role of subject. The noun phrase is headed by the noun *woman*. Single-word nouns, pronouns, gerunds, infinitive phrases used as nouns, and noun clauses are all included within the umbrella term **noun phrase.**

Noun phrase object complement: Some verbs take a noun phrase as a second **complement** following an object, for example, *The committee thought Senator Blather a complete idiot.* The noun phrase *a complete idiot* is a noun phrase used as a complement to the object *Senator Blather*.

Number: The term **number** is used to describe nouns and pronouns. The noun *city* is singular; the noun *cities* is plural. *I* is a singular pronoun; *we* is the corresponding plural pronoun. Verbs also have number in the sense that verbs have different forms in agreement with the number of their subjects. For example, in the sentence *The city is on the plain*, the verb *is* is singular in agreement with its singular subject *city*. In the sentence *The cities are on the plain*, the verb *are* is plural in agreement with its plural subject *cities*. See also **cardinal number** and **ordinal number**.

Object: Objects are **noun phrases** (a collective term for nouns, pronouns, and other nounlike structures) that are the **complements** of action verbs or prepositions. For example, in the sentence *Sherlock checked his watch*, the noun phrase *his watch* is the object of the action verb *checked*. The complements of linking verbs are *not* objects; they are called **predicate nominatives**. For example, in the sentence *Tarzan became a travel consultant*, the noun phrase *a travel consultant* is a predicate nominative (not an object) because it is the complement of the linking verb *became*. Prepositional phrases consist of prepositions and their objects (also called **complements**). In the following examples, prepositions are in bold and their objects are underlined: ***in*** *the back room*, ***near*** *me*, ***after*** *what you said*.

Object complement: Object complements are noun phrases or predicate adjectives that follow objects. Object complements describe or rename objects. For example, in the sentence *Sherlock considered Watson a good sport*, the noun phrase object complement *a good sport* describes *Watson*. In the sentence *Jane considered Tarzan handsome*, the predicate adjective object complement *handsome* describes *Tarzan*.

Ordinal number: Ordinal numbers are *first, second, third*, etc. One way to remember the term **ordinal** is that ordinal numbers refer to the "order" of things. The other form of number is **cardinal** (*one, two, three*, etc.).

Parallelism: The term **parallelism** refers to a series of two or more elements of the same grammatical type, usually joined by a coordinating conjunction. For example, in the sentence *I love reading good books, going to the ballet, and watching NASCAR on television*, there are three parallel **gerund phrases** serving as parallel objects of the verb *love*. Also see **faulty parallelism**.

Participial phrase: Participial phrases are **verbal phrases** headed by either a **present participle** or a **past participle**. Participial phrases are used as adjectives to modify preceding nouns. For example, in the sentence *The woman taking notes at the hearing was a reporter, taking notes at the hearing* is a present participial phrase modifying *woman*. In the sentence *I just finished a book written by a college classmate, written by a college classmate* is a past participial phrase modifying *book*.

Participle: The term **participle** is a cover term for two verb forms: the **present participle** and the **past participle.**

Parts of speech: The conventional **parts of speech** are **noun**, **adjective**, **pronoun**, **verb**, **adverb**, **preposition**, and **conjunction**. Sometimes the **interjection** is included as the eighth part of speech.

Passive voice: The term **passive voice** refers to sentences in which the subject is the recipient of the action of the verb, not the doer of the action (also called the **agent**) as in **active voice** sentences. For example, in the passive voice sentence *Mary was seen by John*, the subject *Mary* is not doing anything. *Mary* is the recipient of the action of the verb *see.* The agent *John* is the one doing the seeing. Passive voice sentences can always be identified by the use of a **helping verb** (usually, but not always, *be*) followed by a **past participle.** In the example, the helping verb *was* is followed by *seen*, the past participle form of *see.*

Past form: Past forms of regular verbs add *-d* or *-ed* onto the **base form**: *call, called*; *walk, walked*; *bake, baked.* Irregular verbs form their past in some other way. Many irregular verbs use vowel changes: *run*, *ran*; *sing*, *sang*; *write*, *wrote.* The most unusual past tense is found in the verb *be*, which has two past tense forms: *was* in the singular and *were* in the plural.

Past participial phrase: Past participial phrases are **verbal phrases** headed by a verb in the **past participle** form. Past participial phrases are used as adjectives. For example, in the sentence *The books written by American authors are on that shelf*, the past participial phrase *written by American authors* modifies the noun *books. Written* is the past participle form of the verb *write.*

Past participle: Past participle verb forms are used in three different constructions: in **perfect tenses** after the helping verb *have* (as in *Santa has seen the list of bad little boys and girls*), in **passive voice** sentences after the helping verb *be* (as in *The list was seen by Santa*), and in **past participial phrases** (as in *The list seen by Santa is the official one*).

Past perfect tense: Past perfect tenses consist of the helping verb *had* (the past form of the verb *have*—hence, the name *past perfect*) followed by a verb in the **past participle** form. For example, the sentence *I had taken some pictures before the boat left* is in the past perfect tense. The past perfect is normally used to describe a past-time event that took place *before* a second, more recent past-time event. In this example, the writer took pictures before the boat left.

Past progressive: Past progressives consist of the helping verb *was* or *were* followed by a verb in the **present participle** form. For example, the sentence *Rudolph was filing his hooves while Santa gave his usual pre-Christmas pep talk* is in the past progressive. The past progressive is used to describe an action that was ongoing (Rudolph's filing his hooves) at some point of time in the past (during Santa's pep talk).

Past tense: Past tenses are used to describe actions that took place at or during some past time, for example, *John borrowed my car last night.*

Perfect tense: The **perfect tenses** refer to action that takes place over a period of time or is frequently repeated. There are three perfect tenses: **present perfect** (*Winston has been checking his maps*), **past perfect** (*Winston had gotten lost once too often*), and **future perfect** (*Winston will have finished packing by now*). The perfect tenses all use *have* as a helping verb followed by a verb in the **past participle** form.

Personal pronoun: There are three sets of **personal pronouns:**

FIRST-PERSON PRONOUNS

Grammatical Function	Singular	Plural
subject	I	we
object	me	us
possessive	mine	ours

SECOND-PERSON PRONOUNS

Grammatical Function	Singular	Plural
subject	you	you
object	you	you
possessive	yours	yours

THIRD-PERSON PRONOUNS

Grammatical Function	Singular	Plural
subject	he, she, it	they
object	him, her, it	them
possessive	his, hers, its	theirs

There is another set of personal pronouns that are used as **noun modifiers** and thus are more accurately classified as **adjectives**: *my, our, your, his, her, its,* and *their*. For example, in the sentence *That is my book*, *my* modifies the noun *book* and is therefore treated as an adjective.

Phrasal preposition: The term **phrasal preposition** is another term for **compound preposition**, for example, *as soon as, up to,* and *in spite of.*

Phrasal verb: Phrasal verbs are compound verbs (often with idiomatic meanings) formed from verbs and prepositions. Phrasal verbs can be either **transitive** or **intransitive.** Here is an example of an intransitive phrasal verb: *Senator Blather finally shut up*. The phrasal verb *shut up* means "stop talking." Transitive phrasal verbs are subdivided into two groups: **separable** and **inseparable**. Here is an example of a separable phrasal verb: *John turned down the offer. Turn down* means "reject." What is unique about separable phrasal verbs is that the preposition can (and in certain cases, must) be moved after the object: *John turned the offer down.* Inseparable phrasal verbs do not allow the preposition to move away from the verb: *John depended on his Palm Pilot.* We cannot say X *John depended his Palm Pilot on.*

Phrase: In traditional grammar, **phrases** are groups of words acting as single parts of speech. The classic example of a phrase is the prepositional phrase. For example, in the sentence *I found the address on the Web, on the Web* is a prepositional phrase acting as an adverb telling where the address was found. In modern grammar, the term **phrase** is used more broadly. A phrase is a noun, a verb, an adjective, or a preposition **head** together with the head's modifiers and complements (if any). By this definition, a phrase can consist of just a single word (as opposed to the traditional definition, which requires a group of words).

Possessive apostrophe: The term **possessive apostrophe** refers to the use of apostrophes to indicate nouns being used as possessives. For example, in the sentence *Mary's lamb was lost again*, the apostrophe tells the reader that the *-s* ending on *Mary* is a possessive *-s*, not a plural *-s*.

Possessive noun: Possessive nouns have an *-'s* or *-s'* ending, for example, *the man's pencil* and *the cooks' paychecks*. Possessive nouns function as modifiers and are thus classified as adjectives.

Possessive pronoun: Possessive pronouns have two forms. One form is used as an adjective to modify a following noun. For example, in the sentence *I lost my porcupine again*, the possessive pronoun *my* modifies the noun *porcupine* and is thus classified as an **adjective**. The other form of possessive pronoun functions as a true **pronoun** that stands in place of a noun. For example, in the sentence *I found mine, mine* functions as the object of *found* and is thus a true pronoun, not an adjective. Here are the forms of the two sets of possessive pronouns:

Adjective: *my, your, his, her, its, our, your, their*
Pronoun: *mine, yours, his, hers, its, ours, yours, theirs*

Predicate: The term **predicate** (also called **complete predicate**) refers to everything in a sentence that is not part of the **complete subject**. In other words, the predicate is the **main verb** together with helping verbs, the main verb's complements, and modifiers (if any).

Predicate adjective: Predicate adjectives are adjectives used after **linking verbs** as **subject complements.** For example, in the sentence *Phineas was lost, lost* is a predicate adjective complement of the linking verb *was.*

Predicate nominative: Predicate nominatives are **noun phrases** used after **linking verbs** as **subject complements.** For example, in the sentence *Popeye was the navigator, navigator* is a predicate nominative complement of the linking verb *was.*

Preposition: Prepositions are "little words" that are used primarily to form **prepositional phrases**, for example, *in the evening, on the deck, by me*, and *after dinner*. Prepositions can also be used to form compound verbs called **phrasal verbs.** For example, in the sentence *Humpty Dumpty passed out, passed out* is a phrasal verb consisting of the verb *passed* plus the preposition *out* meaning "fainted."

Prepositional phrase: Prepositional phrases consist of **prepositions** together with their objects (also called complements), which are typically nouns or pronouns, for example, *by noon, under the tree*, and *near me.* Prepositional phrases play two roles: as adjectives or adverbs. **Adjective prepositional phrases** modify nouns. For example, in the sentence *The car in the left lane cut in front of me*, the prepositional phrase *in the left lane* functions as an adjective modifying the noun *car.* **Adverb prepositional phrases** modify verbs. For example, in the sentence *A car had broken down in the left lane*, the prepositional phrase *in the left lane* functions as an adverb modifying the verb *broke down*, telling *where* the car had broken down.

Present participial phrase: Present participial phrases are **verbal phrases** headed by a verb in the **present participle** form. Present participial phrases are used as adjectives. For example, in the sentence *The children playing in the yard live next door*, the present participial phrase *playing in the yard* modifies the noun *children. Playing* is the present participle form of the verb *play.*

Present participle: Present participles are forms made by adding *-ing* to the **base form** of verbs, for example, *be, being; have, having; go, going*; and *smile, smiling.* Present participles are the only verb forms that are completely regular without a single exception.

Present participle verb phrase complement: Present participle verb phrase complements are complements headed by verbs in the **present participle** form. For example, in the sentence *We heard him mowing the lawn, mowing* is a present participle verb that heads the phrase *mowing the lawn.* The verb *hear* can take the **noun phrase** plus **present participle verb phrase** as one of its complements. That is, when we "hear" we can hear *somebody* (noun phrase) *doing something* (present participle verb phrase).

Present perfect tense: The **present perfect tense** consists of the **present tense** of the helping verb *have* (*has* or *have*) followed by a verb in the **past participle** form, for example, *Watson has held his current job for many years.* The present perfect tense is often used to describe past-time actions that have continued over a period of time.

Present progressive: The **present progressive** consists of the **present tense** form of the verb *be* (*am, is,* or *are*) followed by a verb in the **present participle** form, for example, *Santa is checking his list of naughty boys right now.* The present progressive is often used to describe actions that are taking place at a present moment of time.

Present tense: Present tense verbs use the **present** form in agreement with the subject—for example, *I am, you are,* and *she is.* We use the present tense for generalizations and statements of fact, for example, *Malta is an island in the Mediterranean.* The present tense rarely means "present moment." For example, the sentence about Malta does not mean at this present moment. Malta has *always* been an island in the Mediterranean, not just at the present moment.

Progressive: Progressive is a collective term for three verb constructions that use the verb *be* (in some form) as a helping verb followed by a verb in the **present participle** form. The three constructions are the **present progressive** (*I am working on it*), the **past progressive** (*I was working on it*), and the **future progressive** (*I will be working on it*).

Pronoun: Pronouns are a group of words that can play the role of **noun phrases**. Some pronouns can replace entire noun phrases. For example, the noun phrases in the sentence *The waiters in the restaurant smiled at the cute little boy* can be replaced by **third-person personal pronouns:** *They smiled at him*. There are no fewer than six types of pronouns. The most important group is the **personal pronouns** (*I*, *you*, *he*, *she*, *it*, and *they* in their various forms). The other groups are **demonstrative, indefinite, interrogative, reflexive**, and **relative.**

Pronoun antecedent: Unlike nouns, pronouns have no independent meaning. To be meaningful, pronouns must refer back to some previously mentioned noun. The nouns that pronouns refer back to are called **pronoun antecedents**. For example, in the following sentences, *My aunts live in Chicago. They are my mother's sisters*, the antecedent of the pronoun *they* is *my aunts*. Note that the antecedent does not need to be in the same sentence as the pronoun. Pronouns that do not have proper antecedents are called **vague pronouns.**

Proper noun: Proper nouns are the names of particular individuals, places, or things, as opposed to **common nouns**, the names for categories of individuals, places, or things. For example, *Fred Flintstone* is a proper noun, but *caveman* is a common noun. *Seattle* is a proper noun, but *city* is a common noun. *Empire State Building* is a proper noun, but *tower* is a common noun.

Quantifier: Quantifiers are a subclass of **determiners**. Common quantifiers are *few*, *many*, *much*, *several*, and *some*, for example, *a few beers*, *many children*, *much confusion*, *several ideas*, and *some desserts*. Note that these same words can also be used alone as **pronouns.** For example, in the sentence *Many are called but few are chosen*, *many* and *few* are both pronouns. They are not quantifiers because they do not modify nouns.

Quotation: The term **quotation** can refer to either of two different types of quotation: **direct quotation**, which uses quotation marks to report verbatim what someone said, or **indirect quotation**, which is a paraphrase of what the person said. Quotation marks are not used with an indirect quotation.

Reflexive pronoun: Reflexive pronouns always end in *-self* or *-selves*. The reflexive pronouns are *myself, yourself, himself, herself, itself, ourselves, yourselves*, and *themselves*. Reflexive pronouns must have an **antecedent** in the same sentence. For example, in the sentence *I found myself making the same mistakes*, the antecedent of *myself* is *I*. Reflexive pronouns can also be used as **emphatic pronouns**, which are reflexive pronouns used purely for emphasis. For example, in the sentence *I myself made the same mistakes*, *myself* is an emphatic pronoun. Emphatic pronouns can always be deleted without affecting the grammaticality of the sentence, for example, *I made the same mistakes* (with *myself* deleted).

Regular verb: Regular verbs are the vast majority of verbs that form their **past** and **past participles** with *-d* or *-ed*, for example, *rake, raked, raked*; *walk, walked, walked*.

Relative clause: See **adjective clause**.

Relative pronoun: Relative pronouns are a special group of pronouns that begin **adjective clauses**. The relative pronouns are *who, whom, whose, which*, and *that*. For example, in the sentence *She was in a movie that we saw on TV*, *that* is the relative pronoun beginning the adjective clause *that we saw on TV*. The adjective clause modifies the noun *movie*.

Restrictive adjective clause: Adjective clauses modify nouns. **Restrictive adjective clauses** significantly restrict and redefine the meaning of the nouns they modify. For example, in the sentence *We bought the rug that was on sale*, the adjective clause *that was on sale* is a restrictive clause because it singles out one particular rug (the one that was on sale) from all the other rugs (the ones that were not on sale). Restrictive adjective clauses are never set off with commas. The opposite of restrictive adjective clause is **nonrestrictive adjective clause**.

Restrictive participial phrase: Participial phrases modify nouns. **Restrictive participial phrases** significantly restrict and redefine the meaning of the nouns they modify. For example, in the sentence *The people wearing name tags work for the company*, the participial phrase *wearing name tags* is a restrictive participial phrase because it singles out one particular group of people (the ones with name tags) from all the other people (the ones not wearing name tags). Restrictive participial phrases are never set off with commas. The opposite of restrictive participial phrase is **nonrestrictive participial phrase.**

Run-on sentence: The term **run-on sentence** is a collective term for two independent clauses that have been improperly joined together as a single sentence without benefit of adequate punctuation. The two main types of run-on sentences are **fused sentences** (using no punctuation at all) and **comma splices** (using commas but no coordinating conjunctions).

Second-person pronoun: Second-person pronouns are the personal pronouns *you* (singular), *yours* (singular), *you* (plural), and *yours* (plural). The term *second person* refers to the person or persons being spoken to. The second-person possessive pronoun *your* (both singular and plural) is used to modify nouns and thus functions as an adjective, not a pronoun, for example, *your book.*

Semicolon: A **semicolon** (;) is used in place of a period to join closely related **independent clauses**, for example, *Popeye could always be counted on; he never gave up even when things looked bad.*

Sentence: Sentences consist of at least one **independent clause** (with or without accompanying **dependent clauses**). Sentences are punctuated with periods, exclamation points, or question marks.

Sentences classified by purpose: Sentences classified by purpose fall into four categories: **declarative sentences** (statements), **imperative sentences** (commands), **interrogative sentences** (questions), and **exclamatory sentences** (sentences with exclamation points).

Sentences classified by structure: Sentences classified by structure fall into four categories: **simple sentences** (single **independent clause**, no **dependent clauses**), **compound sentences** (two or more independent clauses), **complex sentences** (single independent clause and one or more dependent clauses), and **compound-complex sentences** (at least two independent clauses and at least one dependent clause).

Simple predicate: The term **simple predicate** is used in traditional grammar for the **main verb** together with any **helping verbs.** The term is rarely used anymore.

Simple sentence: Simple sentences are sentences containing only a single **independent clause** and no **dependent clauses**. *This is a simple sentence.*

Simple subject: The term **simple subject** is used to distinguish the noun in the subject part of the sentence from the noun's modifiers. For example, in the sentence *The young man in the yellow sweater took out his cell phone*, *man* is the simple subject. The entire subject component of the sentence is called the **complete subject**. In the example, *the young man in the yellow sweater* is the complete subject. The term **simple subject** is useful because the simple subject is what the verb actually agrees with. Verbs do not agree with the complete subject, only the simple subject.

Simple tense: In traditional grammar, there are six tenses. The six tenses are broken into two main groups: the three **simple tenses** and the three **perfect tenses**. The three simple tenses are the **present tense**, the **past tense**, and the **future tense**.

Squinting modifier: Squinting modifiers are modifiers that can be interpreted as modifying two different things. For example, in the sentence *Students who practice writing often will benefit*, the reader cannot tell if *often* modifies *practice writing* or if *often* modifies *will benefit*. Squinting modifiers are corrected by moving the modifiers so that there is no confusion about what they modify. In the example, here are two ways of resolving the confusion: *Students who often practice writing will benefit. Students who practice writing will often benefit.*

Subject: Subjects are the doers of the action of the sentence (with **action verbs**) or the **topics** of the sentence (with **linking verbs**). Subjects enter into **subject-verb agreement** with **tensed**, or **finite, verbs**.

Subject complement: Subject complement is a collective term for the two types of **complements** of **linking verbs: predicate adjectives** and **pred-**

icate nominatives. Subject complements are so called because predicate adjectives and predicate nominatives always refer back to the subject. For example, in the sentence *Gloria is famous*, the predicate adjective *famous* describes the subject *Gloria*. Likewise, in the sentence *Santa is a right jolly old elf*, the predicate nominative *a right jolly old elf* describes the subject *Santa*.

Subject of the gerund: Gerunds are **present participles** used as nouns. **Gerund phrases** are phrases headed by gerunds. Gerund phrases are derived from sentences whose subjects can be retained as **subjects of the gerund**. Subjects of the gerund must always be in a possessive form. For example, in the sentence *Tarzan's constant yelling drove all the apes crazy*, the possessive noun *Tarzan's* is the subject of the gerund phrase *Tarzan's constant yelling*.

Subject of the infinitive: Infinitive phrases are phrases headed by **infinitives**. Infinitive phrases are used as nouns, adjectives, or adverbs. Infinitive phrases are reduced forms of sentences. The subjects of these reduced sentences can be retained as **subjects of the infinitive**. Subjects of the infinitive are always the object of the preposition *for*. For example, in the sentence *For Martha to deliver the presents in person was a great treat*, *for Martha* is the subject of the infinitive phrase *for Martha to deliver the presents in person*.

Subject-verb agreement: In all **clauses** (independent and dependent alike), the form of the first verb (also known as the **tensed**, or the **finite**, **verb**) is dependent on the number of the subject. This dependency is known as **subject-verb agreement**. Subject-verb agreement is seen most clearly when the first verb is in the present tense. If the subject is singular, then the verb must also be singular; that is, the verb must be in what is called the **third-person singular -*s* form**. For example, in the sentence *The car needs to be washed*, the verb *needs* is in the third-person singular form in agreement with the singular subject *car*. If the subject is plural, then the verb must be in its plural form without the -*s*: *The cars need to be washed*.

Subordinate clause: See **dependent clause**.

Subordinating conjunction: Subordinating conjunctions are a group of conjunctions used to begin **adverb clauses** (a type of **subordinate clause**—hence the name *subordinating conjunction*). For example, in the sentence *I hung up the phone after I had been on hold for fifteen minutes*, *after* is a subordinating conjunction beginning the subordinate adverb clause *after I had been on hold for fifteen minutes.*

Superlative adjective: Superlative adjectives are formed either by an *-est* ending (for example, *tallest*, *quickest*) or with *most* (for example, *most beautiful*, *most interesting*).

Tense: The term **tense** is used in two different (and somewhat contradictory) ways. (1) **Tense** can mean the "time" in which the action of the verb takes place. In this meaning, there are, of course, three tenses or times: present, past, and future. (2) **Tense** can also be used as the conventional name for various verb constructions built from different **verb forms.** In this meaning, there are six tenses (illustrated with the verb *go*): **present tense** (*go*, *goes*), **past tense** (*went*), **future tense** (*will go*), **present perfect tense** (*has gone*), **past perfect tense** (*had gone*), and **future perfect tense** (*will have gone*).

Tense shifting: The term **tense shifting** refers to a change (or shift) from one tense to another (usually from **present tense** to **past tense,** or vice versa) within a single passage or even within a single sentence. Tense shifting can be either appropriate or inappropriate. Here is an example of appropriate tense shifting: *We ate at an old restaurant that is on the lake.* The writer has shifted from past tense (*ate*) to present tense (*is*). The tense shifting is appropriate in this case because if the writer had written that the restaurant *was* on the lake, the past tense *was* would imply (incorrectly) that the restaurant is no longer there. Here is an example of incorrect tense shifting: X *Whenever the weather changes, my joints started to hurt.* In this case, the writer incorrectly shifts from present tense to past tense. Because the writer is making "timeless" generalizations, the whole sentence should stay in the present tense: *Whenever the weather changes, my joints start to hurt.*

Tensed verb: The term **tensed verb** is used in modern grammar to identify the **present form** or **past form verb** that enters into subject-verb agreement with the subject. The tensed verb is always the first verb in any string of verbs. For example, in the sentence *George has been working out all summer*, *has* is the one and only tensed verb in the sentence. Even in what traditional grammar would call a **future tense** sentence, the first verb is still a tensed verb. For example, in the sentence *Perry will be late again*, *will* is actually the present tense of a **modal verb**. If a sentence contains only a single verb, that verb is also a tensed verb because it enters into subject-verb agreement with the subject. The term **tensed verb** means the same thing as the term **finite verb**.

***That* type noun clause:** The term ***that* type noun clause** refers to a category of **noun clauses** that begin with *that*, *if*, or *whether*. For example, in the sentence *That we will go ahead as planned is not up for debate*, *that* begins the noun clause *that we will go ahead as planned*. The other category of noun clauses is called the ***wh-* type noun clause.**

Third-person pronoun: Third-person pronouns are the **personal pronouns** *he*, *him*, *his*, *she*, *her*, *hers*, *it*, *its*, *they*, *them*, and *theirs*. The third-person pronouns (unlike first- and second-person pronouns) can replace or stand for entire noun phrases. For example, in the sentence *All the bears in the forest gathered to watch Goldilocks leave*, we can replace the subject noun phrase with *they*: *They gathered to watch Goldilocks leave*. When third-person pronouns are used to modify nouns, they are classified as adjectives. For example, in the sentence *The students packed their bags*, the third-person pronoun *their* is functioning as an adjective modifying the noun *bags*.

Third-person singular verb form: The term **third-person singular verb form** refers to the *-s* that is added to present forms of the verb when that verb agrees with a third-person pronoun (or a noun phrase that can be replaced by a third-person pronoun—see the definition of **third-person pronoun**). For example, in the sentence *She drives to the city every day*, the verb *drives* is in the third-person singular form to agree with the third-person singular pronoun *she*. The same holds true for the following sentence:

My friend Louise drives to the city every day. Drives is still considered to be in the third-person singular form because *drives* agrees with the subject noun phrase *my friend Louise*, which can be replaced by the third-person pronoun *she*.

Topic of sentence: The term **topic** is used to describe the nature of the subject in **linking verb** sentences. For example, in the linking verb sentence *The Panama Canal is now too small for many modern ships*, the subject *the Panama Canal* is not the doer of any action as would be the case with most subjects in sentences with action verbs. The linking verb sentence is really about the Panama Canal. In other words, the subject of a linking verb sentence is a topic that the rest of the sentence describes or comments on.

Transitional term: See **conjunctive adverb**.

Transitive verb: Transitive verbs are **action verbs** that require **objects**. For example, in the sentence *Thelma met Louise*, *met* is a transitive verb. If we were to delete the object *Louise*, the sentence would become ungrammatical: X *Thelma met*. The term **transitive** is not usually applied to **linking verbs**.

Vague pronoun: Vague pronouns are pronouns that do not have **antecedents** to give the pronouns meaning. For example, in the sentence *They should do something about airport security*, *they* is a vague pronoun because the reader has no way of knowing what *they* refers to—airports, Congress, the Department of Homeland Security, or the world in general.

Verb: Verbs express action (*Martha sneezed*) or describe the subject (*Martha was not amused*). Only verbs have different forms that express **tense**. That is, only verbs have **present** and **past forms**. For example, the word *watch* could be either a noun or a verb, but the past tense form *watched* can only be a verb.

Verb complement: Verb complements are whatever **complements** are required by the verb to make a complete sentence. For example, in the sentence *Mary loves her lambs*, the noun phrase *her lambs* is the noun phrase complement of the verb *loves*. In traditional grammar, only nouns (and noun substitutes) and predicate adjectives can be complements. In modern grammar, the term **verb complement** is broadened to include any required grammatical element. For example, in modern grammar, adverbials of place can be complements, as in the sentence *The train was at the station*. In this sentence, the adverb prepositional phrase *at the station* is a complement of the verb *was* because if it were deleted, the sentence would become ungrammatical: X *The train was.*

Verbal: Verbals are **infinitives, present participles**, and **past participles** used as other parts of speech. Infinitives (and **infinitive phrases**) can be used as nouns (*To err is human*), adjectives (*a day to remember*), or adverbs (*You must practice to succeed*). Present participles (and **present participial phrases**) can be used as nouns, also called **gerunds** (*Winning is not everything*) and adjectives (*a light shining in the window*). Past participles (and **past participial phrases**) can be used as adjectives (*a book printed in Holland*).

Verbal phrase: Verbal phrases are phrases headed by verbals.

Voice: The term **voice** is used to distinguish **passive** and **active** sentences. A passive sentence is said to be in the **passive voice**. For example, the sentence *Mary was seen by John* is a passive voice sentence. An active sentence is said to be in the **active voice**. For example, the sentence *John saw Mary* is an active voice sentence.

***Wh*- type noun clause:** The term ***wh*- type noun clause** is used in modern grammar to identify a category of **noun clauses** that begin with words such as *who, whom, whose, when, where, why*, etc. Because nearly all the words that begin this type of noun clause happen to begin with *wh*-, this category of noun clauses is called the ***wh*- type noun clause**. For example, in the sentence *What you see is what you get*, both the subject and complement are *wh*- type noun clauses.

Index